Doing business in the
European
Community

To those acknowledged and unacknowledged who contributed to this book and to the generation of European managers, who will create the wealth of the European Business Community.

Doing business in the

European Community

John Drew

Head of International Affairs, Rank Xerox

Butterworths

London Boston
Sydney Wellington Durban Toronto

United Kingdom	**Butterworth & Co (Publishers) Ltd**
London	88 Kingsway, WC2B 6AB
Australia	**Butterworths Pty Ltd**
Sydney	586 Pacific Highway, Chatswood, NSW 2067
	Also at Melbourne, Brisbane, Adelaide and Perth
Canada	**Butterworth & Co (Canada) Ltd**
Toronto	2265 Midland Avenue, Scarborough, Ontario, M1P 4S1
New Zealand	**Butterworths of New Zealand Ltd**
Wellington	T & W Young Building, 77-85 Customhouse Quay, 1, CPO Box 472
South Africa	**Butterworth & Co (South Africa) (Pty) Ltd**
Durban	152-154 Gale Street
USA	**Butterworth (Publishers) Inc**
Boston	10 Tower Office Park, Woburn, Massachusetts 01801

First published 1979

© Butterworth & Co (Publishers) Ltd, 1979

ISBN 0 408 10631 X

British Library Cataloguing in Publication Data

Drew, John
  Doing business in the European Community.
  1. Business enterprises – European Economic
  Community countries
  I. Title
  650'.094   HF5439.E/   79-40243

  ISBN 0–408–10631–X

Typeset by Scribe Design, Medway, Kent
Printed in England by McCorquodale Newton Ltd,
Newton-Le-Willows, Lancs.

Foreword

I warmly welcome the publication of this presentation of how the European Community affects business. It fills a gap in the literature which has existed for some years. I am therefore glad that John Drew's book meets a need felt by managers and businessmen for a short and readable introduction to the European Community.

It is in the interests of us all that businessmen around the world, and particularly in the United Kingdom, should feel, and become, more involved in our common enterprise. I am sure that the potential of British membership of the European Community has been neither fulfilled nor exhausted. There is still a great deal of misunderstanding — for which we in the European Commission must bear our share of responsibility — about how the Community affects business, and how British exporters, indeed all those who do business in the EEC, can make the most of the opportunities provided by the Common Market of the European Community.

The development of policies is a continuing process, sometimes simple, but sometimes inevitably complex. I believe John Drew's book, with its distinguished contributors, will make a major contribution to simplifying the complex and to helping businessmen understand the Community better. I am confident that this publication will encourage its readers to take greater advantage of the possibilities of the Community Market.

Roy Jenkins
President of the Commission of the
European Communities

Acknowledgements

This book owes much to many people, some acknowledged and others not.

My very sincere thanks to those who wrote about their busy Community lives for the book in such a range of lively styles:

Ambassador Lall
Norman Miller
Bill Nichol
Tom Normanton
Jack Peel
Christopher Tugendhat

The Commission in Brussels and the UK office of the Commission in London were unfailingly helpful and generous with their time. My thanks to them also for permission to reproduce photographs and texts.

London Business School students and managers on many of the programmes helped me to develop the material.

Sarah Acton and Samiha Kirke-Smith provided cheerful help, co-ordination and research, not to mention producing the manuscript.

Rebecca encouraged me to write the book and lovingly and patiently put up with having an author in the family. So too did Jason, Emma and David who will number among a new generation of young Europeans.

Contents

Foreword by Roy Jenkins

Community institutions and the decision-making process

1 Business and the European Community

I am firmly convinced that individually we would not
have withstood the storms of world economic development — that is, the crisis that began in 1973 — at all.
Each country alone would have been sucked into
catastrophe. Even the Federal Republic of Germany
would barely have been able to withstand the development. So it is that we must agree it was indeed well
that twenty years ago we founded the European
Community.
Walter Scheel, President of the Federal Republic of
Germany, May 1977.

Successful businesses in the United Kingdom, and many larger companies
throughout the world, will need to devote more time over the next decade to
developing their European operations.

The European Community is like an iceberg and only the tips of its policies
show. The major creative work has been to build an infrastructure of systems,
procedures, committees, formal and informal contacts. These form the solid
base beneath the surface from which policies develop.

Contentious issues naturally receive wide media coverage, but the bulk of the
work is carried out in countless, carefully prepared meetings and negotiations.
The Nine Member States are well on the way to developing a Community framework within which its citizens will live, work and have their being.

The Community now speaks with one voice on a wide number of subjects.
Political, as well as economic views are beginning to converge. The President of
the Commission represents the Community at a growing number of international
meetings.

Business inside the Community needs to take more note of the industrial and
legal framework which is being developed. Business outside the Community
needs to consider the implications of a large market of 260 million consumers
and of trade agreements, quotas, aid and treaties now negotiated centrally in
Brussels and no longer bilaterally with member states.

This book explains some of the implications of the growing political and
economic strength of the Community and suggests ways in which companies
might profit from them. The history of the Community is not written here but
the reasons for setting it up appear in *Box 1*.

Growth of intra-European trade

The next five years are important for British industry, and also for the European
Community. Both will survive, but will they prosper? Britain and the other

3

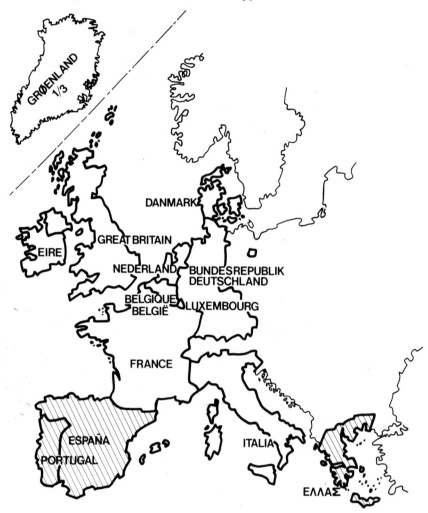

Figure 1 The Nine Member States are conventionally listed in alphabetical order according to the way they are spelt in their own language. Note Belgium is spelt in French and Flemish. Greenland is one-third of its actual size. The applicant countries Greece, Portugal and Spain are shaded. It has yet to be agreed where ΕΛΛΑΣ comes in the alphabet!

Community countries need to export to thrive, as foreign trade represents such a large proportion of their gross national products (GNP). This is not so much the case with 'continental' economies such as the USA, China, India and the USSR, although future energy requirements may change their relative lack of dependence on foreign trade.

As the economic battle for world markets becomes more fierce, an important trend is emerging: world trade is becoming more regional. Intra-European trade increases at a faster rate than its external trade. United Kingdom trade with the Eight is growing in value and volume each year and with France, Germany and Belgium, three of our largest world markets, it is increasing significantly. Current

Box 1

Lest we forget

Reasons for establishing the European Community

(1) Peace in place of war

Following two world wars, started in Europe, the main objective of the founders of the Community was to make war between its members impossible through growing economic and political interdependence.

(2) Political

In a world of super powers individual European states have lost the power and influence they once exercised separately. Only a Community of 260 million citizens carrying on 40 per cent of world trade and speaking with one voice, has sufficient influence and authority effectively to defend and promote the common interests of its member states.

(3) Economic

The progressive removal of tariff and other barriers to trade and the creation of a customs union help to reconcile conflicting economic interests and promote a common economic prosperity. The aim is to prevent the rise of economic nationalism which exacerbated the slump of the 1930s, led to totalitarian regimes, and ultimately to the Second World War.

(4) Defence of democracy

Out of over 140 member states of the United Nations, about 25 are still parliamentary democracies. Seventeen are in Europe and nine form the European Community. The development of the Community into a parliamentary democracy itself will defend and strengthen democracy amongst its member states.

patterns of trade are moving largely in the United Kingdom's favour. This is encouraging as we will only continue to compete in third markets if we can compete with the best products on the Community home market. If a company cannot export successfully to Germany, how can it hope to compete with German products in Kuwait and the Gulf?

Slowness of UK industrial response to the European Community

British industry is largely in favour of the United Kingdom developing as a strong industrial power within the European Community. The Referendum of

Box 2

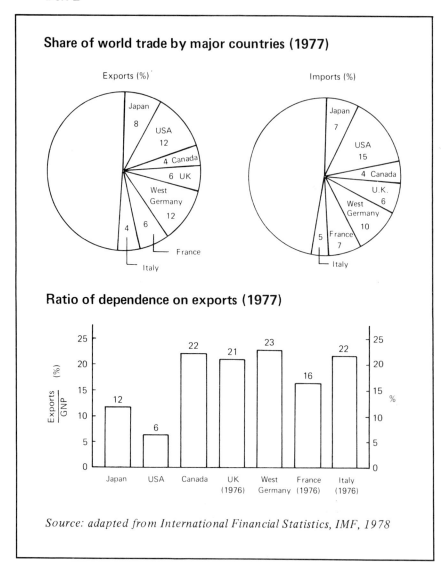

Share of world trade by major countries (1977)

Exports (%)

Japan 8
USA 12
4 Canada
6 UK
West Germany 12
France
Italy
4
6

Imports (%)

Japan 7
USA 15
4 Canada
U.K. 6
West Germany 10
France 7
Italy
5

Ratio of dependence on exports (1977)

Exports/GNP (%)

Japan 12
USA 6
Canada 22
UK (1976) 21
West Germany 23
France (1976) 16
Italy (1976) 22

Source: adapted from International Financial Statistics, IMF, 1978

1975 also showed that nearly 70 per cent of the votes cast were for continued membership. Why then is there relatively little effort, by so many companies, in developing European operations?

While some companies have taken Europe seriously, others have simply paid lip service to the concept of a home market of 260 million people. How many companies can claim to have developed a European awareness in their managers and work force comparable to the importance they believe the Community will

Box 3

Industry's view of the Common Market

Ninety-two per cent of British industrialists are in favour of the United Kingdom's remaining in the European Community. Only one per cent are decidedly against. Thirty-one per cent of industrialists believe that UK withdrawal would lead to greater unemployment in the country.

Source: Daily Telegraph poll of 217 large manufacturing companies, 12 September 1977.

have in the future? Industry must decide on the level of this importance and then inject a corresponding level of effort into developing European operations. This holds true not only for British and other Community companies, but also for those companies outside which trade or invest in the Community. It is, after all, the largest trading bloc in the world and it speaks increasingly with one voice in external trade matters.

Companies need to take the Community seriously at a number of different levels. Too often there is only one Community expert or enthusiast in an organization. Often, development of a company strategy towards the Community is postponed while priority is given to tactical decisions such as whether to put up a factory in Brazil or add another production line to the Belgian subsidiary. If the European Community develops into a home market of 300 million consumers when Greece, Portugal and Spain join, then British companies need to concentrate their production activities in more than one-sixth of it. They cannot afford to have 50 salesmen operating in the UK for every one in other member states. If the European Community is merely an export market like Brazil, then what are its advantages and disadvantages compared to Brazil? There should be some criteria for developing one market rather than another.

International business

Business is difficult enough without having to become involved abroad, unless absolutely necessary. Yet for many companies it is becoming very desirable. The attraction of the Community is that it offers markets with long-term potential, markets which will be less volatile than most in the world during the next twenty years.

To do business successfully a company requires to begin with:

(1) Competitive products;
(2) A good marketing organization;

(3) Reliable sources of information;
(4) A sound strategy for the development of its business.

To succeed in the European Community, it also needs:

(5) A European awareness and competence among its key executives.

Managers do not need to study in too much detail how the European Community operates, or what are the effects of its policies, any more than they need
to know in great detail about national governments and policies. However, they
should be aware of a wide range of Community policies that might affect their
companies' strategic decisions and have specific knowledge about Community
legislation affecting their industry.

The problem is to ensure that a company has the right information, at the
right level, at the right time. An awareness of the broad outlines of competition
policy, for example, is desirable for all managers who contribute to European
operations, however indirectly. They should have sufficient knowledge to brief
outside experts, to enable them to learn and to develop new ideas in a European
context.

Bibliography

Commission of the European Communities UK Office
   European Community. A monthly magazine covering all aspects of the
   European Community, and also political and cultural developments related
   to European unity
   Facts and Figures. A general brochure setting out the aims, institutions and
   policies of the European Community
   Finding out about the European Community. A brief guide to the sources of
   information
   Uniting Europe: A Brief History of European Integration. A pamphlet
Sampson, A. (1968). *The New Europeans*, London: Hodder & Stoughton
Shonfield, A. (1973). *Journey to an Unknown Destination*, London: Penguin

2 The decision-making process : the relationship between the Commission and the Council of Ministers

The Common Market is a process, not a product
Jean Monnet

The key to understanding how the Community works is the relationship between the two major institutions. The *Commission* makes proposals for European laws and the *Council of Ministers* decides whether to accept or reject the proposed legislation. Although the Commission is the only institution which can propose legislation, it can never become law unless the Council of Ministers agrees. The relationship between the two institutions is therefore fundamental to the decision-making process in the Community.

Box 4

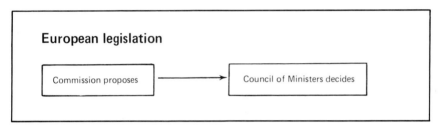

The Commission

Many of the functions of the civil service are performed by the Commission which is also responsible for policy formation, acting as a mediator between the governments of the Nine and executing agreed policies. The Commission staff is headed by thirteen commissioners. Each commissioner is appointed jointly by Member Governments for a renewable four-year term. Senior politicians, or other influential personalities, are usually appointed. In practice, two come from each of the larger countries of the Community and one from each of the others. Commissioners are each responsible for a number of departments known as Directorates-General (see Chapter 3), but they are collectively responsible for proposals put forward to the Council of Ministers. If they cannot reach agreement then they make decisions by a simple majority vote.

Box 5

Special responsibilities of the Members of the Commission

President:	Roy Jenkins	Secretariat-General Legal Service Information Spokesman's Group Security Office
Vice-Presidents:	François-Xavier Ortoli	Economic and Financial Affairs Credit and Investments Statistical Office
	Wilhelm Haferkamp	External Relations
	Finn Olav Gundelach	Agriculture and Fisheries
	Lorenzo Natali	Enlargement Protection of the Environment Nuclear Safety Contacts with Member Governments and public opinion on preparation for direct elections to the European Parliament
	Henk Vredeling	Employment and Social Affairs Tripartite Conference
Members of the Commission:	Claude Cheysson	Development
	Guido Brunner	Energy Research, Science and Education Euratom Scientific and Technical Information Common Research Centre
	Raymond Vouel	Competition
	Antonio Giolitti	Coordination of Community Funds Regional Policy
	Richard Burke	Taxation Consumer Affairs Transport Relations with the European Parliament
	Étienne Davignon	Internal Market Industrial Affairs
	Christopher Tugendhat	Budgets and Financial Control Financial Institutions Personnel and Administration

---

The President of the Commission is the most powerful permanent job in the Community. Roy Jenkins who was appointed in 1977 is responsible for sharing out portfolios among five vice-presidents and the other commissioners. Commission officials can be visited to discuss business in the same way as officials in

Figure 2 The seats of European power. The main Commission building, the Berlaymont, is the X-shaped building on the right. The arrow-shaped Charlemagne building on the left is the Council of Ministers

Box 6

Solemn declaration made by commissioners before the Court of Justice

I solemnly undertake:

To perform my duties in complete independence, in the general interest of the Communities;

In carrying out my duties, neither to seek nor to take instructions from any Government or body;

To refrain from any action incompatible with my duties.

I formally note the undertaking of each Member State to respect this principle and not to seek to influence Members of the Commission in the performance of their task.

I further undertake to respect, both during and after my term of office, the obligations arising therefrom, and in particular the duty to behave with integrity and discretion as regards the acceptance, after I have ceased to hold office, of certain appointments or benefits.

government departments in the United Kingdom, the United States or many other countries. The Commission buildings are in Brussels, close to, but separate from, the Council of Ministers.

The Commission is the European conscience of the Community. Officials make proposals in the interests of the Community as a whole and not in the interests of their own nationality. The two British commissioners have good formal and informal contacts in the United Kingdom which they will use extensively, but they do not represent British interests in the Community any more than the German commissioners represent German interests. Commissioners are sworn in before the Court of Justice (see Chapter 6), and promise to act in the interests of the Community as a whole.

Policies are not conceived in a bureaucratic vacuum. The Commission seeks to propose legislation that will help develop the Community along the lines laid down in the founding Treaty of Rome, and which has a reasonable chance of being accepted by the Council of Ministers. Suggestions for developing policies come from industries, trade associations, pressure groups, member governments and in particular from the four-monthly Council meetings of the heads of state of the Nine (Chapter 6). If broad agreement is reached at a *European Council*, as these meetings are called, it suggests there is a good chance of detailed legislation on the subject being agreed by the Council of Ministers.

Box 7

How many Eurocrats in Brussels?

'The Commission staff is smaller than that of the Wandsworth Borough Council.'
Commission President Roy Jenkins, in the second Sieff Memorial Lecture, at the Royal Institution, London, on 24 November 1977.

'In 1977 there were just over ten and a half thousand Commission staff, compared to about two million central government civil servants in the United Kingdom and 330 000 in Ireland. Over the last three years the United Kingdom civil service has grown at an annual average of 7 per cent, while the Commission – from a vastly lower base, and in an expanding field – has grown by 3.8 per cent. Moreover, within the Commission, under half (5262) are administrative civil servants, as they would be conceived in Britain. 30 per cent of the staff are translators and interpreters, and the rest engaged on scientific research. In short, the numbers are tiny.'

Roy Jenkins, speaking in Edinburgh on 2 March 1978.

As well as specific proposals for legislation, the Commission also sends official communications and guidelines to the Council on a wide range of subjects. The 'Eurocrats' in Brussels, as the popular press calls them, are mostly officials of the Commission. There are in fact relatively few of them — only about 10 000 — of whom the large majority are interpreters, translators, secretarial and administrative staff. There are only about 300 out of 800 senior officials who might need to be contacted for business reasons, and they work in one of the twenty-three Directorates-General and other services which correspond to government departments at the national level.

Box 8

The Commission

Makes policy proposals after consulting experts and interested parties;
Mediates between governments of the Nine;
Carries out policies once agreed by Council of Ministers.

President: (currently Roy Jenkins) is one of the 13 commissioners from the Nine Member States
800 senior civil servants
10 000 total staff

The European conscience of the Community
Multinational, multilingual
Career service but top jobs still tend to be government nominees.

The Council of Ministers

If the *Commission* is the European conscience of the Community, the *Council of Ministers* is the guardian of the interests of individual member countries. A Commission proposal can only become law when all nine governments agree through their representatives at the Council of Ministers.

The Council consists of a minister from each member government, and the ministers change according to the subjects on the agenda. If the proposed legislation deals with transport, then the nine ministers of transport make up the Council; if energy, then the ministers for energy. Ministers represent the interests of their own governments, but try to arrive at agreements which are in the Community interest. When the media suggest, for example, that France or the United Kingdom is blocking a certain proposal, this probably means that a French or UK minister is preventing, on instructions from his government, the proposal from being accepted until satisfactory amendments are made to it.

Voting must be unanimous, although there have been times in the past, and there will almost certainly be renewed demands in the future, for some form of majority voting as provided for in the Treaty. There are, of course, inevitable trade-offs behind the scenes, when one country gives way on one proposal in return for agreement on another. This bargaining procedure is not new and occurs at national and local government levels in most countries. On important subjects, however, it seems unlikely that national governments will give up their effective power of veto in the foreseeable future.

The Council of Ministers meets only for a certain number of days during the year and for the rest of the time the ministers concerned go about their business in the capitals of the Nine. The ministers, unlike the commissioners, are not resident in Brussels and only go there for meetings. Each country takes a six-month turn to chair Council meetings. The minister of foreign affairs is President of the Council during this period. Three commissioners sit in at the Council

Box 9

The Council of Ministers

Guardian of the interests of individual states
One minister from each Member State
Effective veto on Commission proposals
Makes laws by deciding on Commission proposals

Its President is the Foreign Minister of a member state on a six-month rotation
The nine minister members change depending on subject
COREPER — ambassadors of the Nine prepare agenda aided by small permanent Secretariat of the Council

of Ministers to explain proposals when called upon to do so. When the Council is not in session, its meetings are prepared by a small permanent staff, resident in Brussels and located in the Council of Ministers building. The main preparatory work and initial negotiations are carried out by the ambassadors of the Nine accredited to the Community who, with their embassy staffs, are resident in Brussels.

The ambassadors, or representatives as they are called, act as a link between the member countries and the Community. They meet in the Committee of Permanent Representatives (called COREPER) to prepare the agendas for the Council of Ministers and to agree, in advance of the Council meetings, many of the non-contentious proposals which have been put forward by the Commission. They draw up points of difference and agreement on subjects so that when the ministers of the Nine attend Council meetings much has already been agreed and only points still in dispute need to be negotiated.

Box 10

A day in the life of COREPER deputies

Wednesday 10.20. We start our weekly meeting with our Chairman telling us how long we are to work today, what is coming off our agenda because it is not ready, what is essential and cannot be deferred, what sequence we are to follow (so that our helpers can be programmed) and whether he wants to see us for a private meeting on something sensitive.

Our first task – a collection of points, which not being in dispute amongst us can be put down for ministers to adopt without discussion, unless they decide that they need discussion in which case they will come back to us for substantive preparation. We call them 'Part I' points. On Council agendas they appear as 'A points'. Various reservations are expressed but we do not discuss in detail because we are not ourselves prepared. Only points free of reservations – now or later – go forward.

Other business. Time for the Commission or member states to say what they want to be taken later today or on a future agenda. Time to lay down markers about things that are beginning to cause trouble and may need to be done or undone. At this stage we only flag them. Whoever raises them will have a chance later in the day to develop his thoughts on them.

And so on to the main fare. Half a dozen or more subjects which will occupy us until late this evening. Some will be near agreement and need a further push if they are to go through. Some are far from agreement, are brutally jammed, and the question for us is whether they will come out. If collectively we want them to, we will have to find the formulae that resolve our differences.

For each item we have a change of cast. A new team of Commission officials and a new scribe from the Council Secretariat slip into the seats labelled for them and a new helper who knows the subject ranges himself beside each of us. The Commission people defend their propositions, where they have come under attack, but may also show readiness to accept changes in the interest of getting a measure of what they believe in. We, around the table, speak to our instructions. We may expostulate, criticize the Commission or each other, temporize, even filibuster. Some of us, interests not deeply engaged, may more or less switch off and be ready to accept any outcome, or none. Some may try their hands at broking between opposing views – some have high reputations in this art. But this is above all the task of our Chairman. His task is to identify precisely what we are divided upon and then to see how he can narrow the differences. We do not vote because we have no mandate. Our Chairman works for consensus. When he has heard – with patience – what we have to say, he puts to us ways in which we might reconcile our positions. Aided by the Council Secretariat man – who knows the history inside out – he tries out new drafts upon us, or makes procedural suggestions, or seeks to persuade us that we have got it wrong. He marshals majority views or what he may describe as near unanimity. He addresses appeals to those who remain obdurate. Or he says that we all need more time and will come back to it in a week or two, when (he may add) he is confident that we will all be able to show more flexibility. Or he may say that after all it is not ripe and needs more work by the experts in our delegations. Or that it cannot wait any longer and will go very quickly to ministers for them to give political decisions or other impetus – and in submitting it

continued

to them he will also sketch out solutions which seem to him to emerge from our discussion but to which none of the rest of us are committed. This will be the time-honoured 'Presidency compromise'.

For our part we may be able — especially if we have not done well in the argument — to say that we will get it looked at again. Or we may say that there are sticking points which it is no good trying to get away from. Or we may ask if anybody seriously minds there being no decision at all. We may also, within our instructions, find that there are ways of coming to terms either now or *ad referendum*. Joy of joys, we may even find that something on which we thought we were weak corresponds to what everybody else thinks and we may make the quick kill. Less agreeably, deadlock may ensue but cannot be left thus and we leave the subject for the next, knowing that we must come back to it in seven (eight in French counting) inexorable days. If so, it may be time to set out the con-cessions which would have to be made to bring us round, or the con-cessions which are not available for us to make. The conditions that will have to be respected, the linkages that will have to be maintained, the timetables that we cannot depart from, the statements that our Minister will utter when the question comes to the Council.

Any little local alliances formed upon the matter we have just discussed dis-band themselves quietly. We come on to the next and all bets are off. The roles change. Some who did not care on the last item now become noisy participants in the next, and some who were in the middle of it coast along, perhaps taking the oppor-tunity of a quick word with their helpers on what to do about the pre-ceding discussion — how to report it with sufficient precision and brevity and whether to suggest new lines of thought.

The style is distinctive. Lengthy interventions sometimes piling upon each other without much common ground in them and little dialectic. Points often left hanging because nobody terribly wants to tackle them and to face all the implications of doing so. Much verbalizing as dele-gate and Chairman try to state points with precision (itself sometimes hindered by language problems). A good deal of reference to legal (or as the Anglophones say 'legalistic') mat-ters in support, or otherwise, of con-tentions. But the process is the same as happens in any collective — a Christmas club or a municipal autho-rity.

We start by seeing if we fully under-stand each other, preferably by writing down what we are talking about and agreeing that that is what we are talking about. We then estab-lish whether we agree on what we want, or are prepared to say if we do. In this we include how badly any of us want it. If we do not agree on what we want, we then ask ourselves whether there is an alternative that some, most or all of us want. We find this alternative if there is one, by suc-cessive approximation. We go over and over the ground sometimes led by a bright idea, sometimes toiling on. If there is an alternative — and there may not be one that we can or want to find — we again write it down as our text. Depending on the case, it may be a lapidary formula-tion in the light of which we all know exactly where we stand. Or, in another case, it may be enveloped in ambiguity because we prefer to fight again another day, or hope that another day's fight may not after all be necessary. Most of the time, there-fore, we are engaged in what the Belgians (who have more experience of compromises than most) call the policy (or politics) of 'little steps'. We would like to think that they are always forward but there may be dif-ferences of outlook regarding what is the front and what the back.

Bill Nicoll, Deputy Permanent Representative of the United Kingdom Representation (UKREP), October 1978

Even though the bulk of legislation has been agreed beforehand, for legal and constitutional reasons it still has to be placed before the Council of Ministers before it becomes law, and the first part of the agenda consists of a large number of agreed matters which are taken as so-called 'A' points. Unless any minister wishes to contest them, they are agreed automatically at the beginning of the meeting. Thus, for example, a proposal that flashing warning lights be fitted as standard to all European cars built after 1979 might be accepted by the ministers without debate as car manufacturers, consumers, government departments, interest groups, trade associations and other interested parties have all agreed to the legislation beforehand. Only a rubber stamp is required. An agreement on maximum axle weights for trucks might not be so easily agreed, and consequently the ministers of the Nine will debate the position and negotiate any trade-offs. Debate is invariably tense as neither non-contentious proposals, nor proposals that clearly would not have a chance of being accepted, are brought to the negotiating table; also important national interests are often at stake.

UKREP

It is possible to visit the embassy of the permanent representative and talk to the staff of the UK Representation (UKRFP), as it is called. The staff has experts seconded from UK government departments and elsewhere, and they represent Britain in day-to-day relations with the Council and the Commission.

UKREP is different from the British Embassy in Brussels whose ambassador is accredited to the Belgian state and deals with bilateral affairs between Belgium and the United Kingdom. Before the Council meets to discuss a proposal, it has been thoroughly discussed not only by UKREP, but by the British government and Whitehall departments, so that by the time the Council comes to discuss a proposal there is a broad measure of agreement.   The Council also has the benefit of the opinion of the European Parliament and the Economic and Social Committee before beginning its deliberations (see Chapters 5 and 6).

As well as permanent representatives from each of the Nine, resident with their staffs in Brussels, at least 111 countries maintain diplomatic relations with the Community and most of them have offices in Brussels. It is possible for nationals of many countries in the world to meet the ambassador and his staff of their own country's mission to the European Community. The United States and Japan have well-staffed missions in Brussels. British businessmen are advised to contact UKREP, as its staff can provide contacts in the Community at every level, depending on the importance of the subject to be discussed. The most important contacts will probably be with officials in the Directorates-General of the Commission which is the subject of the next chapter.

Bibliography

Broad, R. and Jarret, J. (1972). *Community Europe Today,* London: Wolff
Noel, E. *How the European Communities Institutions Work*, Official Publication

3 The Directorates-General of the Commission

In 1977, the Commission put forward 609 proposals
to the Council, and answered 1013 written and 59
oral questions from members of the European Parliament. The Council held 64 meetings. The Parliament
held 13 plenary sessions, examined 252 session documents and voted 256 resolutions. The Court of Justice
dealt with 162 cases and made 118 rulings.

The Directorates-General of the Commission are where most can be learned
about Community policies affecting business, and where influence can be
effectively brought to bear on officials likely to be of assistance to a company.

One of the major omissions of businessmen in their relations with government,
and that includes the Community, is their failure to visit government officials. It
may seem obvious, but ask yourself when you last visited a government official
to discuss your business or, if you do so regularly, do your colleagues and subordinates? A businessman should also ask if his relationship with the government
is sufficiently well developed. Government involvement in business has been
growing for many years, yet many companies have been slow to recognise the
need to call on governments at all levels.

Box 11

The tasks of an EEC commissioner

The most important day in the week
of a European commissioner is
Wednesday. For that is the day when
he and his twelve colleagues meet —
usually both in the morning and in
the afternoon — to discuss and decide
Commission policy.

The main duty with which the Commission is entrusted by the Treaty of
Rome is to make proposals for Community action to the Council of
Ministers. Most of the discussion at
our meetings therefore — apart from
consideration of internal administrative problems — is about what those
proposals should be.

Each commissioner is given special
responsibility for particular areas of
Community policy and is placed in
personal charge of the departments
within the Commission (called
Directorates-General) which
specialize in those areas. But the
Treaty requires the Commission formally to agree as a body all the
decisions taken in its name. If, therefore, I wish an initiative to be taken
in one of the fields for which I am
responsible I must explain at a Commission meeting what I have in mind
and try to win my colleagues' assent
— indicated, if necessary, by majority
vote. Conversely, of course, the other

continued

commissioners have to try to win my backing for their proposals.

Much of my work between Commission meetings is spent discussing with my 'cabinet' or private office, with the staff in my Directorates-General and with outside experts and interest groups, the exact form and content of the policies which I intend to propose to the Commission in the months ahead.

But perhaps the most demanding of the duties incumbent upon a commissioner are those which arise not *before* but *after* he has had a proposal accepted by the Commission, when he endeavours to steer it successfully through the other institutions involved in the Community's decision-making process.

Nearly all proposals sent from the Commission to the Council are first forwarded to the European Parliament for its opinion. Commissioners therefore have to devote considerable time and effort to explaining and justifying their plans both to Parliament's specialized Committees, which usually meet in Brussels, and also to its plenary sessions, meeting either in Luxembourg or Strasbourg.

That done, a commissioner has to turn his attention to the Community's supreme decision-making body – the Council. In an effort to secure the unanimous agreement of the nine national ministers who make up the Council (any one minister can veto a Commission proposal) a commissioner will usually engage in protracted negotiations with them not only in formal Council sessions, held in Brussels and Luxembourg, but also in informal bilateral meetings in all the Community's national capitals.

Although the Commission has recently achieved some striking successes, it cannot be denied that the number of Commission proposals which the Council rejects or shelves indefinitely is currently very high, and this can make a commissioner's job, at times, a very frustrating one.

In my view, the best hope of increasing the success rate for Commission proposals lies with the Commission's fulfilling much more completely than at present a further task in addition to those I have mentioned. If commissioners are to persuade national ministers to adopt a more positive attitude towards the Community's development then they must be prepared more and more often to step robustly into the area of public debate and argue their case before the widest possible audience.

In the final analysis the conduct of the Community's national governments is largely determined by their perception of the attitudes and expectations of the national electorates to which they are accountable. What the Commission must try to do, therefore, is to explain to those electorates directly, by all the appropriate methods available to it, the substantial concrete benefits which Community action can bring them.

This of course is a political task requiring political skills – but then the Commission is and should remain a political body.

Christopher Tugendhat
EEC Commissioner responsible for
the European Budget, Financial
Institutions and Personnel,
October 1978

Visiting the Commission

Apart from being the conscience of the Community, the Commission acts as its principal information and public relations agent. A Commission official has three good reasons for spending time with visitors: to help them, to learn from them and to show that the Community has a human face. Bureaucrats in Brussels are only faceless to those who never visit them. From those who do, rarely is anything heard but praise for their helpfulness and their receptiveness to ideas.

Of course, not all businessmen can visit the Commission, but I suggest that you do, or that you designate a colleague. Of course, when the corridors of the Berlaymont are crowded with Community businessmen, the system will have to be changed, which will be done more gratefully by a Commission which felt it was more in touch with European business! If you live outside the Community, you should first visit your country's ambassador to the Community and his staff. They will have good contacts among Community officials and help you with any appropriate introductions.

Cabinets of commissioners

In most cases the best contacts are found in the twenty-three Directorates-General of the Commission. The commissioners themselves are always ready to receive senior businessmen who have important business to discuss, but as they have responsibilities and duties similar to ministers in national governments,

Figure 3 The thirteen commissioners. President Jenkins is on the right (high chair back) and clockwise the names are Messrs Noel (Secretary-General), Brunner, Tugendhat, Burke, Cheysson, Gundelach, Natali, Vouel, Davignon, Giolitti, Vredeling and Haferkamp. The Secretary-General of the Commission is on the left of the President. Some of the Chefs de Cabinet are at desks at the back. Interpreters are as usual in evidence behind the glass windows

Box 12

The Directorates-General of the Commission

The Commission is divided into 23 Directorates-General and other services each of which is sub-divided into a number of Directorates with responsibility for a specific area of Commission policy.

DG I External Relations
Director-General: Sir Roy Denman

DG II Economic and Financial Affairs
Director-General: Ugo Mosca

DG III Internal Market and Industrial Affairs
Director-General: Fernand Braun

DG IV Competition
Director-General: Willy Schlieder

DG V Employment and Social Affairs
Director-General: Jean Degimbe

DG VI Agriculture
Director-General: Claude Villain

DG VII Transport
Director-General: Raymond Le Goy

DG VIII Development
Director-General: Klaus Meyer

DG IX Personnel and Administration
Director-General: Pierre Baichère

DG X Spokesman's Group and Information
Director-General: Enzo Perlot

DG XII Research, Science and Education
Director-General: Günter Schuster

DG XIII Scientific and Technical Information
Director-General: Raymond Appleyard

DG XIV Fisheries
Director-General: Eamon Gallagher

DG XV Financial and Fiscal Institutions
Director-General: O Bus Henriksen

DG XVI Regional Policy
Director General: Pierre Mathijsen

DG XVII Energy
Director-General: Leonard Williams

DG XVIII Credit and Investments
Director-General: Antonio Nicoletti

DG XIX Budgets
Director-General: Daniel Strasser

DG XX Financial Control
Director-General: Carlo Facini

Legal Service
Director-General: Claus D. Ehlermann

Statistical Office
Director-General: Aage Dornonville de la Couz

Administration of the Customs Union
Director: Klaus Pingel

Environment and Consumer Protection Service
Director: Michel Carpentier

September 1978

their detailed knowledge of specific subjects must be limited. Many of their views, and those of the Commission, are regularly available in print. Representations on business matters put directly to them, either orally or in writing, will be taken up either by officials of a Directorate-General or by a member of the Commission Cabinet.

The 'Cabinet' system does not exist in the United Kingdom, although the growing use of advisers by ministers is perhaps a move in this direction. The system is well known in France and the United States. Each commissioner when appointed, chooses, for his cabinet and to work with him, a group of people who may be fellow countrymen and women. A Chef de Cabinet may be appointed from outside the Commission and, therefore, is not necessarily a career official.

The 'Chef de Cabinet' holds a powerful position. He is the chief executive assistant of the commissioner. He will often act on the commissioner's behalf and stand in for him at meetings.

Much of the negotiation with the Directorates-General will be carried out by the members of the Cabinet. They will write speeches, prepare drafts, accompany the commissioner on visits, and generally support the work in his sphere of responsibilities. They act as a filter for the commissioner and meet visitors in the same way as any other official of the Commission. It is therefore quite appropriate to call on a member of a Cabinet, who is often an effective substitute for the commissioner himself. Meeting commissioners, like meeting cabinet ministers, will on certain occasions be desirable, but often a meeting with a minister's civil servants, or in the case of the Commission, with members of the Directorates-General, might be equally useful for business purposes. In the Directorates-General there are individuals responsible for different areas of policy who will know most of what is likely to affect business in their subject area.

The Industrial Affairs Directorate-General

A director-general can in some ways be compared to the permanent head of a ministry. The Director-General of DG III, for example, is responsible for co-ordinating the internal market and industrial affairs. He works closely with the

Box 13

Responsibilities of Directorate-General III: Internal Market and Industrial Affairs

Director-General	Fernand Braun
Deputy Director-General (with special responsibility for coordination of regulations and standards)	Pierre Schloesser
Deputy Director-General (with special responsibility for coordination of sectoral measures)	Paolo Cecchini
Adviser	Piero Squartini
Assistant to Director-General	Helmut Schmitt von Sydow

continued

Administrative unit	Head
Directly attached to Deputy Director-General with special responsibility for coordination of regulations and standards	
Secretariat for internal and external work on raw materials	José Nicolai
Directly attached to Deputy Director-General with special responsibility for coordination of regulations and standards	Constantino Friz Chief Adviser
Directorate A	
Industrial affairs I (removal of technical barriers, mechanical engineering, motor vehicles, chemicals and foodstuffs)	Pierre Schloesser
Chief Adviser	
(1) Coordination of removal of technical barriers; motor vehicles and agricultural machinery; electricity, mechanical engineering, metrology and standardization	Jacques Faure
(2) Chemicals, plastics and rubber	Walter Schäfer
(3) Foodstuffs	Anthony Kinch
Directorate B	
Industrial affairs II (public contracts, electronics, data processing, telecommunications and aircraft)	Christopher Layton
Adviser	Leon Alexander Smulian
(1) Liberalization of public contracts; infrastructural industries (railways, telecommunications) and technological policy	Heinrich von Moltke
(2) Data processing and communications; electronics and allied industries	Christian Garric
(3) Aerospace	Ernesto Previdi
Directorate C	
Industrial affairs III (intervention, shipbuilding, textiles, paper and footwear and construction)	Daniele Verdiani
Adviser	Georg Pröpstl
(1) Safeguard measures, removal of non-tariff barriers	Alfonso Mattera
(2) Shipbuilding	Laurus de Jonge
(3) Textiles	Felix Trappeniers
(4) Wood, paper, leather, footwear and other products	Paul Gray
(5) Construction and building materials	Renato Caronna
Directorate D	
Approximation of laws and right of establishment and services	Ivo Schwartz

continued

(1) National law relating to companies and firms   Hermann Niessen

(2) European law relating to companies and firms; and multinationals   Karl Gleichmann

(3) Intellectual property   Bryan Harris

(4) Mutual recognition of diplomas, and access to and pursuit of non-wage-earning activities   Jean-Jacques Beuve-Méry

(5) Passport union, special rights and restriction on free movement of self-employed persons   Karl Heinz Massoth

Directorate E
Steel   Maurice Schaeffer

Chief Adviser   Hans Kutscher

(1) General objectives, forward programmes and market analysis, and crisis measures   Hans Kutscher

(2) Market rules and control reports   John Peters

(3) Production, supply and technology   Otto Becker

(4) Technical research programmes   Peter Rees Vaughan Evans

Directorate F
Commerce; small and medium-sized enterprises; pharmacy; commercial law and economic legislation   Dermott John Devine

(1) Commerce and distribution, and price legislation   Jacques Besnard (acting)

(2) Small and medium-sized enterprises, *artisanat*, and tourism   Peter John Lennon

(3) Pharmacy and economic legislation   Nicolaas Bel

(4) Commercial law, law of procedure, and private international law   Winfred Hauschild

(5) Product liability and fair trading   Hans Claudius Ficker

Directorate G
Industrial restructuring, non-member countries and raw materials   Eckehard Loerke

Special assignments relating to external contacts   Walter George Pacht
Adviser

(1) Industrial and technological problems in relation to non-member countries; industrial cooperation   Jean-Pierre Derisbourg

(2) Secretariat for internal and external work on raw materials   Jose Nicolai

(3) Industrial economy and coordination   –

Unit attached to DG III for administrative purposes
Business Cooperation Centre   Roger Peeters

Source: Directory of the Commission of the European Communities, September 1978. (Available from HMSO or Commission Sales Offices)

commissioners and in particular with the commissioner having special responsibility for industry (*Box 6*). The Directorate-General is divided into a number of Directorates each responsible for specific industries. For example, Directorate B of Industrial Affairs DG III deals with public contracts, electronics, data processing, telecommunications and aircraft — some of the advanced technology industries which the Commission believe should be helped to develop on a Community-wide basis. The director of this directorate, as you can see from *Box 11*, is Christopher Layton. A commission official who is a director would normally be an A2 grade official. A1 grades are director-generals and A2 and A3 grades are senior officials working for them. Most dealings will be with A2 to A4 grades who are the key administrative officials of the Commission. It may well be that for specialist or technical matters A5 and A6 grades are your contacts, or possibly certain B grades. Christopher Layton happens to be British, but those who work in his directorate come from a number of different Community countries. There is no particular advantage in meeting an official who is British, except from the point of view of language and culture, as all officials must take a Community-wide view of their work rather than a national one. The two principal languages of the Community are English and French and most officials speak one of these and many both.

It can be seen from *Box 13* that aerospace (in DG III, Directorate B,3) is dealt with by Ernesto Previdi who is Italian. In his department there may be two or three other officials, as well as some technical and clerical officers. The total numbers are very small, however, in comparison with those working in national governments on different aspects of aerospace. The Commission, therefore, only plays a coordinating and policy-making role. Much of the detailed information on which it bases its policies has to come from national administrations. Commission officials spend a great deal of time briefing and negotiating with national officials. Their task in communicating with national administrations is greatly helped by the nine permanent delegations to the Community described in Chapter 2.

Making contact with Commission officials

About three times a year the Commission produces a directory of its senior officials. *Box 14* is adapted from this directory. It can be obtained from Commission sales agents in about fifteen countries including the USA, Switzerland, Spain and Sweden, as well as direct from the office for official publications in Luxembourg. Details are in Chapter 28.

If a businessman's interests are general and strategic then he will probably want to see one of the listed officials in Brussels. If the interests are more technical and concerned with the application of, or possible timetable for, certain legislation for an industry, then it may be a different official that has to be seen. A telephone call to the key official dealing with particular interests will be as effective a way as any of obtaining a meeting with those who can help. The official will probably arrange a meeting with those colleagues involved in drawing up legislation for your industry. From the commissioner downwards it is unlikely that there are more than a dozen people in the Commission which a

Box 14

Contact with Directorates-General of the Commission

(1) Obtain up-to-date directory of senior officials of the Commission which is issued three times a year. If you are in constant touch with the Commission, obtain an internal telephone directory through a contact. Its circulation is restricted for cost rather than security reasons.

(2) Write to or telephone the official dealing with the subject you are interested in and set up an appointment. Ask him whether there are any of his colleagues it would be appropriate for you to meet at the same time.

(3) Alternatively ask the Commission office in London whether they can set up meetings for you. This is perhaps a better way if the nature of your enquiries requires you to meet a wide selection of officials, many of whom you do not know, or if you do not really know whom you ought to meet.

(4) If your enquiries are technical ones, or if the answers to them may require preparation, write beforehand setting out what you want to know: the official will be better prepared and may have some documentation available for you which will save time. There are many Commission documents which can be of practical value to businessmen but they are not all for sale because of constraints on time and printing. It is often possible to obtain a copy from the official concerned.

(5) Invite the Commission official to visit you in the UK and get him to meet some people from your industry. Commission officials have good travel budgets and respond readily to invitations.

company would find useful to contact on the problems of one industry, unless there were many aspects of Community policies affecting that particular business. In practice only one or two would need to be visited.

Offices of the Commission abroad

It has been suggested that a businessman meets the officials concerned with his area of interest. However, this is only necessary if there is specific business to

Box 15

A working day in the life of the Head of the London office of the Commission

07.30   collected by office car to meet Commissioner at London Airport;

08.30   Commissioner arrives: long conversation during traffic jams;

10.30   reach office: face reading pile of documents, some 10 inches high;

10.35   telephone call from angry British exporter seeking customs documents: re-direct him to the EEC Information Unit at the Department of Industry;

10.37   answer mail: enquiry from Cardiff office about replacement for office station wagon; two applications for jobs in the Community; one request for assistance to hold a regional policy seminar; one application for assistance in official visit to Brussels; one request from Brussels asking for further information about the state of ratification procedure of Mashrek agreements; six requests for appointments to discuss European monetary system proposal; 10 requests for miscellaneous publications.

11.00   dash to Civil Service College to lecture on the Community to a group of trainees;

1.00   lunch with BBC correspondent to discuss series of television programmes on European parliamentary elections;

2.30   appointment with American Professor to arrange visit to London office by 50 students;

3.30   meeting at Cabinet Office to discuss issues of current Community business which may cause embarrassment in the UK;

4.30   first screening of rough cut of film about the Community for distribution to schools;

5.00   visit from senior librarian to discuss whether his library could become a depository library for Community documents;

5.30   meeting with staff to discuss press releases and background reports to be issued during the week;

6.00   series of telephone calls from national newspapers asking for details of Commissioner's programme for the following day;

7.00   reception at the European League for Economic Cooperation;

8.00   dinner with Ambassador from one of the member states together with senior officials of the Foreign Office, etc.

11.30   collapse into bed.

Richard Mayne, October 1978

---

conduct, or if the intention is to influence Commission thinking or learn what projected, or so called 'pipeline', legislation is being considered. If the aim is general background briefing on what is happening in the Community, of concern to industry or commerce, there are more simple and cost-effective ways of doing this. First, there is a team of Commission officials in London, Washington and a number of other centres, one of whose tasks is to be well versed in latest Commission thinking. These officials spend much of their time briefing groups and interested individuals. For example, if a businessman wants to learn more about the way competition policy and industrial policy affect his business, then there are Commission staff available in London, Edinburgh or Cardiff to help, not to mention most European capitals and several non-European capitals. The addresses of these Commission offices are in Chapter 28.

The offices of the Commission are very useful sources for keeping in touch with affairs in the Community, not only through meetings with their staff, but through the publications they produce and their comprehensive libraries. However, the offices do not act as an official channel to the Commission. All normal trade and commercial representations should be directed through the various branches of the Department of Trade or the UK Representation in Brussels, or through similar departments in your country of residence.

Briefing in Brussels

Another option is Directorate-General X in Brussels, the Information Directorate-General and Spokesman's Group. It has a staff of officials responsible for disseminating oral, written and audio-visual information about the Community and its activities. It may be that a briefing from one of its officials for a businessman and his colleagues on a visit to Brussels could be appropriate. This can be arranged by contacting the London, or any, office of the Commission prior to the visit. The advantage of this approach is that it is an information visit and so the need to be briefed is not so important. Time with an official can be wasted by questions on a subject on which a visitor should have been previously briefed.

The Directorates-General, therefore, have a special importance for those who need to learn how the Community may help them to do their business. The involvement of business in Community matters is well developed in some ways, but in others there is still too strong a tendency to transact business at a distance. If more time was spent by companies in cultivating Commission and other Community officials it could not fail to be good for the Community and for business.

Bibliography

Wallace, H., Wallace, W. and Webb, C. (eds.) (1977) *Policy-making in the European Communities*, London: Wiley

4 Community law: Regulations, Directives and Decisions

Community law has precedence over national law if there is a conflict. It stems
either from the treaties themselves, on which the Community is legally based, or
on subsequent derived legislation which is known as secondary legislation and
appears in the form of regulations, directives or decisions. It is not necessary for
a businessman to be familiar with the Community treaties, although he should

Box 16

The instruments of Community Law; Regulations, Directives and Decisions

Primary legislation of the European Community is embodied in the three treaties, the EEC, the Euratom and the European Coal and Steel Community treaties.

Secondary legislation is derived from the treaties through regulations, directives and decisions which are proposed by the Commission and approved by the Council of Ministers.

Regulations or Community laws are legally binding on member countries and are applied directly like national laws. As in the case of any Community law having direct internal effect, in any conflict with national laws, regulations prevail over the national laws of Member States.

Directives are equally binding on member states as regards the aim to be achieved, but leave national authorities to ensure that they are strictly and fully implemented, where necessary, by national legislation.

Directives mainly concern the business community as harmonization of trade and industry is achieved largely by means of directives.

Decisions deal with specific problems and may be addressed to an individual or a company as well as to governments. If addressed to individuals or companies they have direct internal effect and are binding in every respect.

Recommendations and opinions do not have binding force but indicate broad lines of current and future policies and therefore need to be monitored if they concern your industry.

European Coal and Steel Community terminology differs somewhat and if you are involved in these industries you need to know what these differences are. Obtain a copy of the ECSC Treaty from HMSO or ask your nearest Commission office.

be aware in general terms of the powers of the Community to regulate and develop policies which might affect him. This is particularly the case with competition policy, which is described below in Chapter 14, and is one of the policy areas where the Commission has effective powers and can punish companies by heavy fines for infringement of the rules.

There is sometimes confusion about the difference between regulations, directives, decisions and recommendations. This is not helped by the complication of having not one treaty setting up the European Community, but three, nor by the fact that different words are used in two of these treaties for the same type of legislation! *Box 16* gives a definition of the different types of secondary legislation. When in doubt, use 'directive', as most legislation affecting business comes from the European Community in that form.

How a directive becomes law

Directives are laws of the Community, but it is up to individual governments to lay down how they are implemented and to introduce, where necessary, national legislation to ensure that they are. It is useful to know how a directive becomes

Box 17

An open-ended directive on the environment

Of the numerous directives already adopted, one in particular is worth taking a closer look at because of its implications for the environment.

In July 1976 the Nine adopted a directive restricting the marketing and use of certain dangerous substances and preparations. This directive prohibits the marketing and use of these substances in certain products where their use would be dangerous to health or the environment – for example, it bans the use of vinylchloride monomer (a well-known cancer-causing agent) as a propellant in aerosols and prohibits the use of other chemical pollutants.

The importance of this directive is that it is 'open-ended' and other pollutants and dangerous substances can be added to it at any time.

Source: European Community

---

law because a company may need to monitor the progress of directives and influence, directly or indirectly, the way in which they are drawn up (see Chapter 10).

Preparatory work on a directive, for example windscreen wipers for cars, begins in the appropriate Directorate-General. The staff of the Directorate-General will consult with member states through the offices of the permanent representatives of the Nine in Brussels. It will also invite representatives of the national civil services or governments to committee meetings in the Commission. National and European trade associations will also be consulted, and indeed any individual who might be interested in the subject or have a contribution to make. Therefore, the draft directives drawn up in a Directorate-General and put to the commissioners for approval almost always have to take into account the views of member governments and the relevant industries in their countries.

Box 18

Beating tax evasion — a draft directive

To improve efforts at beating international tax evasion, the European Commission has submitted a draft directive to the Council to extend cooperation between tax authorities over VAT collection (similar to cooperation over income tax collection). Three factors have led the Commission to propose these measures: the increase in illegal practices affecting VAT in international trade; the need to avoid double taxation or non-taxation which results from current VAT legislation; the possibility of using such cross-checking to improve collection of income and profit taxes.

Source: Euroforum, Feb 1978

If the commissioners approve of the draft, or after any amendments have been made, it is then proposed by the Commission as a draft directive to the Council of Ministers, thus giving to member states, through the Council of Ministers, the final say on whether the directive becomes law or not. The preparation time for directives can be very short, but in many cases it takes years before proposed legislation is finally accepted and becomes law. Therefore, there is usually plenty of time to make industry's views heard, provided there are good monitoring systems in existence. It pays to have a good system to keep ahead of the competition.

European legislation is rarely, and should never be foisted on industry without warning. The Department of Trade in the United Kingdom regularly publishes lists of directives both those accepted and those in the 'pipeline' (see *Box 70* for an example). Companies can therefore easily monitor the progress of legislation likely to affect them. They can also obtain clear advance information on which to base their own strategies and make any necessary production or marketing changes. Reliable information can be very useful, especially at the 'pipeline' stage when there is still time to influence proposed legislation. For instance, a company developing a new headlight system for trucks will want to know at the earliest possible moment what legislation is planned, even if it is being thought about only in a very general way by the Commission.

Box 19

Canards de Bruxelles

Brussels

Is the EEC Commission in Brussels
made up of fools bent on destroying
the British way of life? In recent
weeks British newspapers have reported that the Commission is trying to
stop British fish-and-chip shops using
traditional vinegar; that it wants to
put an end to Britain's daily milk
deliveries; and that it is trying to
enforce metrication. All quite un-
true; but these stories are widely
believed. Even Mr Jo Grimmond, the
former Liberal leader, got taken in
last year. He wrote to Mr Roy
Jenkins, the President of the Commission, to complain about a number
of EEC directives – most of which
did not exist. One of his grumbles
was that in Orkney the EEC was
making farmers pasteurize their milk.
In fact the culprit was British legislation.

When *The Economist* published an
April-fool story this year suggesting
that the Commission was planning to
harmonize birth rates in the EEC, it
was widely repeated as gospel truth.
It seems that people are prepared to
believe almost anything of those
Brussels bureaucrats. Part of the
reason is the technical nature of
much of the Commission's work,
which generates suspicion through
obscurity. British anti-market ministers such as Mr John Silkin do not
always try hard to put the record
straight.

The EEC could do with a far more
aggressive public relations effort.
There are plenty of selling points
which would be helpful in Britain.
The Commission's efforts to cut the
price of wine and air fares are just
two recent examples.

Source: The Economist, 17 June 1978

The Official Journal

When the Commission proposes legislation to the Council of Ministers, it is
printed in the 'C' series of the Official Journal of the European Communities
(see Chapter 30). The opinion of the European Parliament and the Economic
and Social Committee are sought by the Council (see Chapter 5) and the normal
procedure is then for the proposals to be considered by the Committee of
Permanent Representatives (COREPER). If the proposals are technical ones,
special committees of the Council are set up. They are manned by specialist
civil servants from the Member States and only then referred to COREPER.

Community legislation

The Commission continues to be involved in the negotiation procedure. It has
the right to amend its proposals at any time before they are finally adopted by
the Council. Commissioners sit in at Council meetings. (You can see them on
the lower left-hand side of Figure 4 of the Council of Ministers.) Once adopted

by the Council of Ministers the laws or instruments, as they are called, are published in the 'L' series of the Official Journal. This constitutes effective legal notification to the Member States or other parties concerned.

A good deal of proposed legislation is never accepted by the Council. This is most likely to happen when the Nine cannot agree and prefer to leave their disagreement in the anonymity of a committee rather than have it publicly

Figure 4 The Council of Ministers: The first Council of Ministers after the Community was enlarged from six members to nine.

announced by using a veto in the Council of Ministers. On the other hand, legislation can sometimes go through very quickly. In September 1977 the Commission proposals on a code of conduct for Community firms in South Africa were accepted by the Council very speedily and for those firms they have significant implications. Some large companies were not able to respond immediately to the code because their monitoring systems were not sufficiently developed to understand the implications of it.

Scrutiny of Community legislation by national parliaments

A question frequently asked is how Community legislation is scrutinized by national parliaments. In 1974 a Committee of both Houses of the British Parliament set up scrutiny committees to consider draft Community proposals. These committees report to their respective Houses and can recommend further parliamentary consideration and debate. The government will obviously be influenced by the strength of feeling in these debates, but in fact the last word on Community legislation, short of abrogation of the treaties by a national parliament, lies with the Council of Ministers at whose meetings the United Kingdom is represented by a Minister of the Crown.

The procedure has sometimes been criticized by British members of Parliament who feel that Parliament should have the final say. If all legislation enacted by the Council of Ministers had subsequently to receive the agreement of the Nine parliaments little would ever be achieved at the European level. The Community, like politics, is the art of the possible. Progress can only be made

Box 20

The Commission complains about delays in developing a united Community

'The Commission finds it unsatisfactory that under the present procedure, the long preparation required for directives at the Commission stage, during which every interest likely to be affected is consulted, does not prevent the re-opening of technical discussions within the Council, discussions which last several years on average . . . It is illogical and regrettable that proposals can be held up for years either because their examination in the Council has not even begun or because examination has been suspended without any final decision being taken. It is also unacceptable that the political will in favour of harmonization is held back by quarrels between experts.'

Source: Commission's 5-year plan for monetary and economic union, March 1978

---

pragmatically, by working gradually towards common goals and policies, moving forward where progress seems possible and holding back when it is not. It is generally only possible when the nine countries and interest groups within them are broadly in favour of the proposed legislation. Very little can be bulldozed through a reluctant Community by a minority of the Member States. Although the Parliamentary scrutiny system may not be perfect, the legislation which has emanated from Brussels has been broadly acceptable to the individual countries and has furthered progress towards a genuine Common Market, which remains the common aim of the nine countries.

Bibliography

Official Publications
   Bulletin of the European Communities. Monthly from 1968 to present

Bulletin Supplement. Irregular

European Coal and Steel Community, European Economic Community and European Atomic Energy Community. General report on the activities of the communities. Annual from 1967 to present

The Treaties Establishing the European Communities, Treaties Amending those Treaties, Documents concerning the Accession. 1973

5 The European Parliament and direct elections

It has been said that democracy is the worst form of
government – except all those other forms which
have been tried from time to time
Sir Winston Churchill, House of Commons,
November 1947

The direct elections to the European Parliament of June 1979 are a notable land-
mark in the turbulent history of Europe, and without precedent in the history of
the world. Voters in the Nine can now directly elect representatives to an international parliament. Although the Treaty of Rome provides for direct elections,
it is only now, 25 years later, that the political will exists to carry out its provisions. The European Parliament prior to direct elections had government-
nominated members chosen from the parliaments of the Nine. With direct
elections, it becomes larger and more representative. Its powers will develop, by
custom and precedent, if not by formal legislation and it will become in time
perhaps the most important institution of the Community.

Figure 5 The European Parliament's new Strasbourg seat. Luxembourg and Strasbourg are
the temporary homes of the European Parliament. Neither will give up its claim to be the
permanent seat. Brussels would be easier for members. Some favour the United Kingdom,
but whatever the final choice it will be difficult to make.

Figure 6 The European Parliament: An inside view of a Luxembourg session. President Jenkins of the Commission is addressing the Session. The commissioners have seats allocated on the floor of the Parliament to the right of the speaker

The rate of this development will depend increasingly on the will of the people of the Community rather than the wishes of the Member Governments. European members of Parliament will have more influence and the lobbying of European MPs will become a normal part of the European parliamentary process for individuals, companies and pressure groups.

How Parliament is organized

There are 81 UK members of the European Parliament out of a total of 410. Each represents an electorate of about half a million voters in a constituency which groups together about five neighbouring national constituencies. Although European MPs come largely from the traditional political parties, most of them will not have a dual mandate, that is sitting in both the national and European parliaments. The dual mandate is not legally excluded but political parties are discouraging or forbidding the practice which has proved so onerous to members of the previously nominated European Parliament.

Members do not sit or vote as national delegations but as European party groups. The manifestoes of the European parties proved difficult to draw up

Box 21

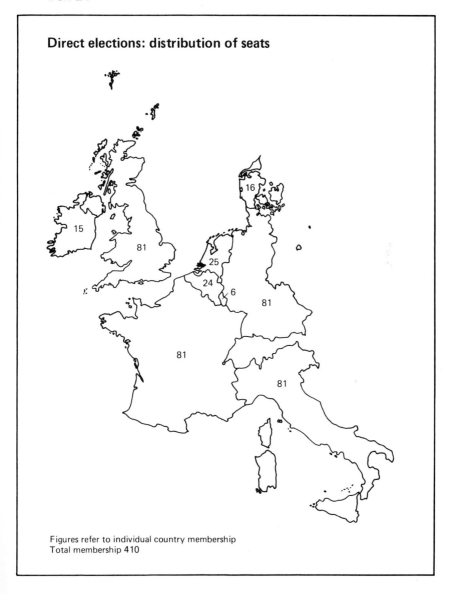

Direct elections: distribution of seats

Figures refer to individual country membership
Total membership 410

because of inevitable national differences of policy and the novelty of the idea. For example, the Christian Democrats have much in common with the Conservatives, but the religious base of the former make total unity difficult. The figure given next to the main political groups in *Box 22* is an estimate of the number of seats the parties would have obtained in 1979 based on 1978 voting patterns in national elections.

Box 22

The political groups and forecast strengths after direct elections

	Forecast
Communists	47
Socialists	131
Christian Democrats	103
European Progressive Democrats	29
European Conservatives	38
Liberal and Democrats	32
Other	31
Total	410

The political groups (1978)
Parliament sits in political
groups, not in national delegations:
Communists on the left, Liberals
on the right

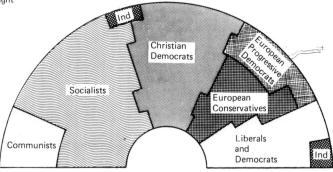

The Socialist group is forecast to be the largest but in practice the
political balance will depend on how the different groups work and
vote together. Where you sit depends on where you stand, but in a
European political sense not in terms of nationality.

Its powers

The powers of the European Parliament are developing steadily and depend very much on the political will of the Community rather than on formal rights based on the Treaty of Rome. Many of the innovations of recent years have established customs and precedents which will one day perhaps form the basis of a formal constitution. The choice facing the Nine, once having decided to go ahead with direct elections, was either to reform the European Parliament first or to elect members and let them become involved in the process. They wisely chose the latter course of action. Much now depends on the calibre and enthusiasm of the directly elected members. The European Parliament does possess, to some extent, the traditional powers of a democratic national parliament.

Traditional Parliament powers	*European Parliament powers*
To dismiss the government	To dismiss the 13 commissioners by a two-thirds majority, provided over half the members vote.
To vote funds	To have the 'last word' on about 20 per cent of the European Community budget allocation and to reject the budget as a whole.
To participate in law making	To give its opinion (not binding) on all proposals for European laws sent from the Commission to the Council. (The opinion has begun to have an indirect influence on the law-making process. The increasingly close cooperation of both the Commission and the Council of Ministers with the Parliament is of significance.)

How it functions: the process of consultation

The hemicycle of the Parliament has seats on the floor of the Chamber set aside not only for the commissioners who regularly attend sessions, but also for

Box 23

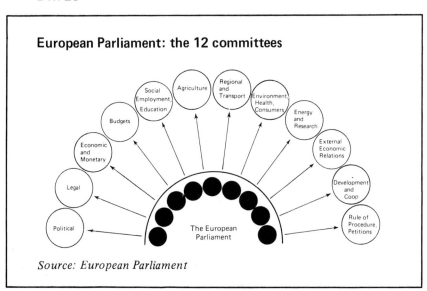

European Parliament: the 12 committees

Source: European Parliament

ministers and officials from the Council of Ministers. Commissioners answer oral and written questions about the work of the Commission and even take part in the discussions of the twelve committees through which the burden of the work of the European Parliament is discharged. The twelve committees (*Box 23*) scrutinize legislation proposed to the Council of Ministers by the Commission.

When a proposal goes to a committee, a 'rapporteur' or spokesman is appointed to prepare draft amendments and ultimately to draw up a final report which is debated in the Parliament. The debate on the formal report to Parliament may lead to further amendments and the commissioner responsible for the subject is usually asked to reply to the debate. The Council of Ministers is often represented and its representative also may speak. The procedure therefore provides much opportunity for formal and informal contacts between the members of the European Parliament, the Commission and the Council. The informal contacts can be very influential and play a significant part in developing the legislation which finally emerges from the Council of Ministers. The relationship of the European Parliament to the other institutions can be seen in *Box 30* in Chapter 6.

The effect of this process is that any legislation proposed by the Commission is scrutinized by a Parliamentary committee. In many cases it is debated and amended in the European Parliament before the Council of Ministers decides whether to agree to the legislation. The weakness of the process is that Parliament's role is advisory only and, legally, the Council of Ministers does not have to accept any proposed amendments if it does not want to. Nevertheless, Parliament's careful scrutiny of proposed legislation means that amendments proposed by Parliament receive careful consideration. Ove the next few years the directly elected Parliament is likely to push for more formal powers.

Parliament and the Commission in formal and informal contacts

Members of Parliament on Parliamentary committees spend a good deal of time with Commission officials. Most of the committee meetings take place in Brussels. The committees are therefore well informed about 'pipeline' activities of the Commission, and often see informal preliminary drafts and hear about proposed new legislation and policies at a very early stage. This pipeline information is important for relations between the two institutions and indeed of interest to anyone wishing to influence the way in which the Common Market operates. It will be too late if action is not taken until legislation is debated by the Council of Ministers or even until it is proposed formally by the Commission. If representations are to be effective they need to be made at the earliest possible stage. The Commission, of course, consults regularly with all interested parties before proposing legislation. But although only the Commission can propose legislation, other institutions can suggest to the Commission that such legislation is formally proposed. In this way Parliament has on occasions been

Box 24

A week in the life of a Member of the European Parliament

A quiet weekend in the constituency – I live there so don't have to travel to it. Saturday morning 9 a.m. to 2 p.m. spent in the constituency association office dispensing help and advice to twelve constituents who have taken the trouble to make an appointment to attend my 'surgery'.

Sunday evening by car to London, call in at the office where an enthusiastic supporter of the European Community wants my advice on whether he should apply to become a candidate for the direct elections.

On Monday, a very full day in 'the House'. Talks with 'Shadow' colleagues, attend two Party committees, give a mass of dictation to 'the girls', 'phone Luxembourg about that Opinion I must do for my Economic and Monetary Affairs Committee on Community textiles. Must stake a claim to a five-minute speech on 'The need for industry to know its war round the Community'. I'm deeply concerned at the way British industry seems to lose out, although its inevitable if they don't take the trouble to know the score. The Germans do, the French do, so must we.

I arrange to meet Geoffrey Howe to discuss the Draft 7th Directive on Value Added Tax. It's depressing how irrelevant Community legislation appears to some from Westminster.

Tuesday. Up at 5.30 a.m., taxi to Heathrow for first flight out to Brussels. At 9.30 a.m. begins the Economic and Monetary Affairs Committee meeting where I'm to lead a discussion on the Commission's proposed Rules for Imports of Textile Products (Doc. 304/78). The agenda is far too full and urgent discussions on EMS with Francois

Xavier Ortoli resulted in my item being deferred another week. EMS discussion is useful but despite intensive questioning I feel certain Ortoli could have revealed much more if he had dared. A private word later confirms this. I'm sure we have to join at the start, being faced with the certainty of Ireland breaking away from the Pound if we don't. What a sickener to see how the UK stands out as the anti-Market odd-ball and the split is just as bad among Labour MEPs as it is in the Parliamentary Labour Party, only the dirty washing look dirtier when washed in front of non-Brit MEPs and commissioners.

Just made lunch with the Director-General of DG XVII, under Finn Gundelach and a key man on the CAP. I need his advice on how Cheshire County Council might get a grant for the Agricultural College at Raeseheath. Most helpful but it's going to be very difficult to prove eligibility.

Had planned for a member of the Directorate-General for External Relations of the Commission to dine with me in the evening to discuss a detailed report I sent to President Roy Jenkins on my tour in the Far East. Unexpectedly he had to change the date because the ASEAN foreign ministers are assembling in Brussels for intensive discussions with the Commission.

Wednesday. Sit in at the Committee on External Trade to hear their views on the promotion of textile imports but must not vote. Extremely worried at unrealistic 'give it to them' attitude, trying to effect amendments to the Commission proposals. Failed, so will table in plenary debate a number of amendments. Work on

continued

two major papers to be presented in Madrid on Thursday.

Friday. Catch flight from Madrid to London and on to Manchester for an evening constituency event and for another 'quiet' weekend.

The day finally over I have some difficulty in getting off to sleep. Never take sleeping pills. Wondering where all this 'mad' way of life will end for me. Yet I am constantly driven by growing concern at the desperately dangerous situation of the Western World. 1937 was deadly and yet no one wanted to face the threats. 1978 is far worse and still no one wants to face the dangers. The only hope lies in speeding up the creation of greater cohesion within the Community and I suppose I can do as much or more than most to achieve this!

Saturday. Topping up my batteries by renewing my contact with people (as opposed to policies and papers). A rather sobering first visit to the Cheadle Hulme Amateur Dramatic Society – Sherriff's 'Journey's End', but not for me, yet, I hope!!

Tom Normanton, November 1978

the prime mover in legislation through what is known as an 'own initiative' report calling on the Commission to take action.

The informal links between the Commission and the Parliament are perhaps as important as those legally established by the Treaty of Rome. Both the Commission and the Council of Ministers have encouraged the growth of the indirect influence of the European Parliament. This is another example of how, given the political will of the Nine countries, significant progress can be made whatever the legal position.

When President Jenkins took office in 1977, one of his first tasks after taking the oath of allegiance before the European Court of Justice (see Chapter 6) was to present to the European Parliament the Commission's plans. His initial speech (almost like the Inaugural Address of the American President) and the subsequent detailed report which he presented, were debated in Parliament. Had Parliament so wished it could have censured the speech and hence indirectly the President and his fellow commissioners.

In fact Parliament has often threatened, but never actually used its power to dismiss the Commission. The reason for this is that members of the Community institutions see that their long-term objective is to make the imperfect mechanism work better and that this aim can best be achieved by a gradual process, by avoiding confrontation rather than by promoting it. 'Europe will be made by little steps' is the philosophy behind this pragmatic, rather than dramatic, approach to organizational development.

Current problems

The formal and informal support being given by the Community to the Parliament will make knowledge of its operations and contacts with its members valuable to companies wishing to influence and monitor the progress of European integration.

Parliament already has a number of important functions (*Box 25*), and direct elections have left its future role open. No-one can be quite sure how it will develop as an institution, but among its current preoccupations are:

(1) *Members of Parliament and direct elections.* Agreement on dates and procedures for direct elections has been a major pre-occupation of the last two

Box 25

The European Parliament

(1) Directly elected. 410 members. Each constituency has about half a million electors.

(2) Has twelve important committees which scrutinize Commission proposals and write reports.

(3) It debates proposed European legislation and proposes amendments.

(4) An advisory role only, except on about 20 per cent of the Community budget. It can reject the whole budget.

(5) Has the ultimate sanction of dismissing the Commission by a two-thirds majority.

(6) Has an informal influence at least as important as its formal powers.

(7) Given the political will, it could become the most important Community institution during the next decade.

years, and even fixing a date was a difficult negotiating problem. Members will be elected for five years in the first instance under national electoral laws. Only at the end of this five-year term will the Community decide on a common method for electing future members. The salaries of MPs also caused problems. Most countries of the Nine pay MPs on scales similar to senior managers and senior civil servants, but others like the United Kingdom pay on middle manager or skilled worker scales.

A European MP has to spend time in his very large constituency, at Parliamentary sessions in Luxembourg and Strasbourg, sitting on committees of the Parliament and making contacts with the Commission in Brussels and at the same time keeping in touch with his national Parliament and Party in the home country. The need to travel throughout the Community, and have a private life, make the job difficult.

(2) *Interpretation and translation.* In one way the European Parliament will never be like a national parliament. Because of the need for interpretation, it lacks the spontaneity and fire of national parliaments. It is difficult to encourage the cut and thrust of parliamentary debate when everything said has to be interpreted into six different languages and everything written has to be translated

Box 26

MPs' pay

	£
Germany	22 700*
Belgium	21 500
France	21 000
Netherlands	19 500
Denmark	11 800
Italy	10 500
Ireland	6 300
UK	6 300
Luxembourg	4 500

*Subsistence, secretarial, office, travel, post and telephone allowances are normally paid in addition.

Source: Hansard, 7 March 1978

before all present can understand it. Language is the greatest non-tariff barrier in the Community and a major obstacle to European unity. It is not possible to impose one language on everyone; Europe cannot be created by force. There would be considerable opposition if individuals were prevented from speaking and writing in their own languages. Much of the detailed legislation needs to be monitored and applied at quite junior levels within the administration of individual countries. It is therefore not possible to ask administrators to apply laws written in a foreign language.

Box 27

European Parliament: problems of simultaneous interpretation

Reproduced by permission of 'Punch'

The enlargement of the Community, to include Greece, Portugal and Spain, adds three more languages, making the problem much more serious. The lack of skilled interpreters and translators will slow the development of the Community at an official level, as well as at the level of industry, commerce and social affairs, and the problem will be with us for at least a generation. From a company point of view multilingual managers need to be trained or hired.

(3) *Where will the European Parliament sit?* Parliament currently moves between Luxembourg and Strasbourg. It needs a permanent home. Strasbourg is favoured by the French and the impressive, but according to some, impractical new building has sufficient space for 410 MPs and their support staff. The

Box 28

A new growth industry?

(1) The interpreter problem

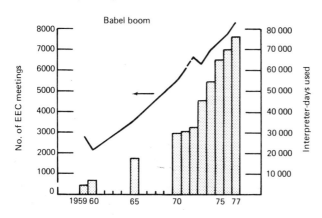

Babel boom

(2) Answer came there none

In an opinion poll* last year young people between 12 and 23 in three countries were asked if they could read a newspaper in another language. They replied as follows:

	None	English	French	German	Spanish	Italian	Others
Germans	53	45	14	–	0	0	3
British	68	–	24	6	1	0	2
French	55	28	–	8	10	3	2

Jugendwerk der Deutschen Shell, Vol 3, 1977

Source: The Economist, August 1978

continued

(3) Now six (occasionally seven) and soon nine Community languages

On formal occasions, Community officials like to use their native language. An Irish judge insisted on Court of Justice proceedings being translated into Gaelic. Irish Commissioners including the present one, Mr Burke, have taken the Solemn Declaration in Gaelic. This excerpt is a translation of Box 7:

mo dhualgaisí do chomlíonadh go lán-neamhspleach ar mhaithe le na Comhphobail:

ag comhlíonadh mo dhualgaisí dom; gan tréoir do lorg, nó do glacadh, ó aon Rialtas nó ó dhream ar bith:

staonadh ó gach bheart a bheadh contrártha le mo dhualgaisí.

Glacaim ar m'áird go foirmeáilte go bhfuil gach Ball-Stát tréis a thógaint air féin claoí lois an bprionnsabal so agus gan aon iarracht a dheanamh ar aon bhall don Choimisiún do chlaonadh ó chomhlíonadh a dhualgaisí.

Fos, glacaim orm féin, ar feadh agus tréis téarma m'oifige, go gclaoidfead le na dualgaisí a eiríos as an oifig sin agus, go sonnraitheach, na dualgaisí maidir le h-iompar cóir discréideach i leith glacadh le poist nó le cochair airitho tréis dom dul as oifig.

Box 29

Computerspeak

The EEC is now leading the world in developing a computer for translations. For the past two years the EEC's computer centre in Luxembourg has been running a pilot programme for French and English. The technology was originally developed by NASA in the United States for translating English into Russian in preparation for the Apollo space hook-up. But the Americans have abandoned this work, and the Europeans have taken over.

The EEC computer is already capable of producing a comprehensible translation, but is still too often baffled by ambiguities. In a recent test, it translated a name, Dr J. van Hoof, as 'le sabot de Dr J. van le camion anglais'. So after the computer has finished with a paper, a human translator has to revise it to eliminate the freaks. But for this he has to refer back to the original text, which can take as long as doing the whole job in the first place. Until the programming can be improved, using a computer for translating important papers is probably uneconomic. But it could soon be worthwhile for working documents, where precise phrasing is not essential.

The EEC has also created a 140 000-word computer bank for translating its own jargon. There are now 40 terminals in Brussels and Luxembourg where inquirers can tap out favourite phrases such as 'monetary compensatory amount' and get an instant rendering in any of the EEC's six languages from the computer. Human translators are finding it jolly useful. But cynics contend that much of the Euroslang, however perfectly translated, still remains incomprehensible.

Source: The Economist, 12 August

Parliament building in Luxembourg is not large enough and a new building is to be constructed. The environmentalist lobby has delayed its start. Many would prefer Parliament to sit in Brussels to save shuttling top level officials and businessmen repeatedly across Europe. There is also a lobby pressing for the European Parliament to be permanently established in London where dockland redevelopments will offer impressive sites near the centre of the City.

Individuals and companies wishing to increase their knowledge and further their interests in the European Parliament can do this directly through their local member of the European Parliament. Other possibilities are through the secretariat of a political group, through the chairman of an appropriate committee or by direct petitioning of the Parliament. Any individual or group can submit a petition to Parliament — even those from outside the Community if the matter is one over which the Community has jurisdiction.

(4) *The future.* The future development of the European Parliament is a key factor in the development of European unity. Its progress should be monitored carefully by interested individuals and companies. It is too early to say how much power it will have. The path leads into unmapped areas of man's search for new ways of living in changing societies. Oliver Cromwell wrote: 'he goes furthest who knows not whither he goes'. Both the certainty and the uncertainty of what he was referring to make it an appropriate comment on a Community institution which could make a united Europe or contribute to its slow decline.

Bibliography

Cocks, Sir Barnett (1973) *The European Parliament,* London: HMSO

Direct Elections to the European Parliament. Report of an all-Party study group commissioned by the European Movement. Study group rapporteur, Ben Patterson

European Parliament Publications
Committee Reports of the European Parliament. Working documents
European Integration and the Future of Parliaments in Europe, 1975
The European Parliament. A booklet
Official Journal of the European Communities: Debates of the European Parliament. Monthly

6 Other Community institutions: the Court of Justice, the Economic and Social Committee, the European Council

Individuals may form communities, but it is
institutions alone that can create a nation
Benjamin Disraeli, Manchester Speech, 1866

So far we have considered four of the Community institutions: the Commission, the Council of Ministers, COREPER (and UKREP) and the European Parliament. It is possible for companies to have both direct and indirect contact with officials, elected representatives or ministers who contribute to the functioning of these institutions. We will look more specifically at ways of making these contacts in Chapter 10. Good contacts and a clear understanding of roles and functions will make for better company strategy formation in a Community context. It will also enable individuals and companies to contribute to the development of the industrial and commercial policies of the Community.

This chapter considers the Court of Justice, the Economic and Social Committee and the European Council. Each plays an important part in the machinery of the European Community but it is the European Council which is slowly emerging as the key institution for making progress towards European unification.

The Court of Justice

The principal function of the Court of Justice is to ensure that European law is observed and interpreted uniformly throughout the Community. It is the ultimate interpreter of the Paris and Rome treaties on which the Community is based and the final arbiter of disputes concerning secondary legislation whenever there is a query or disagreement about the meaning of a particular regulation, directive or decision.

(1) Proceeding against states. If a member state does not fulfill its legal obligations, the Court has jurisdiction over the proceedings brought against that state by another member state, or more usually by the Commission. The Court, however, does not have powers to impose penalties on a member state. Like an international court, it can establish whether there is a breach of an obligation and if there is, request the state concerned to remedy it. As member states consider Community law binding, they always comply with requests from the Court. If they did not, it would imply that they had ceased to adhere to the European Community Treaty obligations, a right which every state reserves. In

Box 30

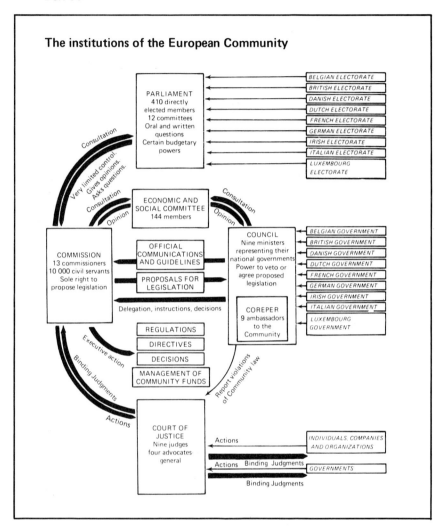

The institutions of the European Community

international law, a treaty is only binding as long as the signatories consider it binding. Although this right is reserved it would obviously be an historic act and a clear indication of change of policies if a state were to ignore the findings of the Court of Justice. The Court of Justice, which sits in Luxembourg, should not be confused with the International Court of Justice which sits at the Hague. The latter is a Court of International Law to which cases are voluntarily referred by countries who wish to resolve their legal differences. The former is the Court specifically set up by the Treaty of Rome to interpret the Community treaties and the secondary legislation derived from them.

52

Figure 7 The European Court of Justice. The Court sits at Luxembourg in a building inaugurated in 1973

Figure 8 A formal Session of the Court of Justice

(2) Review of the legality of Community acts. The Council of Ministers or the Commission can go to the Court if either of these institutions, or a member state, consider that legislation has been passed which is contrary to the letter or the spirit of the Treaties. In this way the Court is able to ensure that none of the institutions exceed their powers.

(3) Settling disputes. The Court is empowered to settle a dispute within the Community, where the dispute is covered by Community law. It rules on disputes between the Community institutions and the officials who work in them, and between individuals, companies or states in disagreement with rulings of the Community institutions. In most instances these disputes are settled between

Box 31

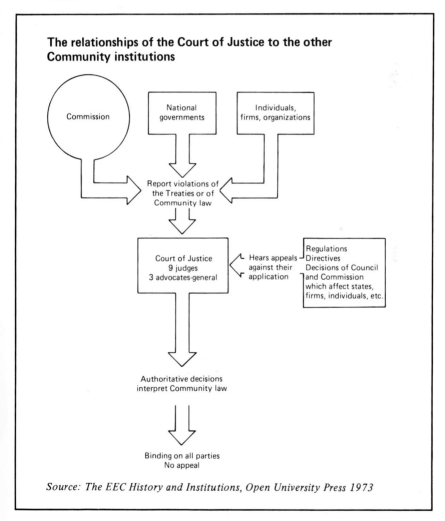

Source: The EEC History and Institutions, Open University Press 1973

the individual or organization concerned and the Community institution, but if they cannot be resolved then the Court acts as final arbiter.

In competition policy for example, the Court plays a major role. Fines imposed by the Commission can be contested and the case referred to the Court of Justice. Many cases are so referred and the Court's decision on the Commission's ruling is final.

(4) Preliminary rulings. The Court will also give, on request from national courts, a legal opinion on points of Community law. It is compulsory to request this opinion when the national court which is called upon to decide an issue of Community law is the court of final appeal on that issue.

(5) The organization of the Court. It consists of nine judges and four advocates-general. There is no official requirement for one judge to come from each of the Nine countries, but over time both they and the advocates-general will tend to come from different member states which gives a balance of nationalities.

In 1978, the Court sent to the Presidents of the Council and the Commission a memorandum which argued that in order to cope with its increasing duties, there needed to be staff increases and changes in structure. It suggested that the full Court need not sit on all cases but only on the more important ones. The number of judges, it proposes, should be increased from nine to twelve, and the advocates-general from four to six. The number of cases heard by the Court has risen considerably:

1957	19
1967	37
1974	110
1977	164
1978	156 (first six months only)

and the number of rulings:

1974	62
1976	88
1977	100
1978	60 (first six months)

The Court argues that the cases being brought before it are of increasing complexity as previous cases have already enabled a whole body of case law to be established.

From a business viewpoint it is unlikely that a company will need to be involved with the Court unless it is large and becomes involved in disputes with the Commission, for example, over aspects of competition policy. The legal foundation of the Community is fundamental to the development of an integrated and united Europe and in that process the Court of Justice plays a central role.

Box 32

Court of Justice cases

These four cases indicate the wide spread of actions before the Court. Nearly 160 cases reached the Court during the first half of 1978.

Case 140/78 – Commission v Italy

2.3.47. The Commission brought an action against Italy on 14 June for a declaration that that member state, by failing to submit in good time reports relating to the use of Community funds allocated to Italy under Regulations (EEC) No. 130/66 on the financing of the common agricultural policy and No. 159/66/EEC on supplementary provisions on the common organization of markets in the fruit and vegetable sector, had failed to fulfil its obligation under those regulations.

Case 141/78 – France v United Kingdom

2.3.48. On 14 June France brought an action before the Court of Justice against the United Kingdom. This is only the second time in the history of the Community in which a member state has instituted proceedings against another member state before the Court. France complained that a UK ministerial order issued in 1977 concerning maximum by-catches authorized for fishing vessels was inconsistent with obligations incumbent on the UK arising under Community fisheries legislation. France relied particularly on the fact that the UK had failed to request the Commission to approve the above-mentioned measure, as provided for in Annex VI of the Hague Agreements on fisheries problems in October 1976, and that the British

measure went further than was required to comply with Recommendation No. 5 drawn up under the North-East Atlantic Fisheries Convention. France alleged, moreover, that the British measure exceeded the powers of a member state basically in view of its excessive effect on the fishery products market and its impact on the Community's external negotiations on fisheries. France also alleged that the British measure was unlawful since it was a national measure which went further than was necessary for conservation purposes.

Case 142/78 – Commission official v Commission

2.3.49. A Commission official brought an action before the Court of Justice on 19 June to obtain the household allowance of which the Commission had earlier deprived him.

Case 143/77 – J. de Cavel, Frankfurt/Main v L. de Cavel, Frankfurt/Main

2.3.50. The plaintiff in divorce proceedings before a French court applied to a German court for an order enforcing the judgment of the French court placing under seal and ordering the seizure of matrimonial property situated in Germany. Since this application was rejected by the lower courts, the Bundesgerichtshof asked the Court of Justice on 19 June to rule on the inapplicability of the Convention on Jurisdiction and the Enforcement of Judgments in Civil and Commercial Matters to the judgment of the French court.
Source: Bulletin of the European Communities, 6-1978

The Economic and Social Committee

The Economic and Social Committee (ECOSOC) is a consultative body of 144 members representing three roughly equal groups, employers, trade unions and 'independents' who are not necessarily committed to either of the other two groups. The independents may be drawn from the professions, the universities, consumer organizations, agricultural or any other appropriate interest groups. The Committee was created by the Treaty of Rome and must be consulted on a wide variety of the subjects dealt with by the Community. Legally, the Commission and the Council do not have to take heed of the opinions or reports which the Committee produces, and therefore its influence is limited. Nevertheless, it does act as a useful sounding board and an indication of what pressure groups and informed public opinion in the Community are thinking. It brings the workings of the Community closer to a group of influential opinion formers on the Committee who come from all the Member Countries.

Purpose

As a two-way communications link it serves a helpful role, a role which is capable of further development. Some officials in Brussels see it as a useful measure of opinion and an aid in gaining public acceptance for proposed legislation. Some consumers, employers and trade unionists see it as a means of indirect communication with the institutions and a possible way of influencing directly and, more important, indirectly the course of Community legislation.

Decisions are reached by ECOSOC in open debate in full sessions rather than by lobbying. Much of its work is carried out by different sections of the Committee, each one dealing with a number of specialized fields rather like the committees of the European Parliament. Members are nominated by national governments. There are 24 members from the United Kingdom and the other large countries, and correspondingly fewer from the smaller countries.

Procedure

Members serve on the Committee for four years with the possibility of renewal. They serve in a personal capacity, although originally selected because of their specialized knowledge or background.

Plenary sessions, of which there are nine each year, are open to the public. At the sessions a section of the Committee may present a draft report which is debated and amended. Much of the detailed work is carried out by small study groups which can be a time-consuming task for some members. There is, therefore, a necessary trade-off between the jobs that members of the Committee have

Box 33

A typical day in the life of a UK member of the Economic and Social Committee (ECOSOC)

Leaving Gatwick about 7.45 (I was up devilishly early) I reached the centre of Brussels just after 10, but in time for the start of a meeting of the Section for Industry, Commerce, Crafts and Services. In the plane, although it was almost too early to talk, I exchanged useful gossip with a Commission official who had been in London on consumer affairs matters, and with a friend on his way to Brussels for a meeting of the accountants' European lobby.

The main topic on the Section's agenda this morning, was the consideration of a rapporteur's draft opinion on a directive dealing with self-employed agents. Having taken into consideration what I have heard from several sources in the UK including the Law Commission, the mail order industry, commodity brokers, the chambers of commerce, and the manufacturers agents organization (which was strongly in favour of the directive), I had come to the view that the Commission was proposing something highly impracticable in some aspects and objectionable in others.

Therefore, during the debate which lasted until the early afternoon, I had frequently to intervene maintaining that the matter should be returned to the Commission on the following grounds: one, the definitions were so imprecise that lawyers in each country would have difficulty in drawing up the implementing legislation; two, the directive referred to a class of persons who although easily identifiable in some Member States was not easily recognizable, and perhaps did not exist, in the UK; and three, as the proposal contained provisions for harmonization in such great detail, it effectively

contravened Article 189 of the Treaty of Rome which states that whereas a directive is binding as to the result to be achieved in each Member State, national authorities should be left the choice of form and method.

When it came to the vote very few of my amendments were carried, and I was given the impression that some colleagues thought I was being 'non-communautaire'. I presume their familiarity with the German law on self-employed agents, from which the directive appears to be copied, led them to ignore my warning that the application of basically 'foreign' systems of law to the UK, and the total neglect of UK legal and commercial practices, would ultimately bring the EEC into disrepute in at least one province of the Community.

I was, however, surprised by the number of colleagues, who voted for me, or who abstained. I suspect that some were attracted by my argument that if directives are too detailed, the powers of national administrations are undermined in contravention of the Treaty. This argument could stand them in good stead on future occasions.

Despite my lack of success at the Section level, I announced that I intended to introduce similar amendments when the directive is discussed at the Plenary Section of ECOSOC to take place later this month. I doubt that I shall win, but my minority opinion will appear in the *Gazette* and form part of the Council papers.

After a thoroughly stimulating but unsuccessful morning, I spent the first part of the afternoon with members of the ECOSOC secretariat

continued

discussing the agenda of the Energy Section meeting which I chair in two days time. On the surface it looks as though it will not be a controversial meeting, except on one point. I make a note to talk to the rapporteur before the meeting to find out how far he will accept an amendment which I intend to make from the chair in an attempt to bring the opposing sides together.

On the way to the airport I had time to stop at the Commission's Berlaymont building for half an hour to discuss with a Chef de Division in DGXV a draft opinion on a tax evasion directive which I have to introduce to the Economic and Finance Section in a month's time.

The 18.20 Caledonia flight back to Gatwick was just long enough to enable me to make a few notes about what I have to do tomorrow, enjoy, what I considered, a well deserved whisky and yet again fail to finish a *Times* crossword. In forty-eight hours back again to Brussels for a similar sort of day, but this time I think I shall be supporting the Commission's papers which the Energy Committee will be considering.

Norman Miller, Member of ECOSOC and Director of Save and Prosper, October 1978

in their home countries and the amount of time they are able to spend on Committee affairs. Senior trade unionists, for example, are unlikely to be able to make more than, at best, regular appearances at plenary sessions.

A success or failure?

There are mixed views about how successful the Committee has been. There are doubts as to whether it is politically effective. It is argued that the opinions of the Committee on various aspects of legislation are often published too late, after the broad outlines of proposed legislation have been agreed. It is therefore unlikely that the Committee's opinions have any real impact.

On the other hand the Community needs to encourage an increasing number of people to become involved in its various activities. The value of the Committee, both as a two-way channel of communication and as a method of involving quite a fairly large number of influential individuals and their assistants in the workings of the Community, should not be decried. The Community is a new type of organization, and it is inevitable that in its formative years, which means for a very long time yet, its institutions will have to develop pragmatically. The role and functions of the Committee will undoubtedly change. It could be that the Committee will find an enhanced role in contributing to policy proposals to solve the economic problems of the next few years. Employment or lack of it, the need to develop new industries, to redeploy and retrain large numbers of individuals will all demand a great deal of serious research and new thinking in a Community context.

The European Council

The European Council is one of the most important mechanisms enabling the Community to develop. These meetings of heads of governments of the Nine take place three times a year. Because they are restricted to the heads of government (who in some cases are also heads of state), and because very few officials take part, considerable progress is often made.

Figure 9 Community leaders meet in London: 1977. Mr James Callaghan (second left) welcomes the European Community leaders to the garden of 10 Downing Street after they had gathered in London for the European Council meeting.

From the left they are: Monsieur Gaston Thorn (Luxembourg); Mr Callaghan; Mr Liam Cosgrave (Eire); Herr Helmut Schmidt (West Germany); President Giscard d'Estaing (France); Mr Anker Joergensen (Denmark); Mr Joop den Uyl (Holland); and Monsieur Leo Tindemans (Belgium). Mr Jenkins, British President of the Commission, has his back to the camera. The President of the Commission is now invited to European Council meetings as a matter of course

Many contentious issues which cannot be solved at Council of Ministers' meetings are thrashed out at the European Council. Its meetings have given great encouragement and political impetus to the other institutions. At the end of each Council, a communiqué is issued giving the broad outlines of what has been agreed. The understandings which are not published are probably of most significance. Agreement in the Council of Ministers on contentious subjects is much easier if the political will exists, and has already been shown to exist at meetings of the European Council.

Meetings of European heads of government were comparatively rare. European Council meetings now enable the leaders of the Nine to get to know one another on a personal level. This inevitably leads to a closer understanding of problems and increases the chances of common solutions being found. Jean Monnet, the *éminence grise*, unknown to most, but probably the key personality in the development of the Community, played an important part in developing the role of the European Council. It may prove to have been his greatest single achievement.

Other institutions: the committee system

There are a number of other organizations, some formally established and others not, which operate in and around the Community institutions. There is a proliferation of committees in the agricultural, social affairs, transport, competition and customs union areas. A standing committee on employment brings together the Commission, governments, employers and unions and meets twice a year. The Social Fund Committee meets at least four times a year and various Community funds such as the Regional Fund and the European Monetary Cooperation Fund meet regularly. The latter could become the nucleus of a future common central banking system. Joint committees have also been established and are described in Chapter 17 below.

The committee system oils the wheels of the Community institutions. It enables them to function relatively smoothly. The views of interested individuals and organizations, of civil services and of governments are taken into consideration in the formulation of new Community policies and the implementation of existing ones. Some of the committees are restricted in their membership to civil servants of the Nine, while others will seek deliberately to have as wide a representation as possible from interested experts.

The role of business in Community committees

The role of business in many of the committees of the Community has not been thought through either by the institutions or by business. Careful consideration should be given to whether it is useful for senior management to be represented on Brussels committees. If it is then to what extent is it for reasons of protocol or ritual. A company must decide at what level it should be represented, if at all. Also it must ask whether involvement in committees does much for the individual and little for the company and whether it helps the industry rather than the company. Also there is the question of how much senior executive time should be given to industry-wide as opposed to company business.

Box 34

The banking institution of the European Community

The European Investment Bank (EIB) was set up in 1958 under the terms of the Treaty of Rome, which established the European Economic Community.

It is a public institution within the Community and has an independent legal status.

Its essential function is to contribute to the balanced development of the Common Market.

For this purpose, it grants long-term loans or gives its guarantee to enterprises, public authorities and financial institutions to finance projects which assist the development of less advanced regions and conversion areas or which serve the interests of the Community as a whole.

Source: Pamphlet on EIB, 1978

Operations in the United Kingdom

Since the UK's accession to the EEC on 1 January 1973, loans totalling the equivalent of almost £975 million have been provided by the European Investment Bank (EIB), which has its headquarters in Luxembourg.

These have gone to support a wide variety of projects ranging from power stations and oilfield installations to steelworks, telecommunications and chemical plants. However, the loans have not been restricted only to large-scale schemes: finance has also been provided to aid small and medium-sized industrial ventures.

Example of 1978 loans

Two more loans, each for £22.9 million, have been granted this year to the Electricity Council, as further support for the Dinorwic pumped storage power station in Wales and for construction of the Hartlepool nuclear power station.

Two loans totalling the equivalent of £31 million have been provided to the National Water Council:

£16 million for on-lending to the North West Water Authority to finance various water supply schemes.
£15 million for on-lending to the Yorkshire Water Authority.

Two loans totalling £13.5 million were made to Grampian Regional Council and Lothian Regional Council to help to finance road schemes in Aberdeen and improvements to water supply, and sewage disposal systems in Aberdeen, Edinburgh and Midlothian.

£5 million was lent to BICC Metals Ltd for modernization of copper refining plant at Prescot, Merseyside, which should lead to lower production costs and substantial energy savings; the project should safeguard about 350 jobs.

Whatever the answers to these questions, from an individual company point of view, it looks as if industry, both employers and employees, will become increasingly involved in the Community decision-making process.

Bibliography

The Court of Justice of the European Communities, European Documentation 1977/2
Information on the Court of Justice of the European Communities. Quarterly Synopsis. Annual

Business in the European Community: exporting, investing, influencing, monitoring

7 Trends in European trade and the response of business

> The members of the Community will in any case have to take a fresh look at their arrangements for export promotion as their commercial relations with the rest of the world become a joint responsibility; they might well decide that it was convenient to hive off this activity from the ordinary work of their embassies and transfer it to a separate organization.
> *Europe: Journey to an Unknown Destination,*
> *Andrew Shonfield, Pelican, 1973*

Many companies still need to respond to the changing pattern of European trade. This chapter describes the pattern, suggests why Community developments are relevant to business and considers the type of companies likely to be affected.

The growth of Community trade

Over recent years intra-Community exports have grown to over 50 per cent of the total exports of the Nine. This trend looks as if it will continue for some time as the barriers to trade in the Community are gradually dismantled. Good quality industrial products are now being produced very cheaply in developing countries and many traditional markets are slowly being eroded. The future of world trade for industrialized nations would seem to lie in high technology exports of both goods and services across the world and in increased and more efficient trade between the OECD countries. Most of these nations are European. Therefore the need for companies to develop a European strategy, whether they are situated in the Community or doing business with it from the outside, becomes almost daily more apparent.

United Kingdom trade with the Community

In recent years there has been a significant growth of UK exports as a percentage of total exports to Community countries:

1960	22
1970	29
1977	37

This growth, although considerable, still leaves the United Kingdom behind the others in intra-Community trade. In countries such as the Netherlands and Belgium over 70 per cent of foreign trade is within the Community. Markets in Western Europe are of growing importance to the United Kingdom, as *Box 35* shows. Ten of the UK's top twelve export markets are European and over 50 per cent of exports now go to Western Europe.

Box 35

Total exports by area of destination 1976

	Exporting country	Total exports (%)	Destination (%)				
			EUR 9	USA	Japan	Rest of world	Among which: ACP
	EUR 9	100	52	6	1	42	3
(1)	FR Germany	100	46	6	1	48	2
(2)	France	100	51	5	1	44	6
(3)	Italy	100	48	7	1	45	2
(4)	Netherlands	100	72	3	1	25	2
(5)	Belgium	100	74	4	1	22	2
(6)	Luxembourg						
(7)	United Kingdom	100	36	10	1	54	6
(8)	Ireland	100	16	7	1	16	2
(9)	Denmark	100	46	6	1	47	2
(10)	Greece	100	50	6	1	43	
(11)	Spain	100	46	12	1	41	
(12)	Portugal	100	52	7	1	41	
(13)	Turkey	100	49	10	2	39	
(14)	Norway	100	56	5	1	39	
(15)	Sweden	100	47	5	1	48	
(16)	Switzerland	100	45	8	3	44	
(17)	Austria	100	47	3	1	50	
(18)	Finland	100	38	5	1	56	
(19)	USSR	100	17	1	3	80	
(20)	USA	100	22	–	9	70	
(21)	Canada	100	12	68	6	14	
(22)	Japan	100	11	24	–	66	

Source: Eurostat 1978: Basic Statistics of the Community

Box 37 shows the UK balance of trade in recent years. Since joining the Community the value of both exports and imports has increased at a faster rate than with the rest of the world. Exports have grown as a proportion of imports from the low point of 1975, and the percentage of coverage of imports by exports continues to improve.

Box 36

UK exports go increasingly to Europe

UK top 20 export markets in 1977

	(£m)	% of total UK exports in 1977	1967
(1) US	3 080	9.4	12.2
(2) West Germany	2 500	7.6	5.3
(3) France	2 140	6.5	4.2
(4) Netherlands	2 130	6.5	3.9
(5) Benelux	1 830	5.6	3.6
(6) Irish Republic	1 640	5.0	3.8
(7) Switzerland	1 420	4.3	2.4
(8) Sweden	1 190	3.6	4.3
(9) Nigeria	1 060	3.2	1.1
(10) Italy	970	3.0	3.0
(11) Denmark	790	2.4	2.8
(12) Norway	760	2.3	2.5
(13) Australia	760	2.3	4.9
(14) Canada	710	2.2	4.2
(15) Iran	650	2.0	0.8
(16) South Africa	580	1.8	5.0
(17) Saudi Arabia	570	1.8	0.3
(18) Japan	460	1.4	1.7
(19) Spain	460	1.4	1.8
(20) Soviet Union	340	1.1	1.2

Distribution of UK exports by area (%)

	1960	1970	1977
Western Europe	34	46	53
(EEC 8)	(22)	(29)	(36)
North America	16	15	12
Other developed	15	12	6
Oil exporting	7	6	13
Other developing	25	17	13
Centrally planned economies	3	4	3
	100	100	100

Source: Department of Trade and The Financial Times, 27 June 1978

Companies likely to be affected by growth of intra-European trade

Businesses that can benefit from the future growth of intra-European trade may be of several types:

(1) The UK company which sees the need to enter the Community market for the first time. Its manufacturing and marketing operations can no longer be confined to one-fifth of the potential home market of 260 million consumers

and it needs to change that situation by either exporting or investing. Many UK companies appreciate that their costs are considerably lower than those of most Community countries but have not yet decided what advantage they should draw from this. Many medium-size companies are in this situation. They have well-established marketing operations or investments abroad but for historic reasons these are in other parts of the world, often Commonwealth countries.

Box 37

United Kingdom trade with the Community

UK balance of trade with the rest of the Community

Balance of payments basis   *Percentage change on previous period*

	Exports fob (£)	*Imports fob (£ million)*	*Visible balance*	*Exports as a proportion of imports (%)*
1970	2 347	2 303	+44	101.9
1971	2 511 (+ 7)	2 696 (+17)	−185	93.1
1972	2 835 (+13)	3 419 (+27)	−584	82.9
1973	3 943 (+39)	5 125 (+50)	−1 182	76.9
1974	5 581 (+42)	7 608 (+48)	−2 027	73.4
1975	6 273 (+12)	8 678 (+14)	−2 405	72.3
1976	9 027 (+44)	11 109 (+28)	−2 082	81.3
1977	11 855 (+31)	13 533 (+22)	−1 678	87.6

British exports to the EEC as % of its imports from the EEC (balance of payment basis)

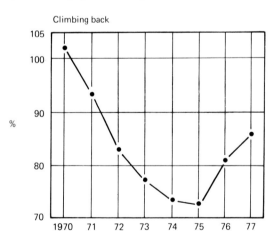

Source: The Economist

continued

UK trade with the rest of the Community by commodity (£ million)

OTS basis

SITC (R2) section	Exports 1976	Exports 1977	Imports 1976	Imports 1977	Crude balance 1976	Crude balance 1977	Exp./Imp. ratio 1976	Exp./Imp. ratio 1977
0 Food and live animals	570	824	1 993	2 268	−1 423	−1 444	29	36
of which								
01 Meat	164	217	501	618	−336	−401	33	35
02 Dairy products	88	64	413	350	−324	−286	21	18
04 Cereals	58	121	418	426	−360	−305	14	28
05 Fruit and veg	38	55	248	300	−210	−245	15	18
06 Sugar	26	31	84	101	−58	−70	31	31
1 Beverages and tobacco	146	183	219	259	−73	−76	67	71
2 Basic materials	406	460	438	478	−32	−17	93	96
3 Fuel	761	1 216	1 000	1 097	−238	+119	76	111
of which								
33 Petroleum and petroleum products	716	1 160	970	1 040	−254	+120	74	112
4 Vegetable oils	18	33	48	63	−30	−30	38	52
5 to 8 Manufactured goods	7 201	9 217	7 664	9 841	−463	−624	94	94
5 Chemicals	1 092	1 398	1 154	1 508	−62	−109	95	93
of which								
58 Plastics	198	246	332	407	−134	−160	60	60
6 Other semi-manufactures	2 123	2 685	2 005	2 523	+119	+162	106	106
of which								
667 Precious stones	476	633	187	279	+289	+354	255	227
67 Iron and steel	235	292	552	570	−317	−278	43	51
7 Machinery and transport equipment	3 144	3 979	3 573	4 608	−430	−629	88	86
of which								
71 to 74 Machinery	1 213	1 520	1 277	1 590	−64	−70	95	96
75 Office machines	365	456	383	478	−18	−22	95	95
76 and 77 Electrical machinery	468	611	519	683	−51	−73	90	89
78 Road vehicles	800	1 069	986	1 529	−186	−460	81	70
8 Miscellaneous manufactures	842	1 156	932	1 203	−91	−48	90	96
9 Other goods	148	194	149	155	−1	+39	99	125
Total 0−9	9 249	12 128	11 510	14 161	−2 261	−2 033	80	86

Source: adapted from Trade and Industry, 19 May 1978

(2) The UK company which has a traditional set of activities within the Community, whether of a marketing or production nature, but which has not looked carefully at this historic situation for some time. A paint company recently found itself in this situation. It had a number of factories near the main continental ports from the time when marine paints had been the major part of its

business. Conditions changed and the marine paint market declined. Although it was already established in the Community in one sense, it was in the wrong parts of it. Moving into domestic and commercial paints meant that its centres of production were now a long distance from the potential outlets. Transport costs for paints are high. The company was faced with the choice of either very heavy transport costs or of selling its factories and setting up nearer major centres of population.

(3) The third type of company is that with its main centre of operations outside the Community. To take advantage of the Community market it needs to look at its operations on a Community-wide scale. Until now it has seen Europe as a number of different national markets. It must now consider the best ways of doing business with a group of countries surrounded by a tariff wall and which negotiates any exceptions to these tariffs or concessions centrally from Brussels.

Whether these three types of company are involved in exporting or direct foreign investment there are certain aspects of Community law and practice which will affect them.

What business needs to know about the Community

Community laws do not impinge very much on the average business from one day to another. Therefore the value to business of detailed knowledge of Community policies must not be exaggerated; it is only one factor among many in export management or investment appraisal. Many managers will operate successfully in Europe with little need to take account of Community aspects of their business. A large firm of accountants in Paris claim that, in their experience, when seeking potential partners or assessing possible takeover situations, Community considerations are not particularly significant. Much more relevant is the current legal, business and political environment in France.

Yet knowledge of Community policies can be of great importance under certain circumstances. The requirement is to establish a system which monitors effectively both current and future Community legislation and trends so that relevant information is presented to decision-makers at the appropriate time and in digestible form. This is not easy. Some companies have ignored European legislation and paid the penalty. Others have erred too much the other way and set up elaborate and unnecessary systems of monitoring Community trends. They have over-informed their management to the extent of overwhelming them.

Some companies have set up European offices separate from the mainstream policy-making functions of the company. As a result senior managers have on occasions been inadequately briefed on important Community matters in spite of the expertise being available in the company. This can sometimes occur when a company or group of companies sets up in Brussels someone who may become very expert, but may be too far removed from the decision-makers to communicate his knowledge and expertise to them.

Companies need to be informed about Community developments because:

(1) Information is needed about new technological standards or proposed business legislation directly affecting the company. It should be obtained as early as possible and ideally at the pipeline stage while there is still an opportunity of influencing the final form of the legislation.
(2) Opportunities may occur for developing new products, processes or markets as a result of proposed new legislation.
(3) Companies need to monitor the broad trends of European legislation because their international marketing and investment strategies will be affected by changes in Community laws.

Keeping abreast of Community developments is not only the problem of decision-makers at senior levels of the company. It may be necessary for middle managers and future senior managers to develop a European awareness if they are to contribute to the strategical thinking of their organizations. The broadening aspects of a manager's development are too often left until he reaches a senior position. Then it may be too late.

Cultivating strategical thinking in managers should be spread over a period of years. It is often more difficult to broaden the experience and knowledge of managers than to deepen it. They should be given wider experience in different functional areas of the company, not necessarily the most obvious functions; an example is the research and development function. In the R & D division of a company there are usually highly skilled, well-trained experts who never get the chance to think about the wider applications of what they are doing. For example a senior designer may be influenced by the realization that the work he is doing is not immutably fixed by current national legislation, and that it could be superseded by Community legislation at any time.

Apart from the practical reasons for ensuring that managers are aware of the implications of European Community trends, there is also a motivational aspect. Broad aspects of policies are often of considerable interest to managers even though they may never be in a position to make specific use of the knowledge. We all like to identify with the great issues of the day which delineate the world in which we work and live. It is reassuring to a manager, both personally and professionally, to learn about the environment in which he operates. The more this environment is subject to change, the more the apparent desire to learn about the influences likely to bring about these changes.

The European Community is one of the influences of change in the present world. Companies, whether they ignore it or adapt to it, are likely to be changed as a result of the Community and the way it is beginning to influence the world economic and business scene. The next two chapters look at general export and investment considerations. The manager already heavily involved in these activities may wish to omit them and continue with later chapters of the book which describe Community policies affecting business and suggest ways in which these policies can be influenced and monitored.

Bibliography

Trade and Industry, London: HMSO. Weekly government publication with section on Community business

8 Export strategies and the European Community

It is often the simple questions which do not get
answered because they do not get asked

Entering strategy

Having decided to rethink its European operations, a company needs to determine the best method of entering the Community market. It will decide this in
the light of its product range and its production, financial and personnel situation. The following options are open to it:

(1) An aggressive sales policy from a home-based manufacturing and sales
    facility. In this case it is necessary to determine the scale of its effort and
    the tactics. Should licencing or service agreements be drawn up with Com-
    munity firms?
(2) Entry from a home-based manufacturing facility by merging with existing
    Community agents, distributors or retailing networks.
(3) Entry from a home-based manufacturing facility but with acquisition of an
    existing distribution system or the establishment of a new one in the target
    countries.
(4) Merger with a local manufacturer who has a distribution network or access
    to such a network. This could be a joint venture with equal partnership or
    a minority holding.
(5) By acquisition of a majority holding in an existing manufacturing and distri-
    bution facility. A joint venture with financial control of the enterprise.
(6) New investment; factories for basic manufacture or plant for assembling
    from components. A wholly owned foreign subsidiary.

The first three options are progressively more costly. As the list of options
continues, what begins as an export sales activity gradually becomes a full-scale
foreign investment. One of the early decisions a company needs is the target
scale of its operations. Although circumstances will change as an export marketing operation develops, it is useful to decide on the provisional size of the
operation the company is prepared to consider and the time scale for the operation. What begins as selling surplus production abroad can end as an operation
on a sufficiently large scale to affect significantly the profitability of a small
company or the division of a larger company in a relatively short period of time.

A major problem for the company, which has not yet made a serious marketing effort in the European Community, is that entering sophisticated markets
is complicated and time-consuming, and the costs are high. Although the Community is in itself a market, it is probably more useful to consider Western

Europe as a whole when looking for business opportunities. Provided that the differences, in terms of actual and potential tariffs and other barriers to trade, are appreciated, it may be more sensible to look, for example, at Norway, Sweden and Denmark as a single market. This is particularly so if the objective is to export rather than invest. Since 1977 tariffs in Europe on industrial goods have been reduced to zero between Community and European Free Trade Association (EFTA) countries. (EFTA is briefly described in the glossary of Chapter 29.) It is therefore of relatively little importance to businesses operating within Western Europe whether their markets are in Sweden or Denmark. If the market opportunity is about equal between these two countries, it must still be in the company's best interests to market within the Community because of any future tariff or other legislative changes. For companies outside the Community the situation is somewhat different as the European Community has a common external tariff (see Chapter 16) while the EFTA countries are free to raise or lower their tariffs individually.

Marketing questions

The following are some of the marketing questions which a company might ask in order to establish a short list of market areas on which to focus attention:

(1)   What is the total European market for the product both in the European Community and in EFTA?
(2)   At what rate is the market for your products growing?
(3)   What is the product market structure by country, and, if possible, by region?
(4)   What are the factors which have influenced market growth and structure?
(5)   Are these factors changing, and if so for what reasons?
(6)   What is the price structure?
(7)   How have prices moved over the past five years and what has influenced these price movements?
(8)   Who are the competitors and what is their size?
(9)   How are they distributed, by country and region?
(10) Where is competition likely to be weakest?

Much of this research can be carried out from the home base. By using official sources of information, which are very good, especially in the United Kingdom and the United States, this work can be done inexpensively. (Useful addresses and contacts are given in Chapter 28.) Most businessmen involved in exporting do not use official government services efficiently, and yet they are the cheapest and often the best way of carrying out basic desk research. Official services are underrated because businessmen too often base their assessment of them on past performance or prejudice. Recently a businessman told me that he never used embassies abroad because of a bad experience in Yugoslavia. The incident, I subsequently discovered, took place in 1952! Incredibly companies often pay for costly advice and consultancy from organizations which themselves use the official government services on behalf of their clients. A more advantageous time for buying in advice is when basic research has been carried out, and when help is needed in the target country to find agents, set up a distribution system or acquire a site.

The small or medium-size firm which contemplates a move into the Community market for the first time often prefers to get its toe wet before taking the plunge. Although the reasons for this are understandable, there are occasions when the experience is costly in terms of the efforts of senior management. Sketchley, the UK dry cleaning firm, made a small initial investment in Brussels, and at the other end of the scale, Marks and Spencer started with only two or three stores in continental Europe. Both companies could have perhaps started with larger investments. The costs for such relatively small operations were high and in the short term hardly justified by the return on the considerable investment of time and money. If the initial operations has been on a larger scale in the event of their failure in the current inflationary climate then sites could probably have been resold or re-let at a profit. Any losses would probably have been recouped on the value of the real estate alone. In addition, fixed costs, overheads and, most important, managerial time would have been apportioned over a larger projected turnover.

Market research

Marketing operations rarely begin at the beginning. In most marketing situations there are already existing products. The problems centre around answering questions such as: Is there a demand for the product? Does the product need to be modified? What specific marketing possibilities exist for it? In which area or countries should a start be made? These are the questions with which a company operating in the Community may need help. Official sources will help to some extent. How many companies are aware, for example, that the British Embassy Commercial Section in Paris has over 30 bilingual product officers throughout France working for British businesses?

The market research is usually done in two stages:

(1) An investigation of the market in general.
(2) Identification of specific business opportunities.

The first can be approached on a Europe-wide basis as regards information sources. As questions become more specific it will be necessary to look for sources of information under national headings. (The main sources of this information are listed in Chapter 28.) Check lists may seem a rather obvious way of ensuring that the groundwork is done, but such simple devices can help a company to think through its marketing decisions.

One simple checklist which has been compiled and refined by a number of managers involved in European operations is given in *Box 38*. The first two parts of the check list on entering strategy and marketing have already been given. Questions on distribution, business policy, legal aspects and investment aspects follow. Perhaps not all of them are necessary, and others could be added to the list.

Box 38

The European market — some considerations for potential exporters

Entering strategy — see text

Marketing questions — see text

Distribution questions

(1) What are the shipping facilities and costs? Port of entry — on-off services and container services?

(2) What are the supportive road/ rail facilities and cost?

(3) What are the tariffs, port and rail clearing charges?

(4) Who are possible clearing agents?

(5) What is the distributive/forwarding agency set-up?

The objective of this research is to determine ability to enter the market.

Business policy questions

(1) What are the current and future growth factors in the markets under consideration? GNP? Net disposable income?

(2) What are the current and forward exchange rates and likely strengths of currencies?

(3) What is the tax structure (including withholding taxes)?

(4) Can profits and dividends be freely remitted?

(5) What are current and likely future trends in wages and salaries in the markets under consideration?

(6) Are there any price controls?

(7) Labour relations and union structure.

(8) Relative productivity factors of different business sectors.

(9) Employees rights — social security payments, pensions, compensation and other benefits?

(10) Engineering and building costs compared to the United Kingdom?

The objective is to establish from these questions a second short list of markets.

Legal questions

(1) Existing and proposed competition and anti-trust regulations?

(2) Existing and proposed company law and European Community regulations?

(3) What are the legal rights of minority shareholders?

(4) What is in the pipeline in the way of legislation on company and competition law?

(5) What are the European Community proposals for harmonization of company law, competition and elimination of non-tariff technical barriers?

The objective is to establish the pitfalls of different methods of achieving entry.

Investment questions

(1) Investment incentives? (Regional policies and capital grants)

(2) Government attitude to mergers and acquisitions?

(3) Banking facilities? Bank charges — working capital, loans, growing facilities?

(4) Attitudes to foreign investors?

Sections to add to the check list could include those on competitors, availability of appropriate personnel, sources of finance, required rates of return on investment. The list is by no means exhaustive but time spent on establishing such a list is not wasted. References at the end of this chapter suggest sources of information and advice on: export marketing decisions; export practice and documentation; marketing in the European Community; markets in the Community; background information on the business climates in the countries of the Community. If anyone makes use of these references he will be well prepared to carry out export marketing in the European Community. Unfortunately the hard work only begins when you get on the ground.

Box 39

Is the European Community a home market?

Many of these aspects of export marketing are as relevant to the European Community as they are to the rest of the world:

Export strategy
Export market research
Export pricing
Distribution alternatives
Advertising
Documentation
Exhibiting abroad
Quotation and payment terms
Finance and insurance

Community aspects of export marketing

A company needs to consider aspects of a specific country in which it seeks a market and also aspects of Community export marketing. The Community aspects are:

(1) The Community, because it has a customs union and an external tariff wall, is a market in itself.
(2) The policies it develops and the laws it draws up regulating business need to be monitored as well as the national laws of individual countries.
(3) Increasingly it will be legislation and policies emanating from Brussels which will be the concern of those operating within the Community, whether from an external base or from one of the countries of the Nine.
(4) Apart from these considerations, marketing in the Community is no different from marketing elsewhere in the world, and the same sort of considerations apply.

In taking marketing decisions, just as in developing an investment decision, time is one of the most valuable commodities and, just as it pays to make check lists, it pays also to work to a strict timetable. Dates for meetings at different levels in the organization should be arranged at the beginning of an export marketing operation. They can always be cancelled but are much more difficult

Box 40

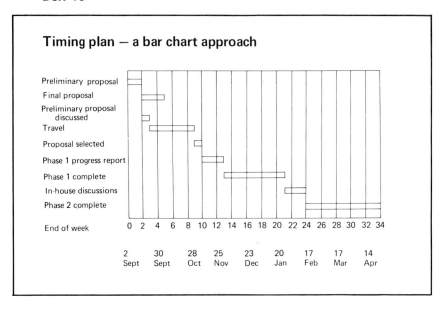

to arrange at short notice. A simple bar chart approach is illustrated in *Box 40*. The considerations which might affect a decision to export to a market in one country rather than another are also relevant to investing in one country or another.

Bibliography

Bolt, Gordon J. (1973) *Marketing in the EEC*, London: Kogan Page
Destination Europe: Exporters Guide to the EEC. BOTB
Economist Intelligence Unit Quarterly Economic Review
Hints to Businessmen. BOTB series on each European Community country
Tookey, Douglas (1975) *Export Marketing Decisions,* Harmondsworth: Penguin
Walker, A.G. (1977) *Export Practice and Documentation*, London: Newnes-
    Butterworths

9 Investment strategies and the European Community

Amid a multitude of projects, no plan is devised
Publilius Synis, Moral Sayings, 100 B.C.

A company often becomes involved in export marketing by chance. A sudden enquiry, a chance opportunity to get rid of surplus production which cannot be sold on the home market, speculative participation in a trade fair in the home country or abroad are some of the ways a company may start its export work. Random factors such as the nationality of the chairman's wife, the country where a manager happens to have been on holiday, that another senior manager comes originally from Italy or Rumania often cause firms to look at a specific export market.

Whether ventures arising from these chance beginnings are successful or not, the likely effect on the company is in many cases only marginal. If the venture fails, the cost is written off and the affair forgotten. If a success, then there is a point when the company has to decide whether to take seriously this initial export effort and to expand it or to invest in setting up a serious export operation, perhaps with manufacturing facilities abroad.

The investment decision

The investment decision affects most functions of a business at many levels. It is perhaps the failure to fully realize this which accounts for many of the difficulties companies experience in developing overseas operations. Often, for example, it is the personnel manager who is the last to know about a projected foreign investment. Yet the task of finding qualified personnel, within the company or outside, and of training them in the appropriate skills to run or coordinate the running of the venture, may require a much longer lead time than raising the finance for the operation. It is more often the finance director than the personnel director who accompanies the chairman on visits to the target country. The finance director must be aware of his responsibility for thinking about the investment from the viewpoint of other colleagues and functions not just in financial terms.

Ways of looking at markets

There are a number of ways of looking at potential investment markets: by continents; country-by-country; regional areas; population centres; language; radio/TV area.

Continents

A large company will sometimes divide the world into continents for the purpose of planning strategy. The problem about planning world strategies is that few companies have trained personnel with sufficient breadth and depth of experience to cope with the development of these strategies. A frequent complaint from subsidiaries of American multinationals in Europe is that the headquarters in the United States do not fully understand the problems of operating in the European or overseas environment. However, criticism of the centre by the periphery is not entirely justified. To win promotion in an American multinational, a manager must have considerable experience of the company at a number of levels and functions in the United States. As a result he may have little opportunity to live and work in other parts of the world. Furthermore, as political pressure for local nationals to run local subsidiaries becomes widespread, there are even fewer opportunities for obtaining overseas experience.

The continental approach breaks down when details of a company's operations or future operations is considered. It is rare for a company to be involved in all the countries of a continent, and if it is, then it probably should not be. Continents are not necessarily economic entities. Shell, for example, sees the UK as separate from the continent of Europe and has different companies to run the two areas. Africa is certainly a very diverse continent. The southern and central Mediterranean and the Arab African countries may not have enough in common to justify a continental approach.

One of the key points in the Betro Trust Report (*Box 41*) is the need to concentrate on key markets. The United Kingdom, for example, exports to some 184 markets in the world. Of these, 100 take 4 per cent and 84 take 96 per cent of UK exports. A company is better advised to direct its resources to its most profitable markets and to cultivate a few others where it can see a rapid rise in demand. It is impossible to service adequately all the markets in the world. Nor is it profitable. Only very large companies need world-wide operations. Many smaller companies would do better to extend their foreign investments by enlarging some and cutting out others. The Betro Trust Report should be required reading for managers involved or interested in overseas operations. It is one of the best reports on export markets and deserves wider circulation.

Country-by-country

For example, a company which manufactures, distributes and launders roller towels and work overalls decided to list and look at all the countries in the world. It proved an exhaustive if not an exhausting exercise. They found that the best three markets were several thousand miles apart. In spite of this they would not all be exploited because of the distance.

Box 41

Concentration on key markets. Recommendations of the Betro Trust Report

(1) Concentration

Even the richest companies have only limited resources to deploy in the export markets. It is more profitable and conducive to faster progress to concentrate talent, effort and scarce cash resources in five or ten of the company's best key markets, for success comes from concentration.

(2) A new manpower policy

Let exports have an equal chance to that accorded to home trade. If a company sells half its output abroad and half at home, it cannot be right that it should have 50 salesmen in the home market and only one for all the export markets. Such a policy discriminates against exports and (even if highly profitable in the short run) will retard continued progress abroad. An investment in export manpower is the best investment British companies can make. The adoption of 'equality' could open an era of prosperity for most companies.

(3) Travel

Nothing can bring prosperity more quickly than increased travel and nothing can take the place of regular and frequent personal contacts for solving problems and developing products and trade. More travel is also the best way to ensure that the agent is not neglected and that the contentious issue of 'after-sales service' will add to – rather than unnecessarily detract from – our trading reputation.

(4) Investment

This is the key to long-term prosperity. Investment, primarily geared to export, will reduce dependence on the static home market and ensure greater stability and faster growth. It is also the most effective answer to the perennial problem of long delivery dates and delivery reliability.

To predict the future is well nigh impossible but an intelligent study of future trends can be very helpful and profitable both for exports and investment.

(5) The vital role of the accountant

The accountant's increasing involvement in exports is vital. He is a dispassionate and logical observer and his review of comparative home and export activities (e.g. pricing, profitability, manpower comparisons, etc.) could lead to a better appreciation of the advantages of exporting. In particular, the detailed study of comparative prices in the major markets can be most rewarding and should be given the highest priority. All the more so since pricing and investment policies are often interrelated.

(6) An approach to an export-led boom

Since 80 per cent of exporters are looking abroad for expansion, this may be the right moment to look afresh at the four significant determinants of export-success:
Concentration
Manpower
Pricing
Travel

If these were now to be given the priority accorded to them by our major competitors they will provide much of the funds and the justification for an *export-led* investment boom.

Source: the Betro Trust Report, Royal Society of Arts, January 1978 Edition

Regional area

This approach is more promising, especially for a company which identifies areas that really have something in common. The European Community is an example, so is North America, Central America and regional groups such as the Andean Pact countries or the African common markets. The strength of these regional groupings needs to be assessed, as some operate more effectively than others. The Middle East is often looked upon as a regional area, but from an investment viewpoint it divides up very easily into different countries: Israel and the Arab countries are divided; the North African countries differ from the Gulf countries, and Saudi Arabia differs politically from Iraq or Syria. Looked at closely it is difficult to see why the Middle East is considered a region at all from

Box 42

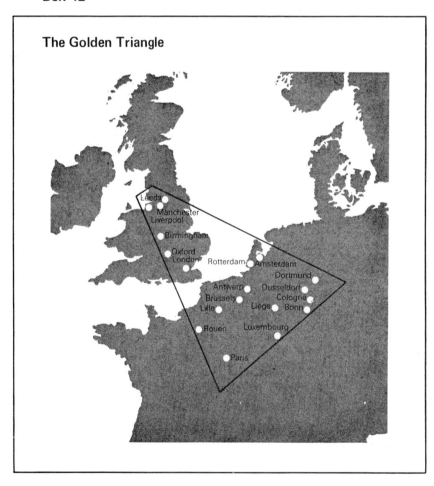

The Golden Triangle

a business point of view, since it is diverse politically, economically, linguistically and culturally. The countries of the European Community are much more closely knit and doing business in all of them is very similar in many ways.

Population centres

This is a more fruitful way of looking at markets. A company will talk about investing in France when perhaps it means it is investing in the Paris area where the largest and richest number of Frenchmen live. The 'Golden Triangle' is an interesting way of looking at a market in terms of population. Over three-fifths of the Community population and its GNP are found in this comparatively small area. It is some five to six times better off than some outlying areas of the Community. This population area will be of particular interest to companies selling or manufacturing for the mass consumer market. While micro-circuits can perhaps be manufactured profitably in the north of Scotland, it will pay to produce domestic paints closer to where they will be applied.

The Roller Towel Company, mentioned above, eventually found that its best way of looking at the world was in terms of population centres. It needed centres of sufficient size to justify setting up an operation — where the population was growing both in size and wealth, and where labour bottlenecks were occurring. The traditional cheap laundering services in these areas would disappear or become expensive as semi-skilled labour was drawn into industry away from these services, thus creating a demand for roller towel and allied services.

Language

Grouping countries by language or culture can be useful especially where knowledge of the language is important. It is cost effective to teach a manager a language that can be used in a number of different countries. For example, if a manager is taught classical Arabic then in a language sense the Middle East becomes a uniform area as classical Arabic can be understood in all of the countries. In the same way French is useful in Luxembourg and parts of Belgium as well as Switzerland and former French colonies from Martinique to Lebanon. Packaging and advertising costs can be reduced by looking at the world in terms of language. As for the Community, English and French are the key languages. Indeed with these two languages a businessman has a good chance of being understood in most parts of the world.

Radio/TV area

This aspect is important for marketing and advertising rather than for investment. Radio Luxembourg now broadcasts in a number of European languages and its message reaches nearly all the inhabitants of the 'Golden Triangle'.

Investment considerations

If a company has decided to invest in the Community, but is not sure in which country it should begin, on what criteria should it base its decision? The check list approach is as good a mechanism as any. If a list of criteria is compiled along the following lines, adding to it and subtracting what is not relevant, then this should provide a basis for a simple but comprehensive approach to the decision. Had certain companies started with such a list, then perhaps the crucial point which upset their investment calculations might not have been overlooked.

Political stability

This must be a key factor. A country which is politically unstable is an investment risk. But do not confuse political stability with the political leanings of the government. For example South Africa and the USSR have been politically stable for the last 25 years. The possibility of the Left coming to power in France in 1977 was not a sufficient reason for thinking, as some did, that the country would become politically unstable. There was little chance of business in general being affected fundamentally by a change of government; the threat of nationalization, even if carried out, was unlikely to have affected foreign investment. Many countries still operate as market economies even when parts of the economy are nationalized. Banking statistics in *Box 43* are surprising to many American businessmen.

Box 43

Public stake in banking

The percentage of deposits received by public sector financial institutions (in the broad sense), i.e. the public stake in banking, varies greatly from country to country. Estimates from the European Commission put this share at:

80% in France
70% in Italy
60% in Germany
50% in Belgium
40% in Holland
30% in Denmark
30% in Switzerland
10% in the UK and Ireland combined

Source: Euroforum, No. 20/78, 23 May 1978, p. 7

The same was true of the United Kingdom when outside investors feared the possible nationalization of North Sea oil. These fears were largely unfounded. The British government had no intention of threatening foreign investment, and if nationalization had occurred there would have been full compensation.

Italy is another country whose political stability is questioned. In fact there is little evidence that a change of government would make a difference to foreign investment in Italy. A communist government in Italy would probably encourage foreign investors.

Thus the main political consideration in any Community country is the effect of a political change on business confidence. Left-wing governments have sometimes had short-term effects on investment confidence, but there is no correlation, in Europe, between the political orientation of the government in power and the profitability of companies during that period.

Economic outlook

On the one hand, there is an advantage to investing in a country when the economy is growing; it is easier to secure a share of the market. On the other hand, it may be easier and cheaper to find a good investment opportunity where the economy of a country is not growing: more businesses may be in difficulty, property prices may be lower and there may be greater labour availability. In 1978 some large companies considered leaving Belgium because of high labour costs and a downturn in the economy. It could be argued, however, that this is a good time to invest in Europe as governments welcome any new investment which preserves jobs.

Attitude to foreign investment

Government attitudes can make a great difference to investment plans. A recent example is the positive attitude of the British government to the takeover of Chrysler by Peugeot. This contrasts with the German government's attitude to the GKN takeover of Sachs. The French government's opposition to takeovers in its food industry, and more recently to the Lucas takeover of Pechinay, has been similar. Foreign investment is time-consuming and expensive. It is therefore necessary for a company to have a clear view of government attitudes so that time is not spent negotiating potential investments which will subsequently prove unacceptable to the government. The European Community also has to be considered, and the Commission must be consulted about large takeovers as Article 86 of the Treaty of Rome, which deals with dominant positions, may be relevant. (See Chapter 14.)

Foreign companies expanding

This is a cheap form of market research. A few years ago a number of large companies left Spain. The political situation at the time did not warrant investment. It may be worthwhile for a smaller company to find out from embassies abroad what companies are moving in or out of a particular country. Many smaller companies have made successful investments by going in on the back of larger ones. If Spain joins the Community, it could become the best potential growth market of the Community during the next ten years. What are the chances of Spain's joining? One way of assessing this is to see how other companies assess the chances and when, and under what conditions, they invest in Spain.

Nationalization, government controls and price controls

The United States fear that European countries are about to nationalize large sections of their industries, is in practice often unfounded. In certain large-scale industries this remains a possibility, but most governments in Europe have enough problems without wishing nationalization on a wider scale, unless it is to protect jobs in a crisis industry. The National Enterprise Board in Britain, for example, proposes to divest itself of its Ferranti interests. This positive move is being made by a Labour government and illustrates a trend in current European thinking on nationalization and business.

Government controls may present a problem. Export or foreign investment opportunities become less attractive when governments are liable to impose controls without warning. The pharmaceutical industry in France might have been a better growth area for UK companies in recent years. French government controls, particularly on prices, made it difficult for British firms to take advantage of favourable exchange rates and to raise their prices in France. Non-tariff or technical barriers can also affect trade. In France, for example, the onus is on the company to prove that medicines do positive good, while in the United Kingdom it is sufficient to show they do not do any positive harm.

Corporate forms

The kind of legal entity to be established will vary from one country to another. The Community is working towards making the process more simple. The Groupement Industriel d'Enterprise (GIE) is a start. This enables two companies in different countries to work together and pool a number of their resources without merging financially. They can form joint marketing or production facilities and apportion the costs between them while still continuing to report separate financial returns to their respective national authorities. The proposed

European company will also be relevant although its chances of reaching the statute book in the near future are slight. The European company will enable European operations to take place without the problems of different tax and legal structures which at present make the integration of firms across national boundaries costly and complicated. The Third Directive on Mergers between public liability companies in the same member states which was adopted in October 1978, is a step towards the proposed agreement on transnational mergers within the Community.

Patent and trade mark protection

As for this aspect of Community investment there is increasingly a Community-level solution. A new European Patent Office has been established in Munich. A Community-wide patent will replace national patents in the future.

Remittability of funds

The freedom of movement of both funds and people is written into the Treaty of Rome. The latter already exists in principle, and each year rules are drawn up to allow different professions to practice freely across the Community. In the case of the United Kingdom and Italy there are still some exceptions to the freedom to invest. Countries outside the Community, however, can remit funds without difficulty. The advantage of investment in the Community, compared to other parts of the world, is that the financial structure is highly developed. It is almost inconceivable that Community countries would ever prevent funds from being remitted. This is not the case in many other countries where investment laws can change overnight with little hope of redress and the risk of considerable losses.

Taxes

At present these are the subject of much debate as the Community countries differ greatly in the incidence of direct and indirect taxation. Taxation levels and exchange rate variations can have a great effect on profits as they can vary in a year and amount to greater than the expected rate of return on the investment. In comparing wage rates of one Community country with another, the incidence of indirect as well as direct taxation needs to be taken into account. VAT rates still vary greatly even though the basis for assessment has recently been harmonized through a Community directive.

Incentives

These are given only when governments believe that a certain region needs them. To invest in Bordeaux or the Mezzogiorno may seem to be advantageous given the incentives offered. But is skilled labour readily available? Do the incentives remain indefinitely or can they be changed from year to year? Careful financial accountants take any initial write-offs they can get. They do not add future incentives to cash flow and other projections unless they are absolutely sure that they cannot be changed by a new government policy.

Capital sources

Many mistakes have been made over foreign financing in recent years largely because of inflation and extreme exchange rate fluctuations. Cheap money may appear cheap from its interest coupon, but what about repayment? Many companies in the United Kingdom rue the day they borrowed in European currencies and used the money for sterling investment. They are now paying back the loans, perhaps in Swiss francs. Some of the most expensive loans of recent years must be those being repayed at four Swiss francs or Deutschmarks to the pound sterling which were borrowed when the rate was nearer eight or ten to the pound. Community loans borrowed in units of account (*Box 44*) based on a basket of currencies and repayable in the same basket may also have proved to be less cheap than the interest rate suggested. The development of the European Currency Unit (ECU) would make investment in the Community less of a risk from an exchange rate fluctuation viewpoint (see Chapter 18).

Box 44

The European unit of account (EUA)

Changeover from the unit of account to the EUA

On account of the severe disturbances in international monetary relationships and the replacement of the system of fixed parities by floating exchange rates, the Community decided to introduce a new unit of account. Whereas the old unit of account (u.a.) was defined by reference to a given weight of fine gold, with fixed parities, the new 'basket' unit of account (EUA) reflects the day-to-day fluctuations between the various currencies on the foreign exchange markets.

A 'basket' unit of account is made up of different national currencies; the European unit of account is thus defined by reference to a sum of

continued

fixed amounts of Member States' currencies. When the EUA was introduced in 1975, these fixed amounts were obviously not chosen at random but took account, among other things, of the size of each Member State's economy.

The value of one EUA is the sum of the values of the following amounts: BFR 3.66, LFR 0.14, DM 0.828, HFL 0.286, UKL 0.0885, DKR 0.217, FF 1.15, LIT 109 and IRL 0.00759.

Depending on whether the rates of these different currencies are those recorded on the market in Brussels, Copenhagen or Paris, etc., the rate of the European unit of account is given in Belgian francs, Danish kroner or French francs, etc. The effect of this definition is that the value of the EUA in any national currency moves in line with changes in the weighted average of exchange rates in all the currencies in the basket; in other words, it reflects the aggregate movement in those currencies (see Table).

The value of the EUA in the Member State's currencies is determined each day by the Commission on the basis of the official exchange rates notified by the Member States' central banks; the value of the EUA is also calculated in a number of other currencies. Rates for the value of the EUA in the various national currencies are published daily. In addition, anyone may contact the Commission to obtain this information.

Scope of the application of the EUA

Since it was devised in 1975, the EUA has been phased into use in various areas of Community activity:

1975: ACP-EEC Lomé Convention (Council Decision of 21 April 1975); balance sheet of the European Investment Bank (Decisions of the Board of Governors dated 18 March 1975 and 10 November 1977);

1976: ECSC operational budget (Commission Decision of 18 December 1975);

1978: General budget of the communities (Financial Regulation of 21 December 1977).

The European unit of account is now used in all areas of Community activity, apart from the common agricultural policy, operations of the European Monetary Cooperation Fund (EMCF), and the customs field. It will be used for customs purposes from 1 January 1979 onwards.

The EUA has also been in use for some time in the fields of banking and commerce.

Values in national currencies of one European unit of account

National currency	1 June 1978	15 June 1978	30 June 1978
Belgian franc and Luxembourg franc	40.245 8	40.429 3	40.695 3
German mark	2.573 18	2.573 84	2.581 01
Dutch guilder	2.758 38	2.759 29	2.777 40
Pound sterling	0 672 698	0.672 029	0.668 451
Danish krone	6.928 59	6.967 65	7.019 62
French franc	5.651 96	5.652 60	5.600 57
Italian lira	1 065.00	1 058.12	1 062.79
Irish pound	0.672 698	0.672 029	0.668 451
United States dollar	1.232 36	1.229 60	1.244 12

Source: adapted from Bulletin of the European Communities, 6–1978

Box 45

Does Belgium benefit or the United Kingdom?

Large Leyland investment in Belgium

Car manufacturers: From 1977 to 1979, Leyland Industries Belgium SA, a subsidiary of British Leyland will increase the car production of its Seneffe plant by 50 per cent, thus bringing production up to 3000 cars per week. The 800 million BF investment will make it possible to create 1350 new jobs, bringing the total of workers in the plant to 3500 people. The extension will be completely financed in Belgium by local interests. The project will benefit from aids provided for in the Belgian law of 30 December 1970 on economic expansion. In the current economic situation, the extension project for the Seneffe plant represents a first-rate gain for Wallonia.

The British group intends to transfer gradually to Seneffe, production of the Austin Allegro Mark 2, which is at present manufactured in Longbridge. About 75 per cent of the components of the Allegro will continue to be produced in Britain. The first phase of the programme will cost 400 million BF and will commence immediately, comprising the extension of the spraying, finishing and assembly installations, as well as collective equipment. This extension programme indicates the British group's wish to increase its penetration of the European market. The Longbridge plant will be used for the new project for a small car.

Does Germany benefit or the United Kingdom?

German firms will reinforce their investments in Great Britain, a survey by the FRG Chamber of Commerce and Industry in Britain confirms. German industry is already represented in Britain by 128 subsidiaries or branches, 48 of which carry out industrial activities. Approximately 90 per cent of the latter intend to expand their activities in the next five years. Among the non-production industries, about a third plan to embark on industrial production during this period. Among the reasons for increasing their investments, German company managers primarily mention the lower production costs, particularly where wages are concerned. The survey also notes that the British subsidiaries of German firms have very few difficulties with their staff: only ten firms have ever had such difficulties.

Source: Agence Europe, 26 January 1977 and 1 December 1977

Personnel, labour, and social considerations

It is not only the availability of labour, but the effect on the home labour force of a foreign investment which needs to be considered. It will be increasingly difficult for British companies to justify taking on labour abroad rather than in the United Kingdom. More efficient communications and closer understanding between European unions will make the investment decision most complex. Careful preparation and consultation with employers will be necessary. Companies need to develop a personnel strategy both to train managers for foreign operations and, equally important, to operate from the home base and establish

Box 46

Fringe benefits and wages need to be carefully assessed

Lower costs at ICI hit West German chemicals

by Leslie Colitt, Berlin, 27 October

West German chemical manufacturers are facing growing competitive pressure from Britain's ICI as a result of wages and fringe benefits for British workers which are said to be less than half those paid to chemical workers in West Germany.

This is the view of top German chemical industry executives, who are gathered in West Berlin for the 100th anniversary of the German Chemical Industry Federation.

Dr. Herbert Gruenewald, chief executive of the Bayer company, notes that comparative wages and social benefits paid per working hour come out to DM19 for the German worker and DM8 for the British worker. 'This explains how ICI can do so well,' he says.

Herr Hans Joachim Langmann of E. Merck says that after a recent tour of British industry his impression is that, 'if social stability can be achieved in Britain, then British industry will make things increasingly tough' for German companies.

Not only are British wages lower, he says, but 30 per cent of the country offers subsidies to industry, and these advantages explain why in spite of low productivity and strikes, companies in the UK do so well.

According to Dr. Rolf Sammet, chairman of the board of Hoechst, the largest of West Germany's chemical concerns, the industry this year will have growth rate of 1 per cent. He compares this with increases in turnover of over 20 per cent in the UK and 10 per cent in the US.

Source: Financial Times, 27 October 1977

---

the boundary relationships with foreign managers in the subsidiary abroad. A knowledge of languages, but perhaps equally useful an awareness of different business cultures, is required.

An understanding of the different attitudes to business of the French or the Italians will be desirable for many managers who will have contact with a new subsidiary in one of those countries. It may be more useful to understand the business culture than the language. It certainly takes less time. As regards language the number of managers who are able to do business in a foreign language is very limited. You can learn to be polite, you can learn to communicate at a basic level, but there is no way you can learn to manage in a foreign language in a few weeks. For someone with good linguistic ability, it will take at least six months of full-time study and a year to eighteen months in the country before he can hope to communicate and manage successfully. Before that time he will be managing through a bilingual secretary or a foreign advisor, which is a different form of management. The boundary between the home company manager and the subsidiary foreign manager, wherever it is drawn, is always crucial. It is on this boundary that many mistakes and misunderstandings occur.

As regards social considerations, the cost of laying off labour can be extremely high in Community countries. These costs need to be carefully checked out particularly in countries such as Italy and, to a lesser extent, France.

Company structure, search procedures, trade policy, Community legislation

You need to consider whether to treat a European investment as a part of your export market or as part of the home market. In what ways do you need to adapt company structure for the acquisition? It is all very well to say that the Community is a home market, but in practice it 'feels' to many of us very much like a foreign market in spite of its proximity and the Community ties. Establishing a search procedure so that no time is wasted is worthwhile (see *Box 40*). Current and future Community legislation needs to be monitored — the subject matter of much of this book.

Exchange rates

Fluctuations can often make or lose more for the company than its operating profit or loss. In 1976 British Leyland made more on exchange rate operations than on business operations. The study of exchange rates and of invoicing, collecting and remitting, lending and borrowing in relation to them has been a subject which has not, in the past, been accorded sufficient attention by senior management.

There follow considerations such as time and distance and competitors. If other things are equal, Calais is closer than Calabria, and both are closer than Canada. The cost of servicing a foreign market increases dramatically with distance, in terms of executive time as well as money.

Having made out a list along the above lines, there is the question of evaluation. By the time the investment decision approaches there is a battery of advice and advisors available within and outside the company. Many of them have

Box 47

The European investment decision

(1) A major step in life cycle of a
   company involving *all* aspects of
   the business.

(2) Ways of looking at markets:
   Continents
   Country by country
   Regional area
   Population centres
   Language
   Radio/TV area

(3) Investment considerations:
   Political stability
   Economic outlook
   Attitude to foreign investment
   Foreign companies expanding
   Nationalization
   Government controls
   Price controls

Corporate forms
Patent and trade mark protection
Remittability of funds
Taxes
Incentives
Capital sources
Personnel
Labour
Trade policy
Social considerations
Company structure
Search procedures
Current and future Community
regional legislation and trade
legislation
Exchange rates
Time
Distance
Competitors

(4) A simple method of evaluating investment opportunities:

	1 Weight (W)	2 Country A	3 Country B	4 1 × 2 (AW)	5 1 × 3 (BW)
Political	5	9	2	45	10
Taxes	2	2	6	4	12
Personnel	1	4	9	4	9
Economic	2	3	5	6	10
	10	18	23	59	41

Note: Country 'A' preferred to Country 'B'

(5) Conclusions:
   The past is not necessarily a guide
   to the future
   Need for detailed analysis and
   research before decision about
   where, when and how to invest

Ideal investment opportunities will
not necessarily be available
Need for method of trading off
one opportunity against another
The role of chance in the investment decision

Source: J.S.N. Drew, London Business School, April 1978

their own particular interests and prejudices and a balanced assessment is
difficult to obtain.

A simple weighting system as in *Box 47* can be useful in deciding between
alternatives. Eliminate all but five or six of the variables of your checklist as they
will not significantly affect the choice, even though they need to be considered.
Give the remainder a weighting according to their general importance to the
investment decision, as in column 1. The weights should add up to ten (or 100
if you wish to give a detailed assessment of the difference between the weights).
Then grade each investment opportunity by country in columns 2 and 3. In the

example Country A is considered politically very stable and is therefore graded 9. Country B is less stable and therefore graded 2. Cross multiplication shows that in this example Country A is preferred to Country B. This rough and ready approach has the advantage of fitting some simple numbers to subjective thinking about the strength of alternative investments. There are various complicated systems which can be developed from a simple approach. In my opinion they are often too sophisticated and there is no evidence that they work any better. Investment decisions like most business decisions, once the necessary careful research and analysis has been made, are based then, to a large extent, on hunch or feel.

The Community as a single market

Foreign investment is that much more difficult than investing in the home country. There are so many extra dimensions. To envisage the European Community as a single market is still more of a hope than a reality. Of course Community markets need to be looked at as a whole: of course there are many advantages of a large heavily populated land area which increasingly has common rules and regulations governing business: of course the development of the Community needs to be monitored by business. Yet in spite of these considerations, exporting or investing in another Community country from the United Kingdom is not much different, as regards the business problems it poses, from investing in another foreign country. It will be a long time before investment in Nice will be as easy as it is in Newcastle. Nevertheless, it is true that the successful company will increasingly have to consider the Community as a home market from an investment and marketing point of view.

However it will remain a difficult part of the home market for many years to come. The methods and procedures for exploiting it will be different from the methods used in the home country base of the company. It is hard at this stage to imagine a company having its European operations totally integrated in its UK home marketing operations. Exchange control and exchange rates will ensure that profits in France, in francs, need to be dealt with more in the way that profits in Brazil, in cruzeiros, are treated rather than like sterling profits in the United Kingdom.

The conclusion is that the markets of the other eight Community countries are foreign markets so far as the UK company is concerned, but that they are and will increasingly be the most important foreign markets. The important difference is in the structure and future development of the European Community. Community markets will need more careful development than other markets because the successful British company of the future will normally have a significant part of its overseas investment and marketing operations in the Community if it is to survive in an increasingly competitive world. For companies outside the Community, the market must increasingly be considered as a whole. It will remain the world's largest importer and therefore vital to companies which need to develop or maintain a strong export or foreign investment capacity.

Bibliography

Royal Society of Arts (1978) *Concentration on Key Markets*, Betro Trust Report

10 How and where to influence decision-making in the Community

Our chief want in life is somebody who shall make us
do what we can
Emerson, The Conduct of Life, 1860

The Community institutions are at least as receptive to business views as national institutions. Some knowledge of the decision-making process and of the pressure points within the system is required so that the limited amount of time and money available for such activities is spent effectively. A planned one-day visit to Brussels by a well briefed senior manager once or twice a year might do more for a company and its industry than a whole research department devoted to monitoring Community activities. The visit might also contribute a little to Community policy-making.

There are two aspects about any contacts in Brussels or indeed in any government department. The first is the function of the particular official and whether he has the authority to solve your particular problem. The second is the calibre of the man as an individual. It is sometimes better to see a man of high calibre who is not exactly in the right position than to deal with the official who is in the right position but is not particularly effective. Only a close observer of an organization will be able to help you with this sort of judgment. It is often very helpful to obtain from acquaintances in one institution their opinion as to the best person to contact in another institution.

Pressure points

The monitoring of Community activities is discussed in Chapter 12. In this chapter the pressure points themselves are considered — where the individual company can put over its point of view in a European context.

Suppose a company is not able to export a perishable product to France successfully because of delays by the French Customs. The company suspects that the delays are more than bureaucratic and in the nature of a non-tariff barrier. Different aspects of this problem can be raised with:

(1)   National trade associations
(2)   National government departments
(3)   National government — your MP or a minister
(4)   The Offices of the Commission in London, Cardiff, Edinburgh, New York or elsewhere

(BIM) and the Institute of Directors. The CBI in particular is now a well-informed and powerful organization on the European scene and will become more so as it develops its resources in this field. CBI reports on different aspects of Community policies and also those of the BIM are worth reading.

National government departments

In each government department, and particularly in the Departments of Trade and Industry, there are a number of senior civil servants whose jobs involve monitoring, drawing up and negotiating policies affecting business in the Community. A telephone call, a letter or a meeting with one of these officials can be a useful way of influencing UK and hence ultimately Community policy on specific issues. Government officials working in this area can often make representations or enquiries in Brussels direct, as many of them are frequent visitors there. They will have direct links with UKREP and, through it, with the Community. They will of course be involved with policy formation for the Government on Community matters.

If British industry had a fraction of the expertise which the senior civil service has on Community affairs, the views of industry, and hence the policies developing in the Community, would reflect more accurately the views of British business. On important Community matters do not go to local offices of the Departments of Trade and Industry. It is better to contact the London Victoria Street office, although it makes good sense to send copies of correspondence to local offices, particularly if you have contact with them on other business matters.

Box 49

The most useful telephone number for business in the Community

EEC Information Unit, Department of Trade and Industry

01-215 4301

Take the telephone call. There is a special EEC information unit which is manned (six lines) by a very competent and well-informed staff. Unfortunately it is not used enough by businessmen. If the problem is a factual one, then an executive officer in a government department will be able to help. If it concerns a matter of policy then it may be necessary to contact a principal or an assistant secretary. An assistant secretary corresponds, approximately, to a senior middle manager in industry or a colonel in the army. He or she will certainly have access to top civil servants or the minister, if your problem warrants it. Occasionally it will be necessary to meet more senior civil servants, but the key official at the policy-making level is usually an assistant secretary.

Too many businessmen do not treat government officials as equals. They either treat them like servants in a country which no longer has servants, or like mandarins in a country which has never had mandarins. The businessman who treats his national or European civil servant in the same way he would treat a potentially useful business contact will learn much to his advantage.

The telephone, the letter and the personal visit are communication tools and thought needs to be given to choosing the one appropriate for your purpose. A telephone call to the key working level official, once you have identified him, may have more effect than letters and visits to ministers which are more time-consuming. On the other hand, if your case is complex and written evidence is required, too much time can be wasted on the telephone. One of the greatest wastes of management time is communicating through the inappropriate medium.

National government

Lobbying MPs can be an effective way of influencing the European Community. An MP has the power to ask questions and obtain an answer from the government department concerned. This can be particularly effective when the problem is complicated and there is uncertainty as to which ministry to approach. It can also be a speedy one, as MP's questions, whether asked in the House of Commons or written as letters to ministers or ministries, are very speedily dealt with. The government of the day is not only the political master of the civil service, but also the paymaster! A 'PQ', as a parliamentary question is called, receives priority treatment throughout the civil service, and other pressing business is dropped in order to answer it.

Companies may think that business–government relations and indeed business–Community relations, can be satisfactorily maintained by the chairman dining with a minister from time to time, or a senior civil servant's being invited on retirement to join the board of the company. Both approaches have their merits, but neither is sufficient in itself. The level of the interface between the company and the government, the intensity of it and the kind of subjects discussed, should be considered carefully. Too often the interface is seen as the responsibility of one or two people on each side. The attitudes to government of others within the company are neither examined nor monitored. Government contacts ought to be encouraged at a number of different levels within the company. Community contacts also need to be developed. How this might be done is discussed in the next chapter.

The local office of the Commission

The Commission offices are not embassies and therefore are not the correct way of expressing to the Community a concern for a problem such as a non-tariff barrier affecting exports to Germany. On the other hand, the offices are staffed by competent Commission officials whose job is to explain the workings of the Commission and its policies. As a source of information and of good advice they are invaluable.

Figure 10 The United Kingdom Office of the Commission, 20 Kensington Palace Gardens. It contains a comprehensive library and should be a first port of call for those interested in following up Community policies. It has a competent staff who can help you directly on Community policies or arrange appointments for you in Brussels

In spite of disclaimers, it may be that senior officials who are made aware of a businessman's particular problem are able to raise the matter on a visit to Brussels or advise the businessman how best to resolve it, even though it is not strictly their job. As a general rule, however, the Commission office whether in London, Tokyo or New York will suggest that your government department takes up the matter directly with the Community.

The United Kingdom Representation in Brussels

The UK Representative to the European Community in Brussels, and his staff, is another useful pressure point. The question of level is important. If a company deals with another company at the wrong level, then it is much more difficult to do business, and this can cause delays or frustration. At too low a level an approach may not receive the attention that it deserves. It may be misunderstood or not passed on to the appropriate level. If the approach is too high, there is a risk of upsetting the person at a lower level, who may be quite competent to deal with the enquiry. Both in the United Kingdom and in the European Community, when influencing or attempting to influence the Community, the same considerations apply. Some industrialists see regional representatives of the Department of Trade on all matters when in fact they should be seeing them on perhaps 90 per cent of those matters. For the remaining 10 per cent they should be in touch with the appropriate official in Whitehall.

At Brussels it is satisfying to be received by the President of the Commission. On most matters, however, he is not the person to deal with. Like all chairmen, the President of the Commission spends much time meeting people for reasons of ritual or protocol. The senior manager could possibly spend his time more usefully nearer the centre of power, relative to his particular problem.

As regards UKREP, it should rarely be necessary to see anyone but a second or first secretary who is likely to be the expert on a particular problem. One may also perhaps wish to meet the counsellor to whom a number of secretaries report. If you have only half a day in Brussels, a telephone call to the relevant UKREP first secretary the week before would secure an appointment to discuss your problem. He may suggest a few contacts in the Commission or elsewhere, and perhaps a meeting with the UKREP counsellor who has supervisory responsibility for your particular area of business. If there is time to write beforehand, or the opportunity to visit the desk officer at the Department of Trade or other relevant department, then your visit to Brussels will be even better prepared.

An alternative is to contact a commissioner or ambassador whom you know. There is nothing against high-level contacts and indeed much can be done through them, but usually not by them. If you ask a commissioner how to appoint an exclusive agent for the Benelux countries, without falling foul of Article 86 of the Treaty, he will suggest an appointment with the Competition Directorate, and in particular the official dealing with exclusive agencies. In discussing exclusive agencies you have wasted a good opportunity to talk with the commissioner about more strategical matters. A direct telephone call to the appropriate official in the Commission Directorate General IV, Directorate B, who would be only too pleased to help you, would have been more effective. Thus, it is not necessary to go to the highest level in Brussels for information or to express an opinion; on occasions it is a positive disadvantage.

Foreign embassies

If a problem is connected with bilateral Community trade, as in the hypothetical case mentioned above, the embassies in London may be of help. Each of the

Eight have embassies in London which have sections either attached to them or as separate organizations, dealing with bilateral trade matters. Also in London the Eight have chambers of commerce offices which may be of assistance. This approach may be particularly useful if the problem is one where a national government can be of more help than the Commission acting on behalf of the Community. Contact with embassies is simple. There is no need for introductions. Businessmen are so accustomed to contacting other businessmen through introductions that they forget that this is not necessary in the case of government officials. A visit, a telephone call or a letter will achieve results, although the results will differ depending on how busy the officials are and the way in which they order their priorities.

The Commission

The remarks about UKREP apply also to the Commission. Commission officials are very approachable. Their job is to propose policies for European legislation based on Community interests. It follows that for any legislation for industry

Box 50

Your business problem in the European Community

Possible pressure points and information sources:

 (1) National trade associations
 (2) National government departments
 (3) National government – your MP or a Minister of the Crown
 (4) The local office of the Commission in London, Cardiff, Edinburgh, New York or elsewhere
 (5) The United Kingdom Representation in Brussels (UKREP)
 (6) Foreign embassies in London
 (7) The Commission
 (8) The European Parliament
 (9) The Economic and Social Committee
(10) A European trade association
(11) The Court of Justice
(12) The media

For factual information contact from the above list:

 (1) If effective; if not then (2)
 (2) Especially EEC Information Unit: 01-215 4301
 (4) London, 01-727 8090. For other addresses, see Chapter 28. General Community information, not specific business enquiries
 (6) For bilateral trade matters

continued

To influence policy making or raise strategic issues, contact: *

(1) For industry-wide representation of views
(2) Relevant government departments at principal or assistant secretary level
(3) For quick action on urgent matters and for political lobbying
(7) To obtain latest Community-wide thinking and to influence those who will draw up Community policies
(8) As (3) but at Community rather than national level
(9) Especially UK members representing industry
(10) For contacts and Europe-wide lobbying on behalf of your industry

Enabling organizations to arrange contacts with Community institutions *

(4) For general information and contacts in Brussels of a general nature
(5) For briefing on latest Community thinking and introductions to the Commission

Final appeal *

(11) But usually through the Commission
(12) If you have a good case, a newsworthy case and all other channels seem blocked.

*The numbers refer to the list of pressure points

they want to collect as many views as possible. The first step in getting to know the Commission is to meet officials dealing with a particular problem. A directory of the European Commission is readily obtainable and worth keeping on your bookshelf (*Box 13*). For those who need one, it is possible to get hold of an internal directory which contains telephone extensions of named individuals. If used effectively you can, from your desk, get in touch with officials throughout the Community. Bureaucracies within governmental or large private or public corporations can often, in the first instance, be better approached by telephone than by meetings. When did you last telephone a government official?

The European Parliament

European MPs have greater influence after the direct elections and should not be left out of the lobbying process. You can contact them individually or through the parties to which they belong. You can meet them in your constituency or in London. They will often be in Brussels attending committees or in Strasbourg or Luxembourg when the European Parliament is in session. The further away from home you are the easier it will be to spend time with them. It may be more difficult to get to Luxembourg or Strasbourg but once you are there, whether you are a European MP or have come to lobby one, there are less distractions than back in the United Kingdom or when sitting on committees in Brussels. Informal contacts with European MPs and officials of the institutions are perhaps more easily made in the buildings of the European Parliament than anywhere else in the Community.

The European MP is not only a useful contact and well-informed about what is going on in the Community, but he can also ask questions both written and oral on your behalf and take up your cause if you can persuade him that it is a good one.

The Economic and Social Committee

While ECOSOC has very limited power, individual members can be useful interlocutors on your behalf. As about one-third of them are businessmen, they will be sympathetic to your problem, particularly if it has implications of a general Community nature. A list of members can be obtained from the Committee Secretariat. As most of them will be resident in their own countries, it may be easier to meet them in the United Kingdom rather than in Brussels where they will always be busy.

European trade associations

Most national trade associations are affiliated to a European-wide association. Like national ones they vary in quality. They are often represented permanently in Brussels, are in regular contact with the Commission and other institutions, and are consulted by them regularly. In particular, the Employers Federation (UNICE) has an important role to play. It represents the combined strength of the CBI, the Patronat of France and the employers associations of the rest of the Nine. It is useful to discover the strength of your European trade association in Brussels and the calibre of its representatives. They can be helpful not only directly but indirectly through the contacts they can obtain for you in the Commission and elsewhere. Some of the secretary-generals of European trade associations are in a good position to be useful in this way. They have wide experience, a broad range of contacts and yet stand outside the official Community machinery.

The Court of Justice

Normally, there will be no wish to consult the Court and indeed in almost every circumstance it would be best to approach the Commission first. In the last resort, of course, the Court of Justice can be petitioned by any country, company or individual on a matter appertaining to a Community law, and it is obliged to respond to petitions.

The Media

If you have a good case and it is good news, then the media may be useful in furthering your interests. The correspondents dealing with Community affairs are very good contacts; they are well-informed and good lobbyists.

There are a wide number of channels through which a businessman can influence the Community. Using the right ones at the right time may have a significant influence on the policies which affect a business. Much can be learnt in the process and this could affect the development of your European business. In Brussels a businessman is more likely to meet European-minded businessmen, and others who might help, than in most other places. In lobbying the problem is one of action rather than inaction, and of using time to good purpose. It is the most scarce resource.

11 Learning more about the Community in your company

Don't just do something, sit there

Government departments necessarily take the Community seriously because European Community legislation has implications for national legislation and policies and vice-versa. No senior or middle level civil servant would claim that knowledge of the Community was irrelevant to him in his current or future work. Many civil servants become involved directly or indirectly with Brussels. The Civil Service College runs courses for junior and senior civil servants on the Community. Relevant documents are circulated around departments and many civil servants visit Brussels, become involved in Community activities and sit on committees of the Commission and the Council.

Slow UK response to challenge of the Community

In industry and commerce, managers on the whole pay lip service to the Community. In many cases they have not seriously considered its significance for their organization. In the short run this matters little, but over time the effects of ignoring the implications of the Common Market will strike home. In August 1978 a report indicated that British car manufacturers had gained little from the Community while other countries had benefited considerably and increased significantly their share of the UK market. The statement needs to be interpreted with care as the effects of the larger Community on trade must be lagged. Increases or decreases in trade either way during the first few years of a country's joining may well depend on conditions prior to accession.

The inference might be that the United Kingdom has not benefited from joining the Community. The implications are, however, much more serious: that UK car manufacturers were not able to take advantage of a home market of 260 million inhabitants in spite of the fact that labour and other costs were significantly cheaper. The general failure of British car manufacturers to develop the Community market during the first years of our joining the European Community can be put down to lack of preparation and strategical planning rather than lack of products. There is no doubt that many of British Leyland's products from the Jaguar to the Mini could have found good markets in the Community had strategies been developed in time.

Britain's membership of the Community is still not always accepted as a fact, and companies do not put enough effort into developing European markets.

Take, for example, the question of language. In ten years time it may be that English will not be sufficient to do business successfully in Europe, and in that case a company would be wise to encourage its managers and technicians to learn French or German.

Box 51

The Chairman of Shell on developing European managers

Since ours are mixed economies and, with stops and starts, are likely to remain so, the European manager needs to *understand the structure of government* – local, national, European and international – which rules his world. To these levels of government we should now add 'regional' also, since devolution to sub-national regional authorities is now becoming a strident demand in some European countries and will certainly complicate the governmental pattern still further. He needs to understand how decisions are made, and how influence can properly be brought to bear, at central and local government level, and within the political system. He needs to see how decisions taken (or not taken) at one level of government produce waves which envelop the other levels. To this end educational and training programmes must increasingly bring together the managements of corporations, both public and private, with officials of government at all levels.

The problems which European countries face over the next decade are formidable. Of course it can be said that their situation is measurably better than even ten years ago; but this very progress carries with it the seeds of further problems, fostered in an expectation of high economic growth, of ever-improving standards of living, and nurtured by the demands of almost irreconcilable sectoral interests. The pressures are social, political and economic, all at the same time. The accommodation of such pressures while still retaining the ability to mobilize complex organizations for action, is essentially the management job. And managers are needed for this complex integration in every sector of society – in corporations, in government entities, in central, regional and local government, in the social services, in the trade unions, and indeed within the political parties themselves.

Source: Pocock Committee Report on the Educational and Training Needs of European Managers. European Foundation for Management Development 1977

Then there are differences in culture. A company should consider whether it is necessary and possible to make employees sensitive to the sensibilities of foreigners. It may be that business could be improved if middle and senior managers were more effective in their dealings with foreigners. If the European Community becomes increasingly important as a trading bloc, and intra-community trade in the United Kingdom increases even to the current level of the other countries, then a company must consider how it will be affected. If French and German subsidiaries develop in the United Kingdom then a company may find itself competing or working with companies controlled from countries about which its managers know very little. It is increasingly the case that managers reach senior positions in organizations without the experience of living abroad and yet need to control foreign operations. It is important that a company knows how managers are to learn about the Community and what they need to learn at different levels of the organization.

A company and the Community

A company will have neither the time, nor the resources, nor would it be cost effective, to educate everyone up to a high standard of competence on the workings of the Community. It is, after all, only a relatively small part of the business scene. I now wish to identify some groups within a company and discuss what sort of knowledge they require about the Community in order to do their jobs more effectively. (In the next chapter I will discuss some of the methods of achieving this knowledge.) What is said here should be taken only as a starting point. The reader may want to divide up his company differently, and add or subtract from these suggestions.

Each category will need to know about different aspects of Community law and policies. The reader may wish to make a distinction throughout between those in any of these categories who will remain in that category and those who are likely to proceed to more senior positions. The high flier may even be a separate category.

Categories of employees and their learning requirements

(1) Employees in general
(2) First line managers — foremen, charge hands
(3) Junior managers
(4) Middle managers
(5) Specialist staff
(6) Senior managers

Employees in general
They need to know the company's views on how the Community will affect them and their jobs over time. At the time of the Referendum in 1976, Cadbury Schweppes, for example, told their employees that they estimated Britain's withdrawal from the Community would cost several thousand jobs. If your company is established in the Community or intends to extend its operations to other Community countries, employees will need to know the reasons for this and the likely effects on them and their jobs. This has implications for those involved with employee communications; they will need to know about the Community themselves.

Should employees be informed more fully about standards of productivity and living standards in other Community countries? There is still a great deal of complacency about British being best, and lack of awareness of the considerably higher living standards and productivity standards of many continental countries compared to the United Kingdom. Employees should have the opportunity to inspect competing products regularly and their prices should be looked at in terms of the hours worked to earn them in the country of origin. (*Box 52*). Publications, films or lectures on aspects of the Community can be

Box 52

Number of hours (h), minutes (') and seconds (") which need to be worked in order to purchase:

	1 litre of milk	1 litre of beer (gravity 1040/ 1049)	1 litre of petrol (premium grade)	1 litre of whisky (ordinary brand)	1 kg of beef (sirloin)	1 kg of salted pasteurized butter
Federal Republic of Germany	5'43"	18'11"	5'15"	2h19'22"	2h23'40"	57' 8"
France	7'37"	13'47"	8'46"	3h53'18"	2h45'53"	1h20'11"
Italy	9'12"	21' 5"	11' 2"	3h21'39"	3h 4'14"	1h49'20"
Netherlands	5'22"	9'16"	5'50"	1h54'28"	1h40' 0"	1h 1'43"
Belgium	5'12"	10'53"	5'31"	2h 8' 2"	2h 0' 2"	54'23"
Luxembourg	6'13"	9' 6"	4'23"	1h35'10"	1h47'31"	53'50"
United Kingdom	6'43"	24' 5"	6'57"	3h29'18"	2h26' 4"	35'20"
Ireland	5'44"	28'30"	7'55"	4h 6'11"	1h43'10"	43'49"
Denmark	4'11"	13' 8"	4'13"	3h15'52"	2h16'33"	39'14"

Sources: survey on the hourly earnings of male workers in industry (October 1975) and survey of consumer prices in the capitals of the member states (October 1975). As the relevant figures for Ireland are not available from Community sources, they have been supplied directly by that country.

obtained free of charge from the offices of the Commission. The in-house magazine or newspaper can also be used for explaining aspects of the company's European strategy. This aspect of employee communications is of great potential importance. The company will need to stress that it is not putting forward a pro- or anti-European line for any reason other than the interests of the company and its employees.

First line managers
They need to have the general briefing suggested in the previous paragraph and also some explanation of Community legislation as it affects industry, and the

reasons for technical specifications being agreed at the Community level to encourage the free movement of goods. Some companies in the United Kingdom have taken first line managers to visit companies on the continent where productivity is much higher. Visits to subsidiaries or companies in other countries can also be made part of incentive schemes, and viewed not only for their direct benefit but also in terms of motivation and recreation.

Junior managers
An occasional in-company talk by managers dealing with the European Community to foster awareness that the Community is of some significance to the company. Also important is identification of a small number of managers with potential to encourage language training and study courses on Community policies. The broadening aspects of company training schemes must not be as neglected as they have been in the past. Satisfied employees will need to be given educational opportunities through the company to learn about the business environment in general, not just the technical aspects of their specific jobs.

Middle managers
It is essential to encourage those likely to succeeed to top management positions to familiarize themselves with the way the Community works and how it makes policies. Certain individuals should be identified as experts on one or two other countries of the Community and encouraged by, for example, subsidized holidays and study tours combined with business, to specialize in the European aspects of the company's business. There is a need to foster the concept of knowledge of European business affairs as part of a potential top manager's equipment in the same way as knowledge of, for example, accounting.

Specialist staff
Some specialists such as corporate planners, business planners, overseas marketing managers and technicians involved with the application of Community regulations within the company will need to study European legislation more closely. It may be necessary to create a section or designate a manager to deal specifically with Community affairs. This expert would be responsible for monitoring Community affairs and liaising with trade associations, government departments and Commission personnel about aspects of the Community likely to affect the business. He would also be responsible for disseminating information about relevant legislation throughout the company, for making sure that the right information was circulated within the company to the right people.

The task would suit a young graduate and, perhaps, could be combined with language training. Funds should be available so that the person involved could visit Whitehall Eurocrats from time to time, and Brussels once a year. The job should be rotated regularly, and be regarded as important for someone with a future in the company. The person should be the Community conscience of the company, and should have appropriate access to senior management. If the communication aspects of the job are not carefully thought through, a company may be left with information which is never used. The danger of specialist departments is that they are unable, in some instances, to integrate their expert knowledge into the management process of the company.

Senior managers
Senior managers need to take the Community, and knowledge about it, seriously and to have sufficient knowledge to be able to contribute to the formation of a European strategy. A once and for all injection of knowledge may be necessary. A company seminar held partly in the United Kingdom and partly in Brussels is a possibility, or a study plan spread over a year with one or two speakers coming from Brussels, Whitehall or the Commission offices in London. Managers from within the company who live in Europe, or whose work involves European business, will also be able to contribute to such seminars.

Developing European awareness in companies

The above suggestions are made to stimulate thinking about what a company or organization should do about the Community. If the European Community has any implications for a company then it is important to ensure that these are taken into account.

Any company which implemented all the above possible courses of action at once would be accused of 'Euromadness'. Indeed some companies in the last few years have made mistakes in Europe. Despite the mistakes most companies would now agree that Community markets are worth penetrating; the opportunities are there and the risk is that someone else, a competitor perhaps, will seize them. To over-concentrate on Community strategy for two years may not be a bad thing for some companies, particularly if the alternative is to continue to ignore it.

The need to learn more about the Community at all levels within the company opens up the wider question of developing managers for senior positions in industry. The United Kingdom lags behind most industrialized nations in the education of its managers for top management positions. There has been rapid improvement, but there is still a feeling that once a manager gets to a top position he has arrived and there is nothing more to learn. This is surprising when one considers that many managers reach top management positions, the board of their company for example, in their forties. They are likely to hold that job for longer than any other job they have had in their lives — perhaps for upwards of twenty years. So why do senior managers often think that training is only for subordinates?

12 Monitoring and contributing to Community developments affecting business

Business in future will shape much more than in the past the ways in which the Community develops

Developments in the Community need to be monitored by companies at the tactical and strategical levels. At the tactical level there are directives and regulations coming into force which might affect business. For example, technical directives about the amount of lead in petrol or the height of bumpers; the suppression of radio interference from power tools or the composition and approval of pesticides. These must be known about if they already exist. If they do not, then it is important to know where they are in the decision-making pipeline. What are their chances of eventually becoming law?

Tactical monitoring

This type of information is available most readily either from a trade association or from the Department of Trade which as well as issuing periodical check lists of regulations and directives, publishes a free monthly supplement to its weekly journal *Trade and Industry*. It is called 'European Community Commentary'. If your trade association is providing a good service (and if it is not you should find out why and demand that it does) you are protected at this tactical level from being surprised by proposals which suddenly become Community law.

Though pipeline information is available in companies knowledge of its existence does not always reach the decision-maker. Some companies have excellent libraries with good reference material on the Community but knowledge of its existence is restricted to the librarian. Some of the material is circulated each week or month but does not necessarily get read by those who need to be informed.

A possible way to prevent this from happening is to ensure that a senior manager has responsibility for supervising the monitoring of Community legislation and that he ensures that those reporting to him are aware of the potential importance of what at first sight might seem like a series of technical standards with no clear relevance to the company's activities. The cost of this basic monitoring is small and the information sources which need to be held are also small. In order to monitor successfully a minimum amount of information needs to be held. Some suggestions are in *Box 53*.

Box 53

A basic library of European Community business information

If a company wishes to maintain a small reference section on the European Community, the following documents and periodicals will form a sound base and cost only a few pounds a year to maintain. Further details are in Chapter 30.

(1) *Trade and Industry*, the official weekly news magazine of the Department of Trade. Regular check list of regulations and directives and articles on aspects of Community business.

(2) *Bulletin of the European Community*. Eleven issues a year plus an index. A comprehensive account of Community developments. Supplements published regularly on important Community policies.

(3) *The Economist*. Weekly section on Europe and the European Community. It will not miss the significance of any major developments and their implications for business. The Economist Intelligence Unit produces good material on European business and is available on subscription.

(4) *The Financial Times*. It has special European pages each day. Read these daily for a couple of years and you will become very expert on the Community.

(5) UK Office of the Commission; briefing and background notes. The best short briefs available anywhere and available free of charge.

(6) *Directory of the Commission.* Names of key officials. Published three times a year.

(7) *Treaties establishing the European Community*. Basic reference text. Available from HMSO.

(8) House of Lords Scrutiny Committee reports on major policies and proposals of the Community. Those from Sub-Committee B in particular will interest industry as they cover trade, industry and treaties. Available from HMSO. Excellent reports.

(9) CBI reports on aspects of Community policies. Specifically designed for business.

(10) European Community Information. Comprehensive *Financial Times* monthly newsletter designed especially for business.

Strategical monitoring

At the strategic level monitoring is more difficult. A company is interested in pipeline information because knowledge of proposed legislation will help with planning. It may also contribute to the development of Community legislation and policies. The development of the company and the development of the Community may go hand in hand. Successful planning of a company's future will depend on accurate forecasts, new products, available sources of finance and the development of national, European and international strategies. It also depends on new ideas.

In some companies it is the chief executive or chairman who develops these ideas, but there is also a wider need to create and maintain a European awareness in senior managers. The production manager needs to think European as much as the finance manager; the computer services manager as much as the marketing manager. A European awareness at an early stage in the development of a product or a service might open up a larger and more profitable market. How can managers learn to think in terms of a 260 million home market when they have traditionally thought of European markets as abroad?

Take one European idea as an example. Some UK companies run their European and overseas operations from a Luxembourg incorporated company for the obvious reason that there are tax advantages to be obtained from operating from Luxembourg. The difference between Luxembourg and Lichtenstein or the Bahamas as tax havens is that Luxembourg is within the Community and therefore safer for a number of reasons. It is a member of the Community and yet there is tacit agreement by the Community that Luxembourg should remain, compared to the other Eight, a tax haven. If this agreement had not existed, then certain funds would have remained outside the Community, or would have been invested outside by Community companies.

In another sense it is not surprising if those possibilities have not been looked into because European awareness among financial managers and accountants (and others) is comparatively new. Less than five years ago fewer than 15 per

Box 54

Monitoring Community developments

A company needs to monitor:

(1) Directives and regulations affecting the industry in which it operates.
(2) Pipeline information. To discover what new legislation is being developed which might affect the industry and to know what stage it has reached.
(3) Broad trends in policies. To be able to view whether the Community is developing into a genuine Common Market and to what extent world trade is becoming more regional and a wide European base therefore necessary or desirable.
(4) Trade between the Community and the rest of the world. The need to know about trade negotiations with third countries which could affect the company's business with a particular country.
(5) Whether and how its managers are developing a European awareness.

cent of the companies represented at the Institute of Chartered Accountants' courses on European investment were invoicing in hard foreign currencies. The main reasons were: 'we are not in the foreign exchange business' or 'our agents in France would realize what we are doing' or 'our out-goings are in sterling and it is therefore better if our incomes are too'. Four years later fewer than 10 per cent on similar courses came from companies which did not invoice in hard foreign currencies.

Flexibility, monitoring and keeping up to date are as necessary in the field of European business as in any other. In fact many companies would have been well advised to have changed back to invoicing in sterling rather than dollars taking a three-year view of the late seventies. Many companies were slow to invoice in foreign currencies because, although someone in the company may have been aware of the potential advantages, the company as a whole, at senior management level, did not welcome and initiate ideas in a European or inter-national sense. Some companies relied heavily on the chief executive. If he was keen on developing European markets, then they were developed. If he was not enthusiastic, then they were ignored.

How to develop European awareness in senior executives at one level seems simple. A daily reading of the European page of *The Financial Times* or *The Times* should be encouraged; a weekly study of *The Economist's* Europe and European Community sections and a monthly clipping service circulated around

Box 55

Management briefing on the European Community: a suggestion

(1) Ten hours of pre-seminar reading on the Community selected from suggestions in this book.
(2) Regular *Economist* and *Financial Times* reading of European pages for six months.
(3) One-day seminar on the European Community.
  (a) The European Community institutions and how they operate
  (b) Community policies affecting business
  (c) Business and business cultural environment in France and Germany
  (d) Company business strategy towards the European Com-munity — a three-year plan.
(4) To follow up, a half-day seminar one year later.
  (a) Developments in the Community over the last year
  (b) Review of action taken on 3(d).
(5) The seminar should begin with board level participation and then further seminars should be developed from it at different levels within the company.

senior managers might be a start. However, in practice this will not work because so many other subjects are required: background subjects; accounting, forecasting, computer applications, international markets, management development, to name but a few.

A European awareness can be better developed by a strong dose of the Community at the beginning and then smaller doses from time to time. A suggestion for a company briefing for its senior executives and a method of follow up is shown in *Box 55*. The advantage of this method is that it enables senior managers not only to learn, but also to develop a European awareness and to monitor European events and activities at the appropriate level. From this type of conference new ideas are developed, and it is often the occasional new idea developed by senior managers together which changes the direction of a company.

Monitoring Community developments which might affect business is relatively simple. The important decision is at what level this should be done in the company and how much time should be spent on it. Time spent on monitoring European Community affairs is probably time well spent, if you believe that the Community is of growing importance to European business.

Contributing to the development of policies is less immediately of value to a company. It can involve considerable senior personnel time and it is difficult to quantify the benefits. Companies are increasingly called upon to contribute to the complex industrial society in which they operate. If this contribution is accepted as inevitable, and indeed desirable, then this aspect of a company's operations must not be neglected.

The Community is very receptive to ideas and contacts with industry. Any company which tries to develop its relations with the Community cannot fail to succeed.

Internal Community policies
which concern business

13 Major policies affecting business

Community policies may or may not affect your
business on Monday morning. The question is will
they affect your Monday morning in five years time?

The first two sections covered the Community decision-making process. They described how the various institutions interact with one another and discussed the problems of exporting, investing and monitoring developments. The primary legislation of the treaties and the secondary legislation of directives, regulations and recommendations form the body of European law which underlies the various policies developed by the Community. The dilemma is that many of the policies, when studied in detail, do not seem to have much day-to-day effect on business. The reader might well wonder how many of the policies described in the following chapters will affect his business on Monday morning.

It is true that not many people in an organization need to know about Community directives in detail. Rather more, however, should be able to contribute over a longer period to their company's European thinking. It will be too late if a company waits until managers reach strategic decision-making levels in the company before encouraging them to learn about the Community. Much of this book, for many managers, is background reading only. Yet it is from wide background knowledge and experience, plus specific detailed expertise, that good strategic thinking develops. Community policies may or may not affect your business on Monday morning. The question is will they affect your Monday morning in five years time?

This section starts with competition policy because it is a policy with teeth which can bite deep into the profits of companies which ignore it. In enforcing the rules of competition laid down by the Community treaties, the European Commission recently has been more vigilant than ever, as the Distillers Company discovered at the end of 1977. The Commission ordered the company to end its practice of applying differential prices to wholesale customers in the United Kingdom depending on whether they were exporting whisky to other Common Market countries or selling it to retailers in the United Kingdom.

Competition policy seems difficult to reconcile with some of the new policies emanating from the Industry Directorate-General of the Commission. These seek to establish cartels, of one kind or another, to protect certain Community industries in crisis. This apparent conflict and the policies developing in the industrial sphere, both for growth industries and for industries in crisis, are discussed in the following chapter.

Trade and commercial policies are at the very heart of the principle of the Common Market. The considerable achievements of these policies are discussed, as also are present concerns and likely future developments.

'Eurobargaining' is still something of a cliché, but there is little doubt that national unions will come to know one another better. European union pressure groups will develop and perhaps transnational unions will be formed, leading to European-wide negotiations on wages, employment conditions and social benefits. A company needs to be aware of future trends to assess what actions, if any, it will need to take and at what time.

The European consumer has recently been championed by the Commission. In this relatively new field of government, legislation is developing rapidly. It is easier for the Community to make progress in new fields of legislation, such as consumerism or technical standards for solar heating, than where a great deal of national legislation already exists and positions are entrenched. It is also easier to develop policies which will take a long time to implement. For instance, the Community has more chance of developing a strategy for the European aircraft industry in the 1990s than it has of coordinating aircraft companies' policies towards the current European Airbus project, or the next decade's demand for military aircraft.

Occasionally a single policy is given widespread publicity, either because significant progress is made or because there are major objections to it. More often progress in developing a policy is made in a steady and unspectacular way through painstaking consultations. These policies may become significant and therefore need to be monitored just as closely as those which are more widely known.

The enlargement of the Community by the accession of Greece, Portugal and Spain, is an example of a fundamental change. Yet this change had less publicity than either the introduction of tachographs into the cabs of trucks or the problems of North Sea fisheries.

In many areas policies are being developed which will be of interest to business. Agricultural policy, for example, is the major developed policy of the Community and in many ways its most important one. From a financial point of view, it uses up the major proportion of the Community's annual budget. From the institutional point of view, it is a highly developed policy which actually works very well in a technical sense. That it needs reforming is agreed by almost all countries and commentators. The mechanisms through which it operates and the complex systems which have been developed indicate, however, that it is possible to operate successfully a transnational policy across the Community.

Economic and Monetary Union was given an unexpected emphasis by President Jenkins soon after he took office in 1977. The French President, Giscard d'Estaing, and the German Chancellor, Helmut Schmidt, gave their considerable political support to it soon afterwards. The policy, which has had a chequered history, has now begun to make significant progress. The great European crisis of unemployment, only now becoming apparent, may have helped it to re-emerge

Box 56

President Jenkins on economic and monetary union

No single European state, however economically strong, now has its own salvation in its hands. Each, if it tries to believe this, is caught in a strait-jacket. Action to stimulate a national economy is undercut either by fears of a fall in the exchange rate or by dependence upon what other governments are doing. I do not claim that greater monetary unity, the drastic reduction of exchange rate uncertainties, would automatically lead to higher employment. But I do believe that there is little hope of returning to acceptable employment levels without such greater stability.

The reasons are simple. First, monetary upheaval has been a major cause of our troubles of the past five years. A world monetary system, as we knew it for the quarter century of Bretton Woods, no longer exists. The stability of the dollar, on which the system depended, underpinned a period of growth and increase in living standards unsurpassed in recorded history. We cannot expect the United States again to carry the central burden in the same way.

Second, Britain lives by trade in a Community which also lives by trade. Not only is the European Community the largest trading bloc in the world but 50 per cent of Community trade is inter-Community trade. And we have suffered immensely from having currency upheavals, not merely external to us as with the United States and Japan,

but in our midst. The result is insufficient financial and trading stability to encourage trade flows and the productive investment necessary to reconstruct and replace threatened industries. This is not balanced by the freedom to float our currency, which has recently been a euphemism for the freedom to sink. And that freedom has been singularly unsuccessful in giving us either higher growth or lower unemployment. It has merely given us higher inflation. Industry needs a surer prospect.

Third, the combination of a more stable international environment for investment and greater financial discipline can give us a sustained prospect of mastering inflation and thus giving real value to wage and salary increases. Too often in the past a spurt of growth, without the backing of overall financial stability, has frittered away the real value of every increase in the pay packet. And this has been true under governments of either party.

Fourth, unless these preconditions are met, the prospect of unemployment will grow and not diminish. Demographic factors, with nine million more young people entering the European labour market over the next five years than there will be old people leaving it, threaten that. Individual national palliative action can make temporary dents in these figures. But it cannot on its own provide a longer-term solution.

Source: ISEC/29/78

---

as a policy capable of further development. It is a policy at the very heart of the idea of a united Community.

Political cooperation has also developed pragmatically. The European Council meets three times a year, and there are regular meetings at foreign minister level. These meetings are of fundamental importance to the development of the Community.

Box 57

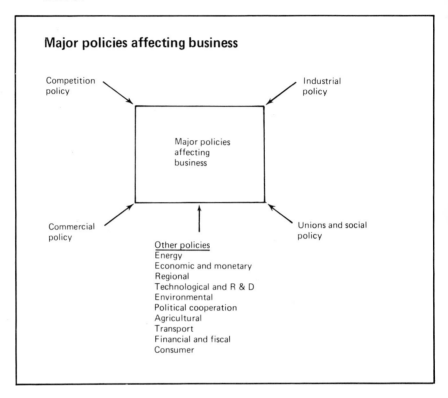

Unfortunately, these policies can only be touched on in this book. However, if you wish to follow up a particular policy in more detail, there are references at the end of some of the chapters to the most important documents, and to commentaries on them. The major internal policies of the Community affecting business are in *Box 57*. External policies are covered in Section Four.

14   Competition policy

Building Europe is like building a gothic cathedral.
The first generation knows that they will never see the
work completed but they go on working
Anthony Sampson, The New Europeans

The competition policy of the Community cannot be ignored by business. The Commission is responsible for controlling the policy and has the power to inflict very heavy fines on companies which infringe it. The principle of free trade is a cornerstone of the Community and the Commission's task is to ensure that the Common Market remains an integrated trading area in which prices are not distorted by trade restrictions, market sharing or monopolies.

The basic rules dealing with restrictions are set out in Articles 85 and 86 of the Treaty. Article 85 prohibits trade agreements which prevent, restrict or distort competition in the Community. Price fixing, market sharing, restriction of production, discriminatory terms of supply, are all prohibited. The policy affects agreements both between firms in the Community and those in third countries, such as the United States and Japan, which trade within the Community. The internal trade of a member state is its own affair. The policing of agreements which affect national but not Community trade is the responsibility of national governments.

Article 85(1) lists the prohibited categories of agreements and Article 85(3) the principal exceptions. Although any agreement which infringes the Article is void, there are a number of exemptions where the agreement between two companies leads to improved production or distribution or promotes technical or economic progress. The Commission grants these exemptions, either on an individual basis or as block exemptions in respect of certain kinds of exclusive dealing. Details of how to apply for an exemption can be obtained from the Department of Trade or by writing to Directorate-General IV at the Commission (the address is in Chapter 28).

Article 86 of the Treaty gives the Commission powers to investigate transnational mergers. It prohibits the use of a dominant position by a company, if this affects trade between member states.

Some cases illustrating different aspects of competition policy follow in *Boxes 59* and *60*. Competition policy is sufficiently complex to warrant legal advice, which must be obtained from experts with good contacts in Brussels and who are familiar with the latest Commission thinking as well as with the realities of business. Cheap advice can be expensive. If a company needs to look carefully at aspects of its present or future policy as regards competition policy, then it should obtain advice before seeking clarification from the Commission. The

Box 58

The Treaty of Rome articles on competition

Article 85

(1) The following shall be prohibited as incompatible with the Common Market: all agreements between undertakings, decisions by associations of undertakings and concerted practices which may affect trade between member states and which have as their object or effect the prevention, restriction or distortion of competition within the Common Market, and in particular those which:

(a) directly or indirectly fix purchase or selling prices or any other trading conditions;

(b) limit or control production, markets, technical development, or investment;

(c) share markets or sources of supply;

(d) apply dissimilar conditions to equivalent transactions with other trading parties, thereby placing them at a competitive disadvantage;

(e) make the conclusion of contracts subject to acceptance by the other parties of supplementary obligations which, by their nature or according to commercial usage, have no connection with the subject of such contracts.

(2) Any agreements or decisions prohibited pursuant to this Article shall be automatically void.

(3) The provisions of paragraph 1 may, however, be declared inapplicable in the case of:
any agreement or category of agreements between undertakings;
any decision or category of decisions by associations of undertakings;
any concerted practice or category of concerted practices;

which contributes to improving the production or distribution of goods or to promoting technical or economic progress, while allowing consumers a fair share of the resulting benefit, and which does not:

(a) impose on the undertakings concerned restrictions which are not indispensable to the attainment of these objectives;

(b) afford such undertakings the possibility of eliminating competition in respect of a substantial part of the products in question.

Article 86

Any abuse by one or more undertakings of a dominant position within the Common Market or in a substantial part of it shall be prohibited as incompatible with the Common Market in so far as it may affect trade between member states. Such abuse may, in particular, consist in:

(a) directly or indirectly imposing unfair purchase or selling prices or other unfair trading conditions;

(b) limiting production, markets or technical development to the prejudice of consumers;

(c) applying dissimilar conditions to equivalent transactions with other trading parties, thereby placing them at a competitive disadvantage;

(d) making the conclusion of contracts subject to acceptance by the other parties of supplementary obligations which, by their nature or according to commercial usage, have no connection with the subject of such contracts.

Source: Treaty establishing the European Economic Community, Rome, 25 March 1957

Box 59

Community law can affect organizations both inside and outside the Community

Competition: Commission this Wednesday carries out checks in premises of German blacksmiths

Brussels (EU), Wednesday 14 December 1977 — The Commission's services paid a surprise visit this Wednesday in Dusseldorf to the offices of the Association of German Mechanical Blacksmiths (Vereinigung deutscher Freiformschmieden). The officials presented themselves armed with a *decision* taken on the basis of Article 14, Paragraph 3 of Regulation 17 EEC, to examine the documents of this association regarding which there are a number of assumptions. They asked to consult the documents concerning relations with other enterprise associations in the EEC, the documents concerning meetings with establishments which form part of this association; the latter's documents on its Zurich office, and notably payments made to that office.

This 'descent' by the Commission's services can be explained by the fact that there are sufficient motives to *suspect the existence in the Common Market of agreements to protect the domestic prices of heavy forge parts of over 4 tonnes* and to limit trade in them between the Member Countries. These agreements and limitations, as well as the assumed distribution of orders, are an infringement of Article 85 of the EEC Treaty. In addition, this association refused to authorize checks last January, arguing that there had been no Commission decision. This has now been given, after the Commission consulted the German Cartels Office (Bundeskartellamt). In its decision, the Commission pointed out that fines can be imposed in the event of the incomplete presentation of the professional documents requested

Competition: anti-dumping: complaint against Kraftliner paper from the United States

Brussels (EU), Wednesday 14 December 1977 — The European Commission is examining an anti-dumping complaint concerning Kraftliners paper imported to the EEC from the United States. The complaint was made by French producers with the support of those of the other Member States. American prices, which determine

market prices, are allegedly considerably lower for export than domestic prices. The Anti-Dumping Committee expressed an *opinion in favour of the opening of a formal procedure,* feeling that sufficient proof has been provided; the Commission should give a decision in the very near future.

Source: Agence Europe, No. 2349, 15 December 1977

---

presentation of a case to the Commission needs to be considered carefully so that the company's position is put in the best possible way.

In 1976 the Commissioner responsible for competition policy said, 'In a year or two's time, I personally feel we shall have all the legislation we need to deal with anti-trust policy in the Community's present economic situation. In future we may well have some big cases, but very few will be as important as the test cases we have had in the past.' The fact that there now exists a substantial amount of case law means that companies in a position where they want clarification of, say, exclusive agencies, can do so without resorting to first principles and test cases. In recent years mistakes have been made usually by those companies which have not known about, or have ignored, competition rules, or who have failed to check whether they applied in a specific case.

Box 60

An Italian court asks the European Court of Justice for a ruling

Football: Europe 1 — Italy 0

In the Europe v Italy match the referee's decision was final: Italian football teams can employ players from any Community country.

The question was raised by a dispute between a Mr Mantero and a Mr Dona. Mr Dona was instructed by Mr Mantero to make enquiries in footballing circles abroad in an attempt to find a young player for the Rovigo team. Mr Dona inserted an advertisement in the Belgian sports press but Mr Mantero refused to interview the applicants – or repay the cost of the advertisement – on the grounds that the Italian Football Federation's rules specifiy that only members of the Federation can play in matches, membership in theory being restricted to Italian nationals.

The case was referred to an Italian court which in turn referred it to the Court of Justice of the European Communities. In its recent judgment the Court of Justice found that any national rules or code of practice which reserves the right to participate in football matches to national professionals or semi-professionals is incompatible with the Treaty of Rome.

The Court stated once again that the Treaty prohibits any form of discrimination against a person providing services based either on his nationality or on the fact that he is resident in a Community country other than the country in which he provides services.

The only exception to the rule that the Court could accept was the exclusion of foreign players from certain matches for non-economic, in other words purely sporting, reasons.

Source: Euroforum, No. 30/76, 27 July 1976, p. 4

In addition to maintaining and developing the Common Market and preventing large companies from abusing their economic power, competition policy has a third aim. This is to encourage firms to rationalize production and distribution and to keep up with technical and scientific developments. The concentration of industry is regularly monitored throughout the Community and reported on each year, in April, when a comprehensive document is produced by the Commission. *Box 65* is taken from the introduction to the 1978 report. The report shows that in the four years 1973–6 nearly 20 000 companies, 40 per cent of which were international, were involved in these activities.

Competition policy covers a number of different subjects, the scope of which is outlined in the rest of this chapter. Each subject is potentially of significance to companies operating in the Community. Because much of the policy is based on legal interpretations of the treaties and subsequent secondary legislation and case law, company legal advisors need to be aware of the implications of the

Box 61

What use is competition policy?

The Treaty of Rome which is the basis of the European Community stipulates that a system should be set up to ensure that competition within the Common Market does not become distorted.

The three principal objectives are:

To create a single market for the benefit of industry and consumers. This is not simply a question of removing customs offices at the borders and enabling goods to travel unhindered throughout the Nine. It is necessary to prevent companies from setting up 'invisible frontiers' through restrictive agreements and cartels;

To prevent the abuse of economic power. When companies dominate a market and have eliminated their competitors it is then up to Community regulations to ensure that the companies do not abuse the economic power they have;

Encouraging companies to rationalize and change with progress. By ensuring commercial rivalry, competition policy aims to encourage the competitivity of European industry in world markets.

policy. The bibliography at the end of the chapter supplements the necessarily brief treatment and should be referred to by managers interested in the ramifications of the policy on their business.

Market sharing agreements
Many of the Commission's actions have been in this field. In 1969, the Commission imposed fines for the first time on six European manufacturers who set up an international quinine cartel which maintained prices and quota arrangements so that each had exclusive control over its respective domestic market. Together they accounted for half the world and 80 per cent of the Community market. There are brief accounts of a number of cases in the books on Community law mentioned at the end of this chapter.

Exclusive agreements
Not only horizontal agreements between competitors, but also vertical agreements between manufacturers are prohibited if they restrict business freedom. A

Box 62

The Commission on Competition policy, 1978

The economy of Europe is undergoing a difficult period of transition. Much structural weakness has become apparent or become worse following a reduction in demand accompanied by increased pressure of imports. If structural change is essential in order to reach a new economic balance, it is as well to realize that this will be difficult to achieve in a climate of poor economic growth unless clear perspectives are maintained.

The role of the Commission must therefore be to promote and establish structural change within a socially acceptable framework. The illusion must be resisted that enterprises can protect themselves against those necessary changes by coming to terms with their competitors or by seeking excessive protection from national authorities.

Competition policy plays an important role in the application of the basic rules which govern the integration of markets. The flow of trade creates the need for constant structural adaptation. The maintenance of non-competitive behaviour or anti-competitive practices, on the other hand, leads to partitioning of markets in the sectors directly involved, which then tends to spill over into related sectors in the downstream markets.

It is no coincidence that these simple but basic rules should be challenged at a time when the forces of competition seem to demand excessive sacrifices in certain sectors, particularly so far as employment is concerned, following a lasting slowing-down in the growth of or a switch

in demand. Private arrangements for organizing markets or government intervention affecting the competitive ability of undertakings have the object of softening the rigours of market forces. If some of these measures are prompted by the market, others on the other hand substitute themselves for the market, the decisions in such cases being centralized, whether they concern production capacities or govern production itself or prices.

Whatever the means chosen to 'organize' a sector, that is to say protect it from competition, one should bear in mind that the direct or implicit object is always to re-establish at least temporarily an artificial profitability by raising prices. Thus the cost of the salvage operation is supported by the market, that is the user, the processor and finally the ultimate consumer or the taxpayer. Measures for organizing the market therefore tend to have repercussions and to spread, especially to later stages in the manufacturing process, particularly when these remain exposed to the competitive pressures of imports.

Accordingly it is essential that public intervention in the markets should be governed by the rules and procedures which correspond best with the common interest in the sense of the Treaty. In particular, restrictions of competition should be part of a plan for reinforcing competitivity not only in the sector concerned but in the Community economy as a whole. The latter cannot support indefinitely the high costs of poorly adapted structures.

Source: Seventh Commission Report on Competition Policy, April 1978

manufacturer cannot supply a single dealer exclusively in one specific part of the Community unless he can obtain agreement from the Commission that it is in the interests of the consumer.

The German firm Grundig discovered that its agreement with its sole distributor in France, Consten, infringed Article 85(1). It did not qualify for exemption because the parties gave each other absolute territorial protection. Grundig equipment could be sold in France only by Consten; no other Grundig dealer could export to France. The case arose because a third company bought wholesale Grundig tape recorders in Germany and imported them into France for resale at well under Consten's prices. Consten tried, unsuccessfully, to prevent the imports. In some cases it is often on the complaint of a third party that the cases come to light. It was through the complaint of a Scottish whisky distributor that the Distillers Company was prevented by the Commission from charging differential prices to wholesalers in the United Kingdom depending on whether they were buying the whisky for the UK home market or for export.

Industrial property rights
The Commission opposes the use of trademarks, patent licences and know-how agreements as a means of market protection. Drawing the line is, however, very difficult. In the Grundig–Consten case (1966) it was decided that trademark rights could not be used to protect a national market by preventing another distributor from importing products bearing the same trademark.

Problems of notification
Agreements liable to fall within the scope of the competition rules must be notified before they are put into effect, so that the Commission can state in advance whether they are consistent with the rules of the Common Market. As case law developed a number of general guidelines emerged. For example, there are block exemptions, in particular for small firms with an annual turnover of less than 20 million units of account, provided also that the products involved constitute no more than 5 per cent of the volume of business of the particular market. There are also cooperation agreements to help small business to work more effectively and to increase their competitiveness. They have enabled firms to exchange information, carry out joint market research, cooperate on financial matters and jointly use production, storage and transport equipment as well as joint advertising and common labelling.

Dominant position
A number of companies have abused their dominant position under Article 86 of the Treaty and as a result have had either to divest themselves of companies which they had taken over or pay fines until certain practices were discontinued. This Article is of critical importance to companies which are likely to find themselves in a dominant position in their industry, but for the vast majority of companies it is unlikely that they will need to be concerned with its provisions.

Merger control

Large companies with annual sales of over 200 million units of account make up over 50 per cent of all Community sales. Europe's fifty largest companies alone account for 25 per cent of total sales. The Commission is therefore keen to be involved in the approval of mergers before they take place. This has caused problems because, it is argued, prior notification of a merger could often prevent it taking place. There would be considerable uncertainty while awaiting the Commission's approval.

State aids

The Commission is also involved in safeguarding the Community interest as regards state aids, state monopolies of a commercial character and nationalized undertakings. The Commission has made slower progress on state aids, which are based on Articles 92 to 94 of the Treaty, as the direct interests of member governments are involved.

In looking at state aids the Commission has been guided by three principles: (1) national aids must be compatible with the general Community interest; (2) they must make an effective contribution to improving the structure of a given industry or region while encroaching as little as possible on competition; (3) they may be justified not only on purely economic grounds but also for social reasons; for example the maintenance of employment or to support backward regions.

In practice, the Commission has had difficulty in applying its rights in this area. In times of economic recession companies pressure governments for aid, and in many cases all that the Community has been able to demand is prior notice and discussion of these aids and confirmation that they will be selective, temporary, degressive and 'transparent', that is clearly quantifiable.

Competition v cartels

The conflict within the Community on the question of competition versus cartels is considerable. It takes place both within the Commission, where Directorates-General have different responsibilities, and between different countries depending on political and economic pressures put on the governments by different industries. There are arguments on both sides. The conflict is achieving one important result, namely to bring industrial policy more to the forefront. This conflict is the subject of the next chapter.

Although there is no basic contradiction between competition policy and industrial or regional policy, conflicts can arise where individual member states provide unreasonable assistance to individual industries or firms, or improperly attract investment to specific regions through excessive regional aids. The Commission's power to control such measures may clash with the internal affairs of member states. Sometimes there are direct confrontations which, occasionally, can only be resolved by the Court of Justice which is the final arbiter in all competition cases, as it is in all interpretations of the treaties. In

Box 63

Cartels, anyone?

Brussels

Free competition and opposition to cartels have always been a cornerstone of EEC policy. But Viscount Étienne Davignon, the EEC's Industry Commissioner, is proposing to modify the EEC's competition rules to legalize cartels for industries in crisis.

Europe's steel industry already has a cartel, Eurofer, but this is a special case. Under the 1952 Paris treaty the EEC Commission has special powers to set minimum prices and production quotas during a crisis. Other cartels, however, need to be squared with the competition rules of the Treaty of Rome.

Article 85 of the Treaty of Rome says that the only cartels which can be approved at present have to 'allow consumers a fair share of the benefit' and must not 'eliminate competition' for their products. Viscount Davignon suggests that the Article should be modifed, allowing the Commission to approve cartels if the Council of Ministers agrees that the industry is in crisis.

The Industry Commissioner is having to overcome stiff opposition to this change from Mr Raymond Vouel, the EEC's competition supremo. Mr Vouel wants to keep the Council out of what until now has been exclusively a Commission responsibility, and would prefer not to see competition policy used as an instrument of the dirigiste policies favoured by Viscount Davignon. The proposal may also still run into trouble with the Germans in the Council of Ministers.

Industries eyeing cartels include zinc producers, makers of women's tights and string manufacturers, all hit by overcapacity after over-optimistic investments. The French are pushing hard to include paper and pulp makers, but so far without much response from the other Member States. Dutch, Italian and French petrochemical firms are keen on a cartel too, but the idea has been scotched by the German and British competitors, who reckon that they can survive in better shape uncartelized.

They could yet change their minds. Commodity plastics plants are still running at 30 per cent below capacity, and plant is expanding faster than demand. Big new plants in the advanced developing countries, particularly in OPEC, could also hit them hard. Commission officials say there is little excuse for a cartel in what is still a growth industry. But managers argue that investment has to be on such a large scale for a plant to be competitive that they need to know in advance about other firms' investment plans, or face overcapacity.

This sort of voluntary investment cartel is exactly what Mr Guido Brunner, the German Energy Commissioner, is proposing for Europe's oil refineries, which are also suffering from overcapacity. But not many other industries can meet the special conditions required for a successful cartel: that all major producers should want to join and that production should be fairly concentrated. Ideally, Commission officials say, all the chairmen should be able to sit round a dinner table — an idea that would have struck horror into the hearts of the EEC's founding fathers.

Source: adapted from The Economist, 27 May 1978

Box 64

National and international operations in the EEC, 1973–76

| | Type of operation | | Breakdown of operations by number of firms involved | |
Year	Number of operations	Number of firms involved	Bilateral operations	Multilateral operations
National operations				
1973	641	1 632	544	97
1974	923	2 206	789	134
1975	1 586	4 061	1 387	199
1976	1 326	3 211	1 137	189
International operations				
1973	997	2 151	751	246
1974	812	2 024	578	234
1975	695	1 909	484	211
1976	731	1 884	502	229
Total				
1973	1 638	3 783	1 295	343
1974	1 735	4 230	1 367	368
1975	2 281	5 970	1 871	410
1976	2 057	5 095	1 639	418

(Operations include takeovers and mergers, store purchase and joint ventures)

The table sets out the actual numbers of national and international takeovers and mergers, acquisitions and joint ventures that took place in the EEC from 1973 to 1976.

A minimum of two firms were involved in each operation and the actual number of firms involved is shown in a separate column. The total column of the 'Number of firms involved' takes account of the fact that a given firm may have been involved in more than one operation in the course of the report period.

The breakdown in the last two columns of the table gives the number of national and international operations involving only two firms (bilateral operations) and those involving more than two firms (multilateral operations).

The reason for the absence of international takeovers or mergers is that the company law of the Member States does not allow cross-frontier firms.

The total number of operations fell from 2281 to 2057 between 1975 and 1976; this was the first fall since 1973. In each of the years considered, share purchase was the most frequent form of operation, followed by joint ventures, and lastly by takeovers and mergers. In 1976, 65 per cent of all operations were share purchase, 28 per cent were joint ventures and only 7 per cent were takeovers and mergers. The development of the total number of operations broken down by number of firms involved shows that between 1973 and 1975 bilateral operations increased in number, only to fall in 1976, whereas the number of multilateral operations kept rising throughout the period. In 1976, 80 per cent of all operations were bilateral.

Source: Seventh Report on Competition Policy, April 1978

recent times, however, there is evidence that hard-pressed national governments are glad to have the Commission on their side when trying to resist the demands for assistance from a particular region or industry.

Concentration of industry

The Competition Directorate-General of the Commission also monitors the progress of concentration trends on a country-by-country and industry-by-industry basis. This is to enable it to judge whether specific mergers or arrangements are compatible with the principle of the Common Market. A substantial

Box 65

How to pay a fine

European sugar producers were fined by the European Commission not so long ago for contravening the Community's competition rules. The fines actually given (as prescribed by the European Court of Justice) were expressed in units of account (equal to 0.88867088 grams of fine gold), and the text actually gave the value in national currency. Two French companies who were fined have agreed to pay the fine, but pay it in Lire equivalent to the value of the fine in units of account.

The Commission has informed the two companies, Générale Sucrière and Beghin-Say, that the payments are not enough and that if the companies wish to pay in Lire, they should pay in Lire equivalent of the fine expressed in French francs.

The companies have contested this. The Court of Justice has however ruled that the companies should pay the fine as expressed in French francs. The reference to units of account is only for the purpose of enabling the European Commission to deliver fines. The Commission has now requested the two companies to pay their debts in French francs.

Source: Euroforum, No. 14/77, 5 April 1977

part of the Annual Report on Competition Policy is concerned with details of concentration. These statistics can be a useful source of information on what is happening in industries within the Community. *Box 64* gives some statistics of a general nature, but the Seventh Report on Competition Policy from which the table is taken provides, for example, lists of the twenty most profitable companies, in such industries as food and beverages, in the United Kingdom. It also lists markets in the Community where the market leader holds more than 25 per cent of the total national market. Current trends in distribution and concentration in individual states are also given.

Competition policy is the first of the policies affecting business to be outlined; this is because of its immediate impact on many aspects of business in the Community. While its effect on the small firm is likely to be minimal, it could have very significant implications on even the medium-size organization.

It would be very costly, for example, to appoint exclusive agents in a number of territories and help them sell the goods through an expensive promotion campaign across a number of Community countries only to find that the costs of this campaign could not be covered by the higher prices for the product. Any third party would have the right to buy the goods from other parts of the Community and could undersell in the territories where the company and its agents were making a special marketing effort based on an expected high margin of gross profit.

The policy is complex and there are ways that a company can obtain exemption or temporary protection in order to establish itself in a market. However, it needs expertise and careful planning to take advantage of the complexities.

Bibliography

Cawthra, B.I. (1972) *Restrictive Agreements in the EEC*, London: Butterworths
Cunningham, J. (1973) *The Competition Law in the EEC*, London: Kogan Page
Layton, C. (1971) *Cross-Frontiers Mergers in Europe*, Bath: Bath University Press
Official Publications
Annual Report on Competition Policy. From 1972 to present

15 Industrial and sectoral policies

The machine does not isolate man from the great
problems of nature but plunges him more deeply
into them
Saint Exupery, Wind, Sand and Stars, 1939

In one sense industrial policy is very general. It consists of a framework of general Community policies within whose parameters industry operates. In another sense it is very specific and consists of a number of rules affecting specific industries, products and systems. Unlike policies such as agriculture and transport, there is no reference to industrial policy in the Treaty of Rome. Certainly the problems of coal and steel existed when the Treaty was being worked out in the second half of the 1950s, but the European Coal and Steel Community, which was established by the Treaty of Paris in 1953, had already helped to resolve them. The authors of the Treaty of Rome did not envisage any problems of adaptation which industry could not itself deal with.

At its lowest level, the industrial policy of the Community is the creation of industrial free trade within the Common Market. Its first major success was the gradual abolition of tariffs over a period of years. Tariffs came to an end on 1 July 1977, when the final tariff cuts took place and goods could move freely from one country to another. Attempts to remove non-tariff barriers to trade have been less successful and the process will continue for some time. The removing of technical obstacles to trade and the harmonization of legislation on a wide range of subjects affecting industry is also a continuing task.

Industry, competition and pragmatism

This harmonization will not be complete before the expected enlargement enables Greece, Portugal and Spain to join the Community. This event will create, as did the United Kingdom, Ireland and Denmark, the need for a further round of transitional arrangements and gradual abolition of tariffs. A rather pragmatic industrial policy is being developed which adapts to changing conditions and makes progress slowly, sometimes in one area of activity, sometimes in another. Its ultimate aim remains the creation of a European integrated industrial base.

Industrial policy is particularly interlinked with competition policy. The latter aims to create competitive conditions for Community industry by removing any arrangements which distort the free competitive market. Yet the growing emphasis on sectoral policies for industries in crisis is, in many ways, in

Box 66

President Jenkins on industry

Europe's industry is the principal creator of wealth; and the role of the Community is to create conditions in which manufacturing industry and commerce can prosper. The freeing of trade within Europe's internal market has contributed to economic expansion over the last two decades.

We must pursue the practical work of removing barriers to trade through harmonizing company law, competition law, and taxes. These are useful bricks with which to build economic integration in Europe. But we must not lose sight of the practical objectives of our programme. We should not indulge in a bureaucratic game of harmonization for harmonization's sake. Unless we can be sure that our proposals will lead to more trade, and better conditions for producers or consumers, there is no point in making them.

As well as setting the overall framework for industrial integration the Community has to take action in individual sectors such as steel and shipbuilding where Europe's vital interests are at stake. We all realize that in the storms which have lashed these industries over the last few years – storms which have by no means abated yet – national solutions offer scant protection. Europe as a whole must act to sustain its competitive position.

We also have a role to play in industries such as textiles and footwear which are in difficulties because of increased competition from the Third World. Here we have a double responsibility. We have a duty to cooperate in a sensible international division of labour. We must respect the needs of producer countries with far less sophisticated resources than our own. But we should not impose excessive and sudden strains on our own industries, and we have a right to ask for cooperation and equality of effort from other industrial countries of the world.

At a different level we have, I believe, an even more important role in the area of advanced technology – the aircraft and computer industries provide two obvious spectacular examples – but there are others where the private sector cannot undertake investment on the necessary scale, where state intervention is therefore indispensable, and where common action promises significant economies of scale. A Community strategy for these sectors is urgently required, and one of the main priorities of our industrial policy will be to achieve such a strategy.

From speech to European Parliament on presentation of General Report for 1976 and the Commission's programme for 1977, 8 February 1977

direct opposition to competition policy as a general solution to sectoral problems is sought by some form of cartel arrangement.

The businessman will be interested in other aspects of the Community's work which affect industry and commerce. For example, the harmonization of Community company law, the encouragement of mergers through the proposed European company statute and the embryonic attempts of the so called 'marriage bureau' to encourage small businesses to join together across national boundaries.

Community-wide strategy of companies

The willingness of companies to adapt their strategy and organization to the larger market has been more limited than originally hoped. In retrospect this might have been foreseen, particularly in the case of smaller companies. In the United States, for example, many small companies do not consider it necessary to have a national marketing operation. If they do, they will experience fewer legal, cultural and linguistic problems than similar European companies. The

Box 67

Looking for a business partner?

Marriage bureau: good record

The Community's industrial 'marriage bureau' or Business Coopera-tion Centre was set up to search out firms wishing to make coopera-tion agreements across Community frontiers.

According to its latest annual report, most requests for assistance in 1977 came from the United Kingdom where small and medium-sized companies are trying to expand into the continent where they have little experience. Interest in transnational agreements has also increased in France in parallel with France's export drive. German interest in European cooperation has slightly decreased and it would seem they are more interested in third countries. The most popular countries for making agreements with are Germany, France and the Benelux. The Centre's activity in 1977 was as follows:

Information : 515 requests
Partner research : 84 requests and 894 replies
Contacts established: 75
Agreements confirmed : 18

Source: Euroforum, 1978 and Business Cooperation Centre 1978 annual report

legal problems of transfrontier mergers and the growing amount of restrictive legislation have not helped. Industry is too often criticized for not being entre-preneurial when many of its activities are being curbed almost before they have begun.

On the other hand, some larger firms are already heavily involved throughout the Community. The bid by Peugeot to buy European Chrysler, and British Petroleum acquisitions in Germany, in 1978 shows this process taking place. It is, perhaps, not as fast as some would consider desirable, but faster than might have been expected 50 years ago. The market has become Community-wide while industrial structures remain largely on a national scale.

Sometimes when an entrepreneurial effort is made it is thwarted by the political will of member states. For example, one large food manufacturer has decided to halt further developments in Europe because it feels there are better opportunities elsewhere, in places where the entrepreneur is still welcome.

The Colonna Memorandum

The Colonna Memorandum (March 1970) is perhaps the most comprehensive statement about Community industrial policy. The Commission gives three reasons why such a policy is required.

(1) To improve the working of the single Community market through enhanced industrial integration.
(2) To assure continued economic growth by helping companies and industries to adapt themselves to changing conditions.
(3) To achieve a reasonable degree of economic and technological independence from the Community's major trading partners.

Box 68

The Commission on industrial affairs

Internal market and industrial affairs

Main developments

The Commission responded to the persistence of the structural crisis by intensifying its endeavours to consolidate and accelerate the unification of the internal market and customs union and by developing specific policies to help individual industries adapt to the new competitive position in world trade.

Much effort was accordingly devoted to preventing or pursuing breaches of the treaties as regards free movement of goods, to removing technical barriers to trade and to encouraging the introduction of Community and international standards. Progress was made in the harmonization of legislation, particularly in relation to companies and industrial property. Valuable progress was made on right

of establishment and in the implementation of legal provisions to open up public contracts.

Community measures to help individual industries were taken upon a number of occasions, each time geared to specific requirements. Since 1 January there has been a plan to put the internal steel market on a sound basis, with measures to regulate prices and volumes of business; a start has also been made on changing the industry's structure, with impressive amounts of Community money to help. Negotiations with the Community's trading partners and stricter application of its GATT-based anti-dumping arrangements are helping to attenuate the disruptive effect of imports on domestic prices,

continued

though the actual volume of import business is fairly stable. Steel policy as a whole has been concerted regularly and fully with the governments of the Member States and with manufacturers, workers and users (through the EGSC Consultative Committee).

The steady deterioration of the employment situation in the textiles industry under the pressure of excessive imports led the Commission first to recommend then to conduct complex negotiations with the chief supplier countries with a view to stabilizing the Community market while leaving room for imports to grow at 'normal' rates. When agreements had been signed with these countries, renewal of the Multifibre Arrangement in 1978 became possible. The Commission has also announced structural measures to help the industry adapt.

Community shipbuilders are faced with a dramatic decline in demand as a result of large-scale excess capacity worldwide, and the Commission has proposed structural reforms while seeking to stimulate demand and place international competition on a healthier footing.

For the first time appropriations (of 20 million EUC in 1978) have been entered in the Community budget to cover interest relief grants and investment premiums in the Community's industrial restructuring and conversion scheme, initially for textiles and shipbuilding.

The first-ever Council meeting devoted to telecommunications was held.

In aerospace and data processing, Community research programmes, concerted with the manufacturers, were set in motion. But in aerospace, attention gradually narrowed and is now concentrated on a joint programme for the construction of large civil aircraft.

In other industries, particularly the motor industry, significant steps have been taken towards the establishment of a genuine Community market; without this there is no hope for satisfactory industrial expansion.

Eleventh General Report of the Commission of the European Communities, February 1978

Two further objectives might now be added:

(4) To achieve a better geographical distribution of industry and hence of economic growth within the Community.
(5) To protect the environment.

The Colonna Memorandum is an example of a comprehensive study which was never seriously taken up by the Council of Ministers. As Commissioner Tugendhat points out in *Box 11* this can make the Commission's job very frustrating.

Enhanced industrial integration

This first objective has been achieved only to a limited extent, although there is frequent news of British companies extending their operations in the Community through joint ventures. *Box 64* (page 134) shows that the number of national and international takeovers, mergers, acquisitions and joint ventures was considerable

Figures 11 (above) and 12 (opposite) Europe by Stealth. When the Community's first satellite misfired and fell into the sea off Cape Kennedy and when the European Community's yacht with crew members from the Nine fails to win a race, the Press stress the specific failure rather than the general success. That the Community should enter joint teams for sporting events and fire joint satellites into space so soon after a century of devastating European wars may strike future historians as a rather fast rate of European integration.

during the years 1973–6. The total number of operations fell in 1976, but even then was over 2000. The ratio of national to international operations was roughly two to one. Many industrialists and commentators consider that the move towards European integration is rather slow, but it is significant that

during the above years one operation in every two was cross-frontier. Furthermore, the table is not cumulative. There have been therefore over 8000 international operations in the Community during 1973—6, which compares with about 11 000 within the member countries.

Helping companies and industries to adapt to changing conditions

Helping companies and industries to adapt to changing conditions is at the moment a prominent part of Community thinking on industrial policy. Economic recession has placed increasing emphasis on supporting the so called 'crisis' industries such as steel, textiles, shipbuilding and footwear. Increasing competition from developing countries and state trading countries has forced these industries to demand help from the Community. This help is particularly demanded as regards external competition, as in trade arrangements with countries outside the Community it is the Commission alone which has the right to negotiate on behalf of member states (see Chapters 24 and 26). On occasions individual countries of the Nine find that the Commission's regulatory powers are an advantage. It can help protect their industries against fierce international competition at a time when there is a world-wide retreat from free trade.

The Commission's objective in these difficult circumstances is to persuade member countries to adhere to the basic Community principles of fair and free competition, and to ensure that where markets are contracting the flow of trade is regulated and markets are shared equitably. On the one hand, individual industries and member states call for increased protection and, in some cases, the establishment of cartels. On the other hand, the Community proclaims to the world, through the General Agreement on Trade and Tariffs (GATT) and the Organization for Economic Cooperation and Development (OECD), the need for continued free trade.

The situation in some of the crisis industries, and the Commission's attempts to improve the situation, is as follows:

(1) *Textiles.* The Multi-fibre Agreement (MFA) which ran from 1974 to 1977 was designed progressively to liberalize world trade, but by the time it expired in 1977 there was an unprecedented boom in textile and clothing imports. The Community's own textile and clothing industries were severely threatened.

In return for extending the MFA for a further four years, the Community insisted on bilateral agreements with major textile suppliers to restrict the flow of imports. The restraints consist of quotas, ceilings on imports and consultative arrangements on a number of 'sensitive' products. The agreed annual growth rate for imports ranged from 0.25 per cent to 6 per cent. The negotiations were carried out by the Commission on behalf of the Member States and were most complicated. As many as twenty-six states were affected and nearly all were negotiating bilateral agreements in Brussels at the end of 1977. These were major negotiations for the Commission and it cast a number of officials into new roles.

Similar problems to those in the textile industry are likely to occur in other industries during the next few years. Although the Community wants to encourage free trade, and in particular imports from developing countries, there is a limit to the rate at which it can bring this about. It is politically and socially inconceivable to achieve this at the cost of running down, to near zero, those industries within the Community already in severe crisis. The contraction of the textile industry has already been drastic with tens of thousands of jobs lost. With unemployment in the Community running at about six million (January 1979), a major problem is emerging. Developing countries want to export manufactured

Box 69

Textiles: crisis trends

Between 1973 and 1976 imports of textiles into the Community in terms of tonnage increased by 80 per cent. In 1976 the value of imports rose to an impressive 9.3 billion dollars.

The impact of such imports is only to be expected: 3500 factories have had to close down between 1973 and 1976, and half a million jobs have been lost, 15 per cent of the total work force in this sector.

If things stay as they are, 1 600 000 jobs will be lost between now and 1982, which is humanly, socially, economically and politically unacceptable for the European Community. To avoid this, the Community has just introduced measures to limit the imports of cotton fibre and clothing from certain non-Community countries.

The synthetic fibre industry is in such difficulties through over-capacity that the European Commission has just sent a letter to the governments of the Nine requesting that no further aid be given to the industry over the next two years for the construction of additional capacity. The Commission intends to keep track of events by receiving regular information from individual synthetic fibre producers about the market situation facing the firms concerned.

Source: Euroforum, 18 July 1977

goods from factories which, in many instances, have been built with Community aid. While most Community governments accept that industries, such as the textile industry, need to be restructured, there has to be some curb on imports from low-cost third countries. In theory these will be of a temporary nature. However, even modernized countries in the Community, in less advanced areas of manufacturing and technology, may be unable to compete with low-technology industries in developing countries, where social conditions and wages are a fraction of those in the industrialized countries.

(2) *Steel.* The situation is perhaps even more severe in this sector. The present forecast is that thousands of jobs will be lost in steel and shipbuilding over the next few years, in spite of steadily declining numbers for over a decade.

The Commission has direct powers under the Treaty of Paris, which set up the European Coal and Steel Community, to regulate the internal market. These powers include the authority to decide national production quotas and fix prices, although it is unlikely that they will ever be used. However, at the beginning of 1977 the Commission set voluntary production quotas and guideline prices for major Community steel companies, and compulsory minimum prices in some products. In addition to the attempt to raise minimum prices within the Community, the Commission has taken action to protect the Community from

Box 70

Arms and the Market

Parliament debates industrial aspects of defence

The long awaited and controversial report by Egon Klepsch (CD/Ger) and Tom Normanton (Con/UK) on armament production in Europe was voted through with only one amendment on Wednesday 14 June. It called on the Commission to prepare an action programme 'for the development and production of conventional armaments within the framework of the common industrial policy'.

The Community treaties say nothing about defence; and many members were doubtful whether involvement in the subject was wise. In December 1975, however, Parliament voted through a report by Lord Gladwyn (Lib/UK) on the defence aspects of foreign policy coordination (now increasingly a Community matter). This time the starting point was industrial policy.

As the principal rapporteur, Christian Democrat (People's Party) leader Egon Klepsch, noted: 'It is not possible to think in terms of a common industrial policy which does not include the military as well as civil aspect of certain key industries – in particular the construction of aircraft frames and engines, shipbuilding and electronics'. The military market, for example, accounted for 62 per cent of aircraft industry sales by Community states.

Further, a 'common market' in armaments would save everyone a lot of money. 'One of the main problems for Western Europe is that we have too many armaments industries producing too many different types of weapons in circumstances of considerable financial waste'.

What about the objection – made during the debate by a number of Socialist members – that defence was best left to other organizations like NATO? Only the Community, replied Mr. Klepsch, had the power to act in the industrial field.

But purely military matters were not absent from the debate. Conservative leader Geoffrey Rippon (UK) argued that the balance of the forces in Europe was not merely a question of the arms in existence – as important was production capacity. The Soviet Union, for example, could probably produce 1000 battle tanks annually. 'How can this compare with the economics of French production of AMX30 main battle tanks, probably of 150 tanks annually, or British Chieftain tank production of, say, 200 annually . . .?'

Commissioner Davignon, replying to the debate, accepted that arms procurement was a legitimate subject for the Community to tackle. Among those unconvinced were the French Communists, who suggested that the whole emphasis on industry was merely a cloak for the development of a full common defence policy.

Interestingly enough, however, their view was not shared by the Italian Communists, who all voted for the report. It seemed that even a sizeable part of the Parliament's left was impressed by Tom Normanton's warning that, unless European nations got together, the result would be total dependence on the US.

Source: European Parliament No. 48, July 1978

cheap steel imports by invoking anti-dumping measures against countries which export to the Community at less than 5 per cent under minimum prices. The Commission has invoked these powers, in particular against those countries which were not prepared to negotiate with the Community on voluntary export limitations.

As in the case of textiles, the Commission has been able to demand that third countries either negotiate restrictive export levels to the Community or lose even their current levels. The restrictions on free trade, which these measures represent, indicate a change in world attitudes. Again, it indicates the importance of the Community as a large home market. Manufacturers will find it increasingly difficult to export certain goods to third countries. As the problems of unemployment, the shortage of raw materials and the growing stream of manufactured goods from Third World countries increases, new pressures will emerge.

Box 71

Shipbuilding in crisis

Table 1 Production in grt as a percentage of world total

	1955	1960	1965	1970	1975	1976
EEC	70.0	51.1	31.3	25.6	23.3	22.6
AWES	80.0	73.8	50.8	40.5	38.5	37.5
Japan	12.0	21.4	41.5	48.1	50.6	46.7
Rest of the world	8.0	4.8	7.7	11.4	10.9	15.8

Table 2 1975 production and 1980 production forecast based on foreseeable demand

	1975 grt	1975 cgrt	1980 grt	1980 cgrt
EEC	7.8	4.4		2.4
Rest of AWES	5.3	3.2		1.5
AWES	13.1	7.6		3.9
Japan	17.0	7.7		3.9
Rest of the world	4.2	4.2		4.0
Total, world	34.3	19.5	10.4	11.8

grt is gross registered tons
cgrt is compensated gross registered tons

Source: AWES: Association of West European Shipbuilders (Community countries + Norway, Sweden, Finland, Spain and Portugal). Quoted from Shipbuilding Reorganization Programme, Bulletin of the European Communities, July 1977.

Developing countries will restrict access to their markets for goods they can now produce themselves. Within the Community manufacturers will continue to find markets for their products.

(3) *Shipbuilding and shipping.* Community shipping is threatened by the increasing (it is alleged unfair) competition from the state trading countries of Eastern Europe and the policy of an increasing number of countries to insist on carrying their trade in their own ships. The shipbuilding industry is in crisis: in 1976 orders fell by 40 per cent and by a further 20 per cent in 1977. One of the reasons is that the developing countries are producing ships very much cheaper than is possible in Europe. Japan also is threatened by the emergence of Brazil, Mexico and in particular South Korea which, it is forecast, will build one-third of the world's tonnage by 1981.

Member states, while accepting the need drastically to cut both Community shipbuilding capacity and the labour force, and the need to restructure the industry, are not able to agrèe about the size of the cuts. Politically, it is very difficult for individual countries to make these cuts even though they become inevitable as there are so few new orders for Community yards. Ships have been built, often speculatively, for many years but this cannot continue.

In 1978, the Council adopted a directive on coordinating state aids to Shipbuilding which gave the Commission the right to monitor state subsidies. The Commission under its Commissioner for Industry, Viscount Davignon, a Belgian, is clear that short-term national efforts to prolong the life of inefficient yards, or to continue the building of speculative ships, is doomed to failure and can only lead to further problems in the industry. It has proposed a Community strategy to make yards more competitive. This must be linked with adequate social provisions for workers who lose their jobs and the creation of new jobs for those affected by the new techniques and modernization. The Commission proposal is an example of how Community-wide policies should be developed, but the political situation within member states makes it difficult to agree on Community-wide solutions.

While an excellent policy in theory, the problem is complex. There are not many, if any, new jobs available in the shipbuilding areas of the Community. Job creation is not easy and extremely costly. Further modernization of shipyards in the Community means that even more jobs will be lost. There is no point in having the most modern yards in the world if there is no demand for ships, at any price.

As regards relations with Japan the Community has made some progress. The Japanese government has agreed to urge its shipbuilders to increase prices by 5 per cent, but this only partially reduces the gap in prices, which is estimated at 40 per cent. Japan has also agreed to reduce the number of hours worked by 30 per cent in 1978, and is to allow only a maximum of 1½ ships to be under construction in any one yard at a time. But already Japan complains that by cutting capacity and raising prices, Community shipbuilders are being kept afloat by more and more subsidies. In the meantime, South Korea is undercutting

Japanese prices by large amounts as labour costs are only a fraction of those in Japan. The situation is complex and the Community is not successfully tackling it at the moment. However, the future must lie in Community action if there is to be any hope of regulating shipbuilding. Individual European nations by themselves do not have sufficient weight in the world.

(4) *Footwear.* The number of shoes imported in 1977 was over 300 million pairs — one pair at least for each citizen of the Community. Most of the shoes came from Hong Kong, Taiwan and South Korea. Countries such as the United States, Canada, Australia and Japan have already restricted imports. There is pressure on the Community to do the same in order to preserve the indigenous shoe industry. The Council has agreed that the Commission continue talks with the main supplier countries in view of an Irish demand to take protective measures to prevent the virtual disappearance of her shoe industry. In 1977 the Commission set up a joint committee of employers and unions to study the social and economic problems of the industry. This was the first time that official contacts had been established between the two sides of an industry for which the Treaty of Rome does not specifically prescribe a common policy.

Since May 1978 the Commission has been operating a prior automatic licence surveillance system. It is a temporary measure, but indicates how, in footwear, as in other industries, the Community is aware of the need to protect the industry while at the same time conforming as much as possible to the concept of free and fair trade.

(5) *Other industries.* The man-made fibre industry which produces nearly 50 per cent of all textile fibre consumption is also in difficulty. Community companies lost nearly $2.5 billion between 1975 and 1978. They have slashed labour forces and closed plants, and hopes were that the industry could again become profitable. Encouraged by Commissioner Davignon, eleven of the major fibre producers, responsible for over 80 per cent of the market, signed a cartel arrangement which froze market shares and agreed to cut some 400 000 tonnes of capacity. This crisis cartel could have been the first of a series as both petrochemicals and plastics have potentially similar problems. However, in July 1978 the commissioners could not agree to the Davignon plan and it looks as if the cartel will be examined in the light of existing Community rules on competition. This could lead to a ban or a considerable dilution of the provisions of the cartel.

Community economic and technological independence

The third aim of industrial policy — to give a reasonable degree of economic and technological independence to the Community — is proving even more difficult to achieve than that of helping firms adapt to changing conditions. Member States are quite willing to look at the advantages of joint action for those industries which are in difficulty, but when it comes to the high-technology industries of the future there is still much national self-interest. Nowhere can this be seen

Box 72

ECOSOC's views on a Community policy for industry

What is 'industrial policy'? Does the Community need one? What should it do? So many questions that nearly five years after Britain joined to reap – as many thought – industrial rewards from agricultural losses, still remain unclear. At its last plenary session after long preparatory work, the Economic and Social Committee tried to provide some answers.

First question: does it exist? Answer: yes, most governments have one. What is more, one country's policy may be in conflict with other's – and thus public money wasted and problems exported from one country to another. So there is a role for the Community.

What can the Community do? So far it's tried to act as umpire. In some respects it's done well – e.g. removing tariffs and technical barriers. But in others – like government help to new or ailing industries – ECOSOC feels it must do better. Excuses abound: times are tough, unemployment is high, competition is fierce. Yet is it right, fair or even economic for long established and efficient Danish textile firms to be thrown out of business by competition from brand new subsidized Italian ones? Or for that matter for the British government to compete with the French government in bailing out their respective motor manufacturers.

Judgements in matters of this sort are highly sensitive and politically charged. Broad criteria can help. Thus aids to industry must be phased out and never become permanent. Equally, intervention should be the exception not the rule. Even so, decisions on what is fair remain very awkward which helps excuse the Commission sometimes turning a blind eye to uncricket-like behaviour.

ECOSOC wants the game to be more open. It insists that reports be drawn up at regular intervals setting out the effects on capacity and employment of different government aids: and that these reports be submitted to it and the Parliament for comment.

In ECOSOC's view a common industrial policy was never more necessary than now. The adjustments which have to be made to fit in to the changing world economy have barely begun. With lower growth rates than before they will be harder to carry through. Preserving the status quo is an ostrich-like strategy. So the Community must push for change and help it along, including new EEC loans to help with investment.

An uncomfortable view, however realistic. Which might be taken to explain the opposition, principally from ECOSOC trades union members, to the opinion. Yet their quarrel, as expressed in debate, was not with the diagnosis, but rather with the cure. For they felt the proposals too weak and wanted more detailed planning, especially by sectors, to carry things through.

Thus widespread agreement on the need for a stronger Community policy in this key field – of European solutions for European-scale problems as put by one French member – was discoloured by what the French employer M. de Precigout described as a religious war. And as René Bonéty of the trades union group said, 'religious wars end up destroying religion itself'.

Source: European Movement: Facts, October 1977

more clearly than in the aerospace industry where the Commission has regularly proposed major initiatives for concerted action only to find its proposals acceptable only in part. The major US producers of civil aircraft, realizing the need to cooperate with European companies, have made a number of offers for joint ventures which cut across suggested cooperation schemes in the Nine. As a result, some governments and aircraft industries in the Commission are reluctant to enter wholeheartedly into European projects if there are prospects of higher employment and development work with US manufacturers.

Although frustrating for those who wish to see European industry develop rapidly, there is perhaps something to be said for this pragmatic and gradual move towards a European aerospace industry. In order to encourage Europeans to buy American planes, US companies have had to encourage them by increasing the proportion of the planes, whether wings, engines or technology, that are of European origin. Thus the European aerospace industry is making remarkably steady progress, not only through increasing cooperation between its companies and countries but because of the larger contribution it is making to the American aircraft industry. Between 1970 and 1976, total turnover (civil, military and space) at constant prices and 1970 exchange rates rose by 40 per cent which is an annual rate of growth of nearly 6 per cent. American turnover dropped by 26 per cent during the same period. As a result, the size of the

Box 73

The JET programme and the European airbus

JET originally was the joint engineering team set up by the four systems manufacturers, British Aerospace, Aerospatiale, MBB, VFW-Fokker, to study a short/medium-haul narrow-bodied aeroplane equipped with two engines in the 10-14 t thrust category. The same letters are currently used to identify this aircraft (Joint European Transport). The Franco-American CFM 56 engine is suitable as a modern technology engine for versions JET 1 and JET 2 (see below) of this project.

The four companies have prepared an initial design for an aeroplane which would satisfy the market needs

evaluated by another working party, the joint marketing team, and joint teams are currently marketing this project to the airlines.

This aircraft, which would come into service at the beginning of 1983 could be produced in two different versions, a 136 seater (JET 1) and a 163 seater (JET 2), to meet the demand which is represented by these capacities. Their respective ranges would be 2400 km and 3100 km.

Worldwide market forecasts for this category of aircraft up to 1990 and the sales prospects for the two versions of the European project would be as follows:

	Europe	USA	Rest of the Western World	Total
Total demand	400	400	400	1200
Sales prospects	200	80−100	100−120	380−420

continued

The basic model would be the JET 2 which is intended to meet the requirements of most airlines and whose seat/mile cost is optimized for short and medium ranges. The smaller JET 1, which could be available concurrently, would be aimed at those companies who need a reduced capacity with lower aircraft mile cost.

The trend emerging can therefore be summarized as follows:

(1) The European aircraft range might look like this:

	Seating capacity single class (34 inches)	Range (km)
JET 1	136	2400
JET 2	163	3100
(JET 3)	(188)	(3300)
A 300 B10	214–217	3300–5370
A 300 B2	269	3300
A 300 B4	269	4600

As it has been decided to develop a longer-range version of the A300 B4, the European range of aircraft would offer an ample spread of capacities and ranges, from 136 seats and 2400 km to about 269 seats and 5500 km, and the airlines would have at their disposal two basic aircraft (Airbus and JET) each offering different capacities and performances, with the commonality of equipment extending throughout the range. This would therefore be a way of satisfying the airlines' most keenly felt requirement, i.e. a very large measure of homogeneity in the different types of aircraft making up their fleets.

Source: adapted from Commission communication to the Council with a view to concerted action on aircraft programmes, Com (78) 211, 23 June 1978

European aircraft industry, relative to that of America, rose from 18.5 per cent in 1970 to 35 per cent in 1976.

The aerospace industry is perhaps the only one where foundations have been laid for a sectoral industrial policy although no firm decisions have been made. It is one of a select group of advanced-technology industries which are vital to future economic development. Progress with the European Airbus has been considerable and there is also potential for the JET (Joint European Transport) project which would cover the short/medium-haul narrow-bodied aircraft category. This aircraft will come into service at the beginning of 1983 in two different versions – a 136 seater (JET 1) and a 163 seater (JET 2).

Although cooperation is at present limited, there are encouraging signs for the future. The new multi-role combat aircraft, the Tornado, is to be produced in large numbers and is a cooperative venture between Britain, Germany and Belgium. It is increasingly evident that large-scale operations whether in aerospace, computers or electronics can only now be carried out where there is cooperation either between Community companies or between countries, or often both. Large markets are necessary to justify the huge investments involved.

Projects can be carried out only by large multinational companies or by governments through aid and help to coordinate their industries. The future success of such industries depends on increasing cooperation. From this cooperation, European unity will further develop. Each year there are more companies and individuals in the Community gaining experience of working together across national boundaries.

Strategy for growth
In June 1978 the Commission produced its report on structural aspects of growth. It sees the need for a two-pronged strategy to adapt to the new international division of labour. The performance of companies in difficulty must be

Figure 13 All wired up and ready to go. One of the most complicated cable harnesses made for a European satellite – involving 2000 cables with 280 connectors strapped to 650 metal bases – has been completed for Europe's first geostationary satellite 'GEOS'.

Box 74

The Commission's report on structural aspects of growth: excerpt on electronic/data processing, June 1978

39. In the future, the competitiveness of European industry will depend on its ability to mobilize new technologies, to improve productivity and to supply capital equipment to the world.

This is an area dominated – particularly where the production of machines and subcontracting is concerned – by small and medium-sized enterprises, with all the advantages of structure and employment that this implies. Consequently, general measures for improving the environment of these enterprises, for innovation and for research and development, will be particularly fruitful. Nevertheless, in some sectors, the public authorities must assume a direct stimulatory role.

Encouragement may also have to be given to different industries to co-operate in the development of new types of production systems which an individual sector is incapable of developing of its own.

Some member states have already adopted measures in this field, but a common effort is needed to avoid distortions within the Common Market and to enhance the thrust for growth in the Community as a whole.

In some key industries, particularly electronics/data-processing and aero-space, public authorities in most industrialized countries intervene to promote research and development and create markets, partly to satisfy defence or other national public needs, partly because they consider these industries critical to economic growth and development.

(a) The electronics/data-processing complex

40. The most important of the

sectors aided in this way is the electronics/data-processing complex, which is as vital a motor of economic development in the second half of the twentieth century as the steam engine was in nineteenth century Britain or electricity in the United States and Europe in the first half of this century.

This industry has three characteristic features:

41. *The computer systems industry,* non-existent in 1950, employs some 200 000 people in the Community today, while some four times that number are employed by user industries. The industry, growing at present by some 15 per cent per year, is expected to employ some 400 000 people directly and another 1 500 000 in users by the mid-1980s.

In the computer industry, national support programmes have helped to keep national industries alive. They have not yet achieved the aim set out in the Council resolution of 1974 of creating a 'viable and competitive industry' capable of standing on its own feet by the early 1980s. Adoption by the Council of the Commission's proposals for a four-year programme for data-processing will be a modest but essential step towards fulfilment of the resolution.

Before current national programmes come to an end in 1979 and 1980, it will be essential for further measures to be concerted at a European level so that from 1980 onwards they form part of a systematic common effort.

42. *The telecommunications infrastructure.* In our day, good and cheap communications are critical to the development of economic union. They are essential, in particular, to

continued

the development of outlying regions, to the integration of new Member States in an enlarged Community, and to the rapid development of the myriad new forms of service of an information society.

New challenges are emerging. As telecommunications switching becomes electronic – in essence a computer – and the telephone and television become terminals of computer systems, the two industries are becoming one. Although the move from electro-mechanical to electronic systems, and the use of integrated circuits, is reducing the manpower required for the production of telecommunications hardware, it will dramatically increase the importance of an efficient Europe-wide infrastructure to the development of a vast range of new information services equipment.

The EURONET network has provided a first step. This is a pilot network organized by the Community and put into effect by national administrations that is designed to ensure the effective dissemination of technical and scientific information.

In the Community, continued industrial efficiency on the world market depends on a loosening of the existing ties between industry and the national public telecommunications services, through a policy of opening up public contracts without delay, and by the development of common technology.

43. *Electronic circuit technology.*
The third critical element in the new computer industries is the advanced electronic circuit technology which now makes it possible to make available in a pocket calculator the computing power of the early computers, and which by the early 1980s will make available on a chip, the size of a ten-penny piece, today's large computer or a telephone exchange which in previous generations occupied a large building.

Already today the Community imports 90 per cent of its integrated circuit requirements, reflecting the commercial and technological lead of competitors.

To meet this situation, industrial agreements have been concluded between European companies and foreign industries directly or indirectly subsidized by their governments.

In view of the foreseeable impact of advanced components on other branches of industry, it is essential to forestall the dangers either of a duplication of effort as a result of unco-ordinated national programmes or of the abusive creation of a dominant position.

The implications of the choices for European industry are so fundamental that a Community debate at political level on the desirability of a long-term technology programme is both necessary and urgent.

improved. Innovation must be encouraged to satisfy needs at home, to increase or maintain the Community's share in world trade and to retain a substantial role in the development of new technologies.

The Commission forecasts that the greatest scope for new jobs will be in the tertiary sector of health, education, training, engineering and consultancy. By encouraging the further development of the Common Market, supplying funds and other support for research and development on a Community scale, providing support for medium-size and small enterprises and for education and training, the Commission hopes to contribute to a European growth strategy. In particular it identifies the electronics/data-processing complex as the most important sector, as vital to economic development in the late twentieth century as the steam engine in the nineteenth century or electricity at the beginning of this century.

There is nothing very new in the Commission report but it does underline an acceptance of the changing economic conditions and the need to adapt, not as individual countries, but as a Community, if the benefits of scale and pooled resources are to be gained.

Box 75

A new role for Europe's industry

Finally, we pose the problems that may dominate the European industrial debate in the coming decades.

First: what shall be the *international strategy* of European industry? Should it attempt to integrate more deeply its production and marketing with the energy-rich, materials-rich countries of the developing world (North Africa, the Middle East)? What would be the alternative?

Secondly: should European industry seek to develop a distinctive international character based on a very high investment on *research and development*? What form should such a strategy take? Should it be basic or applied? Traditional or advanced? For manufacturing or for the increasingly dominant service sector?

Thirdly: what should be the attitude of European industry towards the movement for greater *participation and decentralization* of decision-making? Should it break down its present decision structures and stress more democratic procedures? Should it encourage the participation of workers at the centre or on the shop floor?

Fourthly: how far should the *pattern of industrial development* within Europe be extended from the traditional industrial areas to the rural periphery? How far should it be encouraged to remain in older industrial areas – including the older central cities – where it is now rapidly declining?

Fifthly: what should be the relationship to *national or international planning systems*? Should the present degree of relationship, or non-relationship with national governments continue? Or should there be a move towards industrial cooperation inside a European system of industrial planning, superseding many of the national powers?

Sixthly: should the present system of *financing of industry* – mainly through private funding, partly through direct state funding – continue? Or should a conscious effort be made to tap new sources, either by extended equity markets or by more direct participation on the part of workers?

We give no answers here because we do not know them. Nor do we think that European societies will necessarily know them. But our strong presumption is that, around the year 2000, European industry will be moving into new institutional relations with state and international organizations, new modes of finance, new patterns of internal organization – and above all, a new basic rationality.

Source: Peter Hall, Europe 2000, p. 154, Duckworth 1977

Better geographical distribution of industry and environmental protection

The fourth and fifth aims of industrial policy, to achieve a better geographical distribution of industry and hence of economic growth within the Community and the protection of the environment, both involve regional policy and environmental policy which are discussed in Chapter 20. While certain limited strides have been made in regional policy, in one specific area it will be difficult to reconcile industrial policy and regional policy. The large industrial countries of the Nine may be very interested in working together on high-technology programmes and using Community funds for this. Some of the small countries may not be so keen, especially if there is no spin-off for them. With the accession of countries such as Portugal and Greece, the problem will become more severe. It is fundamental to regional policy that industries are encouraged in, for example, Northern Ireland, Britanny, Scotland and the Mezzogiorno. It is difficult, however, to see how the high-technology industries, already established in the major countries, are likely to accept the principle of developing these industries in other areas for social and employment reasons when they are already well-established in the more prosperous areas of the Community.

Community industrial policy is rather wide-ranging in its implications. In many cases it is not possible to identify its present importance for any particular business. What is clear is that if the Community continues to develop, then much of the present distortion of competition between industries of member states will end. Technical barriers to trade, preferences for domestic producers when public contracts are placed, different legal systems and tax laws, financial arrangements and access to capital markets, all of these will be appropriately ended, developed or improved upon to establish the common industrial base which will be the foundation of wealth creation within the Community.

Bibliography

Denton, G. (In preparation) *Industrial Policy in Britain, France and Germany*, Federal Trust

House of Lords Select Committee reports on different industries. List available from HMSO, London

Industrial Policy in the Community, Commission Memorandum 1970

16 The Customs Union and the Common Commercial Policy

The World has narrowed to a neighbourhood before it
has broadened into a brotherhood
Lyndon B. Johnson, New York, December 1963

The Customs Union is fundamental to the Common Market. It has two objectives:

(1) Abolition of customs barriers between countries of the Community to promote the development of internal trade.
(2) Regulation of the Common Customs Tariff (CCT) which surrounds the Community. Variations in this affect external trade with third countries.

External trade relations, which are the responsibility of the Community institutions, have two aspects:

(1) The Common Customs Tariff
(2) The Common Commercial Policy. This is the policy of member states to

Box 76

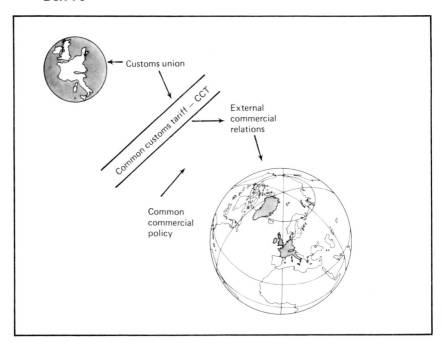

conduct their formal commercial and trade relations as a single economic Community. The Commission negotiates trade agreements on behalf of the Member States both with third countries and with international organizations. The relationship of these three aspects of trade policy is shown in *Box 65*. They are important parameters within which the Community's internal and external trade takes place. The parameters are drawn up by the Community and only the Community can change them. Changes can have a significant effect on intra- and extra-Community trade; hence their importance to business planning.

The Customs Union

The Customs Union is more than a free trade area. It involves:

(1) The abolition of customs duties and charges and all restrictions affecting trade between member states.
(2) Common customs legislation.
(3) Pooling of customs revenue.
(4) A common customs tariff applicable at the external frontiers of the Union.

The abolition of customs duties

On 1 July 1977 the transitional period for the Customs Union came to an end. The last customs duty barriers between the United Kingdom, Denmark and Ireland and the original Six were abolished.

The process of gradually reducing the customs duty between member states was thus successfully completed for the second time. The original six members had gone through the same process themselves in the 1960s. If the Community is enlarged to twelve countries, then Greece, Spain and Portugal will need to do the same during their respective transitional periods.

Although quotas and tariffs are now eliminated between the Nine, the Treaty contains safeguard clauses which enable countries in severe difficulty to introduce temporary measures to protect their markets. They must have the prior authorization of the Commission although this rule is not always adhered to. France, for example, took measures against Italian wine imports in 1977 and only afterwards negotiated Commission approval.

Common customs legislation

As tariffs were dismantled within the Community, the need for harmonizing legislation and procedures became more apparent. It has proved a slow process. Goods moving from one country to another still have to overcome formidable

Box 77

VAT and income tax rates in the Community (%) February 1978

VAT rates in the different Community countries vary between 4 per cent and 40 per cent. The rates are constantly changing and need to be monitored.

	Normal	Intermediate	High	Reduced	Zero
Ireland	20		35/40	10	X
Belgium	18	14	25	6	X
Netherlands	18			4	X
France	18		33	7	
Denmark	15				X
Italy	14	18	35	1/3/9	X
Germany	11			5.5	
Luxembourg	10			5/2	
United Kingdom	8		12.5		X

It is easy to see why nationals of some Community countries come to shop in the United Kingdom. Rates of VAT are low and income taxes in the countries from which they come are low. Conversely, the UK citizen abroad finds both direct and indirect taxes working against his financial interest.

Income tax percentage rates February 1978

Country	Starting rate	Maximum rate
Denmark	42.2	66.4
United Kingdom	34	*83
Federal Republic of Germany	22	56
Netherlands	20	72
Ireland	20	60
Luxembourg	18	57
Belgium	10	72
Italy	10	72
France	5	60

*98% where the investment income surcharge applies

problems of documentation. Delays at frontiers still exist. Some of the delays are inevitable because of the differences between countries in the rates of value added tax (VAT), in policies on the control of dangerous drugs and other substances, in the level of health regulations, such as rabies control, and in the collection of trade statistics.

Obstacles to trade are therefore still considerable. Although in most cases the obstacles are not deliberately used to prevent goods from circulating freely, there is a risk that small companies in particular will be discouraged by the complexities of export documentation and that Community markets will not be opened up as widely as intended. Customs law within the Community remains fragmentary and there is no political will among the Member States to bring about the necessary changes. The Commission has attempted to bring about the approximation of customs law through its introduction of directives. However, unlike regulations, directives do not have a direct effect on the laws of member states. National authorities are therefore free to choose the methods of applying the directives. This inevitably leads to the use of traditional channels based on existing customs arrangements and documentation.

Technical barriers in industry are a type of non-tariff barrier, however some progress is being made towards abolishing them. Most countries, for the purpose of consumer protection, or because of the effect on the environment, regulate the quality, safety or technical characteristics of products. The aim of this legislation may be identical but the means can vary considerably. Therefore it can be very difficult and costly to move goods from one country to another; standards need to be harmonized. An electrical appliance without an earth wire may be acceptable in one country whereas in another it may be illegal. The colour of live wire coverings may differ, or in some countries a colour code may not even be necessary.

The Community has never harmonized legislation for the sake of harmonization, but since 1969 there has been an ambitious programme to remove technical barriers to trade. A list of the directives already adopted and in the pipeline is published every three months in the magazine *Trade and Industry*. It is an important source of information for businessmen. More than 100 of these directives have been approved and another fifty or so are in the pipeline. It is estimated that about 300 directives will be needed to harmonize existing technologies and processes. It has taken ten years for about half of the work to be carried out and it is likely to be another ten before the programme is complete.

However, this does not take account of the legislation which will be required for new processes and technologies. As industries and trade associations work closer with one another and with the Community institutions, channels of effective communication will develop to ensure that technical standards are discussed at as early a stage as possible. Any national legislation which is planned will be discussed at Community level in order to prevent parallel legislation from being drawn up and to ensure that national legislation is compatible, if not identical, with Community legislation.

With *public contracts* some progress has also been made. Each state tends to reserve public supply and works contracts for its national enterprises, but the exclusion of other Community companies is clearly a restriction on the free movement of goods. These contracts average about 10 per cent of the gross domestic product in Community countries; therefore the extension of tendering for public contracts is considered an important task. A number of directives, with regard to this, have already been issued and large contracts (over 200 000

Box 78

Article 100: checklist of draft and adopted directives

Subject	Reference of directive or latest draft received	Status (where applicable)
Motor vehicles		
Type approval*	70/156/EEC of 6.2.70	Directive (*OJ* 23.2.70)
	COM(76)721 FINAL	Commission amending proposal (*OJ* 2.2.77)
	78/315/EEC of 21.12.77	Directive (*OJ* 28.3.78)
Rear registration plates	70/222/EEC of 20.3.70	Directive (*OJ* 6.4.70)
Sound level and exhaust system	70/157/EEC of 6.2.70	Diective (*OJ* 23.2.70)
	Adapted to technical progress by 73/350/EEC of 7.11.73	Commission directive (*OJ* 22.11.73)
	77/212/EEC of 8.3.77	Directive amending 70/157/EEC (*OJ* 12.3.77)
Fuel tanks and rear protective devices	70/221/EEC of 20.3.70	Directive (*OJ* 6.4.70)
	XI/249/75	Preliminary draft for adaptation to technical progress
	XI/260/75 Rev 2	Preliminary draft for further adaptation to technical progress
Audible warning devices	70/388/EEC of 27.7.70	Directive (*OJ* 10.8.70)
Air pollution by gases from positive ignition (spark ignition) engines	70/220/EEC of 20.3.70 Adapted to technical progress by 74/290/EEC of 28.4.74	Directive (*OJ* 6.4.70) Directive (*OJ* 15.6.74)
	77/102/EEC of 30.11.76	Commission directive adapting 70/220/EEC (*OJ* 3.2.77 L32)
Steering equipment	70/311/EEC of 8.6.70	Directive (*OJ* 18.5.70)
Doors	70/387/EEC of 27.7.70	Directive (*OJ* 10.8.70)
Direction indicator lamps	76/759/EEC of 27.7.76	Directive (*OJ* 27.9.76)
Suppression of radio interference produced by spark ignition engines	72/245/EEC of 20.6.72	Directive (*OJ* 6.7.72)
Installation of lighting and light signalling devices	76/756/EEC of 27.7.76	Directive (*OJ* 27.9.76)
Windscreen-wiper and windscreen-washer systems	COM(76)571 FINAL	Commission proposal Directives adopted but not yet published

Source: Trade and Industry, 4 August 1978. This list covers three pages and is a regular three-monthly feature. Only a small part is reproduced here.

units of account which is about £130 000) have to be published in the Official Journal. Out of the 55 000 public contracts placed each year in the United Kingdom, about 600 would fall into this category. This makes the Official Journal required reading for those interested in supplying goods to the public enterprises of other Community countries. Details of the Official Journal and of *Trade and Industry* mentioned above are given in Chapter 30.

Pooling of customs revenue

The revenues collected on imports into the Community, irrespective of where they are collected, are pooled and together with agricultural levies and a proportion of VAT, used to finance the Community budget. The budget is outlined in *Box 98*.

Common Customs Tariff

When the Community was founded in 1957, there were considerable differences between the customs duties of different member states. National tariffs were amalgamated and there were something like 20 000 tariff headings. Considerable work by the Community institutions led to the application of the Common Customs Tariff (CCT) by 1960 which had about 3000 headings. The CCT was applied in full by the Six in 1968 and by the Nine in 1977. The CCT now has about 3700 headings. It also provides a basis for the nomenclature for External Trading Statistics (NIMEXE) which has over 6000 headings. The CCT is now an integral part of the external trade relations of the Community and any amendments to it must be made by the Council of Ministers. The arithmetical mean of tariffs in the industrial sector is: European Community 7 per cent; Japan 10 per cent; United States 13 per cent.

The Common Commercial Policy

Since 1970, the Community alone has been responsible for negotiating tariff agreements with third countries. When a bilateral agreement between one of the Member States and a third country lapses, the Commission takes over responsibility for negotiations. The Council of Ministers has insisted that the negotiations for the Community should be conducted by the Commission. This prevents the development of a dialogue with individual Council of Ministers members. The Commission is limited in its negotiations in that the Council of Ministers must give it a mandate. On occasions Commission officials do negotiate with a third country but refer back throughout negotiations to the Council of Ministers. The important point of principle is that if the Community is to negotiate as one then it must be the Commission which carries out the negotiations.

The Common Commercial Policy develops naturally from the Common Customs Tariff. Much of the Policy is implemented by negotiating trade agreements with third countries. The agreements involve, among other things, amending the provisions of the CCT to take account of changes in the trade, commercial and political relations between a third country and the Community. Technical, industrial and financial cooperation agreements may still be negotiated by individual member states.

External trade negotiations

Before the Community negotiates with a third country, it needs to agree a common position. This is developed by member states through the Council of Ministers, through consultation with the European Parliament and through informal discussion with the Commission. The Commission is then empowered to conduct the negotiations on behalf of the Community, but continues to take into account the interests of individual member states.

The work involved in negotiating trade agreements is considerable and as they are invariably for specific periods of time, there are regular renegotiations.

By mid-1977, the Community had made 74 trade and cooperation agreements with 92 countries. These agreements have been formed for trade, and for historical and geographical reasons. It is not surprising that there are so many agreements when, for example, in 1975, Community imports from third countries accounted for nearly 25 per cent of world trade outside the state trading countries. The agreements cover the EFTA countries, the Mediterranean countries, South American countries, Asian countries and the 54 countries from Africa, the Caribbean and Pacific (ACP countries) which are signatories of the Lomé Convention (see Chapter 24).

Although the details of these agreements may not be of interest to business, it is of value to be aware, for strategical planning, of the relationships between the Community and specific countries. Where there are strong trade and commercial agreements, combined with a political commitment to develop trade and other relations, there are likely to be good business opportunities.

Trade protection

The CCT and the Common Commercial Policy enable the Community to regulate its external trade. The Community is also able to authorize temporary protective measures when specific industries are threatened. Anti-dumping duties are sometimes applied to protect Community industry. These measures, and other temporary measures, may be applied whenever Community industries are threatened by unfair competition, either through dumping or export subsidies. The definition of unfair competition is a complicated one which depends on political pressures as well as on the legal interpretation of existing rules. In recent years this aspect of the Community's external trade has become increasingly important. As with the CCT, the significance of anti-dumping and other protectionist measures is that the Community has now developed sophisticated mechanisms for varying at short notice the provisions of current policies.

For example, a Canadian company once argued that the tariffs around the Community were so low that it did not matter whether its new subsidiary was located in Norway, which is not in the Community, or in Ireland, which is.

Although existing Community tariff levels are not a major business problem, in a world economic crisis they could be raised very high, very quickly. Companies outside the Community therefore need to take into account future tariff levels when planning investment or the development of markets in the Community.

Box 79

The House of Lords Select Committee on the Common Commercial Policy

General conclusions of the Committee

58. The Committee would like to emphasize to the House the outward looking character of the Community as evidenced by the number and variety of trade and cooperation agreements negotiated by the Community with both developed and developing countries. The general effect of these links has been to establish the Community as the largest single trading bloc in the world.

Despite the enormous trading power of the Community (greater than either the United States or Japan) there is a tendency for the news media to emphasize the Community's internal problems with the result that the importance of the Common Commercial Policy is often overlooked; indeed it is probably unknown to the general public. It may be that political and monetary union are no nearer now than they have been since the accession of the United Kingdom, but the Community has undoubtedly succeeded in establishing itself as a major influence in world trade, in international organizations such as GATT and UNCTAD, and in the North-South dialogue.

This position is a consequence of the Community's great power as a trading bloc and has been consolidated by its capacity to speak with a single voice in international gatherings in accordance with the Common Commercial Policy, and by the development of the Community's network of external agreements. The Community has not exploited this position of power in relations with developing countries, but has tried to use it in such a way as to increase the level of mutually beneficial trade between the Community and developing countries in the future.

In a situation of world economic recession it is perhaps unlikely that the Community will seek to expand the scope of its external relations in the immediate future. In the present circumstances, it will be of great importance to the health of the Common Commercial Policy in the longer term to ensure that, at least until the economic situation improves, every effort should be made to coordinate internal and external policies. The developing countries wish to expand their production and their exports. Their capacity to export goods to the Community is expanding faster than the capacity of Community markets to absorb them. Consequently it will remain particularly important until Community markets expand again to take account of the size of import concessions granted to developing countries and their effect on the Community policies for the internal market.

From 40th Report of the House of Lords Select Committee on the European Communities, Session 1976–77, (HL 226): EEC Common Commercial Policy

GATT and UNCTAD

The Community seeks to present a combined front at negotiations in the General Agreement on Tariffs and Trade (GATT) and the United Nations Conference on Trade and Development (UNCTAD).

The GATT negotiations of the Dillon and Kennedy Rounds made substantial progress in reducing world tariff levels. The Tokyo Round of negotiations which began in 1975 lays particular emphasis on the need to reduce non-tariff barriers. It aims to include agricultural products in the negotiations and also to treat tropical products as a special and priority sector. The Community's aim is to reduce tariffs by an average weighting of about 40 per cent over eight years. It also wants preferential treatment for developing countries and special preferences for the least developed ones. The Community is particularly hopeful that the Tokyo Round will stimulate world trade and improve the present unfavourable balance of trade between the Community and the United States (see Chapter 22). The refusal of the Community at the end of 1978 to continue the GATT negotiations until the US Senate withdrew its threat of countervailing duties on certain Community agricultural exports is a further example of the growing political and economic power of the Community (see Chapter 22).

The Community has played an important part in the textile negotiations which were concluded, within the framework of the GATT Multi-fibre Agreement (MFA), with twenty-six countries at the end of 1977. The MFA allows for the continuation of discrimanatory restrictions on imports of textiles and export of clothing, in return for the agreement of the Community countries not to cut back existing quota levels and to phase out certain restrictions which cannot be justified under the terms of the MFA.

As most of the producers of fibres and textiles are low-cost developing countries, disappointment has been expressed by these countries that restrictions of any kind should continue. The defence of the developed countries, the Community in particular, is that without these restrictions imports would have continued to increase at such a rate that the whole of the indigenous textile industry, and the jobs in it, both of which are already declining at a rapid rate, would have been wiped out. This would have been politically unacceptable.

As regards UNCTAD, the UNCTAD IV meeting in 1976 in Nairobi dealt with commodities and the suggestion of a common fund to finance buffer stocks and help the producers of commodities most of whom came from developing countries. The Community supported the idea of a common fund and this was confirmed by the European Council of Ministers meeting in Rome in March 1977.

The Generalized System of Preferences

The Community was first, in 1971, to introduce the Generalized System of Preferences (GSP) which had been agreed at UNCTAD. Japan followed soon afterwards and then the United States in 1976. This system of tariff preferences has four basic principles:

(1) Non-reciprocal. The poorer countries do not have to offer any concessions in return.
(2) Autonomous. Preferences are granted without any negotiations.
(3) Non-discriminatory. The preferences are granted to all developing countries.
(4) Generalized. All industrialized countries are expected to grant them.

The GSP extended to 112 developing countries by 1977 and covered a wide spectrum of processed agricultural products, manufactured and semi-manufactured goods. Total tariff exemption is granted in some cases, and the tariff reductions in others depends on the degree of sensitivity of the product. Where there is a quota restriction on a sensitive product, the total volume of preferential imports is divided up among all those countries which want to export to the Community in order to give a share to all, not just to those countries which make the products at the lowest cost.

The theoretical amount of goods qualifying for concessions in 1978 was estimated at over 5000 million units of account for industrial products and 1300 million units of account for agricultural goods. In practice, this amount is not imported into the Community. This is partly because beneficiary countries do not exploit, or are unaware of, the possibilities. The GSP marks a turning point in world trade and the formal recognition of the needs of developing countries. Its development is still only embryonic but it reflects the Community's policy of working towards a more equitable distribution of the world's wealth.

Business and the Common Commercial Policy

Business both inside and outside the Community needs to take account of the Common Commercial Policy. At the working level, negotiations between the Community and third countries about quotas and tariffs on specific products need to be monitored and, if necessary, influenced through discussion with national and Community authorities. Companies and industries can be affected very quickly by these changes. An Indian company, which manufactured textiles, discovered in February 1978 that when it attempted to export $100 000 worth of shirts to Italy, the quotas already had been taken up for the first six months of the year. The special order could not be sold elsewhere and was therefore a complete loss. That the quota system needed to be applied more rationally was no compensation for their loss. Therefore, companies need to be sufficiently well-informed to be able to work with government officials to ensure that such difficulties are avoided.

At a more strategic level, the patterns of Community exports and their likely future trends are of significance to those planning future business activities whether in companies inside or outside the Community. The commercial relations of the world's largest trading bloc will become more coordinated during the next decade.

Bibliography

The Customs Union. European Documentation 1977

EEC Commercial Policy. House of Lords Select Committee on the European Communities 40th Report 1977, London: HMSO

Customs Union. House of Lords Select Committee on the European Communities 2nd Report 1978, London: HMSO

Review of the GATT Multilateral Trade Negotiations, Information Directorate-General, February 1978

17 The unions and social policy

> I believe that some historic new stimulus is required to
> reverse convincingly present trends in unemployment,
> in flagging investment and in weak growth. We have
> 6½ million unemployed now in the Community. This
> is bad enough. But what is not so widely recognized
> is the extent to which demographic trends over the
> period from now to the mid-1980s is going to more
> than redouble the task of job creation before us.
> Between now and 1984 25 million young people are
> going to reach the age of 16, while only 15 million are
> going to pass the age of 65. Demographic trends are
> thus going to add 10 million persons to the Com-
> munity labour potential – almost 10 per cent of the
> present total.
> *President Jenkins, December 1977*

Social policy is not so familiar in the United Kingdom as it is on the continent
and yet what it covers is of great importance to the Community. The Commission has a Directorate-General for Employment and Social Affairs. *Box 80*
shows its activities. Social affairs covers health, social security, housing, education, environment, employment, employers and unions.

The objectives of Community social policy are;

(1) Full and better employment throughout the Community.
(2) The improvement of living and working conditions.
(3) The involvement of both sides of industry in economic and social policy
     decisions and the participation of workers in industry.

These objectives were spelled out by the Council of Ministers in 1974 when it
accepted the Commission's Social Action Programme. This contained nearly
forty separate proposals which were to be achieved during the three years to
1977.

The Treaty of Rome says so little about social policy that nearly all developments have depended on the political will of member states. During the first two
years of the Social Action Programme much progress was made. In 1974 the
Council of Ministers agreed to establish the European Vocational Training
Centre and the Foundation for Improved Living and Working Conditions. There
were important directives on equal pay and mass dismissals. In addition, work
was begun on provisions for handicapped workers and safety regulations. This
was followed in 1975 by the adoption of a poverty programme, the agreement in
principle to a 40-hour week and four weeks annual holidays with pay. The
programme for migrant workers in the Community was established and there
were extensions of the Social Fund to help young workers under the age of 25.

169

Box 80

Directorate-General V

Employment and Social Affairs

Directorate A

General social policy guidelines

(1) Reports, analyses and general matters
(2) Wages, incomes and social welfare
(3) Social protection and social security
(4) European social budget

Directorate B

Employment and vocational training

(1) Coordination of national employment policies
(2) Employment forecasts: employment aspects of economic policies
(3) Community employment projects and employment aspects of the other Community policies
(4) Bureau for questions concerning women's employment
(5) Vocational guidance and training

Directorate C

European Social Fund

(1) Regulations, coordination and sectoral operations

(2) Operations concerning categories of workers, readaptation and ECSC conversion
(3) Regional operations and technical progress
(4) Finance and administration
(5) Preparatory work and analyses

Directorate D

Working conditions and migrant worker policies

(1) Working conditions and housing
(2) Action programme for migrant workers, freedom of movement and European Coordination Office
(3) Social security for migrant workers

Directorate E

Industrial relations and labour law

(1) Industrial relations and labour law
(2) Joint Committees

Directorate F

Health and safety

These actions, among others, led to a mood of optimism. It looked as if a Community social policy was being successfully developed. But progress slowed down in 1976 as member states became increasingly concerned with national social problems. The gap between the weaker and stronger members of the Community emerged. Different social policy objectives and priorities of member states became apparent, often reflecting political attitudes of the Nine Governments.

Many activities in the social policy area are important not only because they directly affect groups of individuals within the Community. If the Community is to develop successfully it will need to pay increasing attention to its public relations. Its actions will have to be explained more effectively to the world. Many of the provisions of a social policy, because they are to do with conditions of employment, improving working conditions and providing better jobs, can help to reflect the human face of the Community. If the human side of Community enterprise is neglected, the institutions will stand as monuments of little use or as ornaments on a side road of European history. There are, however, signs of new Community initiatives to combat unemployment and to protect industries in crisis. These actions could revive the role of social policy. What is required to further them is political will and greater resources at the Community level.

The Social Fund

The Social Fund was established in 1960 to assist in combating structural causes of unemployment. It has increased its resources from about £30 million in 1971 to £250 m in 1975, and to nearly £400 m in 1978. The rules of the Social Fund

Box 81

Help from the European Social Fund?

What kinds of schemes are helped?

As a result of an initiative taken by the Chamber of Commerce in Reggio Emilia in Italy, 225 unemployed young people are currently training as managers of supermarkets, shopping centres and tourist agencies. The students are aged between 18 and 25 and, although they have school certificates, are lacking in any other qualification to equip them for a job.

The distribution sector in Italy seriously lacks qualified staff, which is why the Reggio Chamber of Commerce has set up a special centre to teach the trainees general economics, statistics, marketing and publicity. They will also spend two months of their 11-month course gaining practical experience by working in a local business. At the end of it all, the course organizers undertake to find the trainees their first jobs in the distribution sector.

Recently a British firm in Northern Ireland, which manufactured knitwear and hosiery, embarked on a scheme to train 335 unemployed

people in Londonderry to work as cutters, stitchers, pressers and inspectors.

The company has been established in Northern Ireland for nearly thirty years, and now plans to open a new factory in the heart of Ulster's most troubled area. The factory will be manned largely by former members of Londonderry's unemployed. They will be trained for the job over a three-year period with financial help from the European Social Fund.

The Department of Employment publishes its own detailed booklet, 'The European Social Fund – A Guide to Possible Applicants'. Copies of the booklet and advice on applications can be readily obtained from the Social Fund Division, Department of Employment, 32 St James Square, London SW1. Contact with the Department is strongly advised and may save potential applicants wasting valuable effort in formulating claims.

were revised at the beginning of 1978 so that it could be directed to helping the hardest hit regions of the Community, and in particular those groups suffering most from unemployment: the young, women over 25, textile workers, clothing workers and migrant workers.

The Fund does not reimburse national governments for money they would have spent in any case. It attempts to encourage governments to spend more than they would normally do when helping to train and place workers in the right jobs. More than two million workers have so far been retrained with the help of the Social Fund which, like the Regional Development Fund, the funds from the European Coal and Steel Community and the European Investment Bank, is still relatively modest in size. Demands on the various funds greatly exceed the amounts they have to disburse. The amounts themselves are often only a fraction of the amounts spent by national administrations in the same policy areas. Nevertheless, the functioning of these funds, and the ways in which the moneys are used, has provided a European framework for cooperation. Mechanisms have been established and can be adapted with ease to distribute any increased funds accorded by Member Governments.

Industry in the United Kingdom is a major recipient of disbursements from the social and regional funds, but, in spite of simplified procedures for applying for these funds, the disbursements are still in practice made in close collaboration with national governments. Therefore, from the businessman's point of view, it is probably better in the first instance to seek any aids or grants direct from national governments. If Community funds are available the national administration will be able to suggest ways in which they can be tapped. Many of them can only be obtained together with matching funds from a member government or with its approval or support.

Full and better employment

During 1977 and 1978 as unemployment in the Community rose to over six million, the governments of the Nine accepted that the problem would need to be tackled at least on a Community, if not on a world, scale. Community initiatives were given a new emphasis. At 6 per cent, unemployment was higher than it had been since the establishment of the Community. In particular, the level of unemployment among the young rose very steeply to almost two million under the age of 25, almost 40 per cent of the total unemployed. The Commission has recognized youth unemployment as a serious problem. Imagine what society will be like with a substantial number of men and women in their late twenties who have never had a job. This prospect is extremely depressing, and the effort to avert the problem is negligible. The Commission, acting as the European conscience of the Community, is publicizing the matter and making some progress.

Community funds are one way of alleviating the situation, but the amounts are relatively small. During 1975–77, however, the Social Fund allocated 280 million units of account for vocational training compared with 400 million units of account by the Member States.

Box 82

The Commission's Director of Industrial Relations: a typical day

Not being by nature razor-sharp early in the morning, and Belgian drivers tending to be fast and aggressive, the shock therapy of driving into Brussels every morning ensures an adrenalin-charged start to my typical day. Gulping a quick coffee I check my day's appointments and a dictating session clears urgent letters on the closed shop, worker participation and the rights of commercial travellers. Meanwhile, a clutch of telephone calls brings a request from the Commissioner's Cabinet for a background paper on comparative labour standards and invitations to speak on industrial relations in Madrid and environmental pollution in Manchester. A colleague glides in with a bulging file and an eager face to brief me on a plenary session of a transport joint committee at which I am presiding later in the morning.

A flurry of raindrops slash the office windows and I grasp my umbrella. Ten minutes later I am shaking hands with the fifty participants of the Transport Joint Committee. It is 10 a.m. and at least we're friends to begin with. After sliding into the President's chair, I make an opening statement which I hope sounds lucid, clip on my earphones and spend the morning guiding the discussion towards acceptable compromises. My Directorate provides the secretariat for the eight Joint Committees already operating and there are at least ten others in prospect. They add a Euro-dimension to industrial relations. I sometimes feel these committees achieve more than the much publicized Summit meetings, which tend to suffer from being too prestigious and not sufficiently practical (my apologies to the President). Great expectations not realized soon turn to cynicism.

Lunchtime finds me back in Berlaymont hosting a lunch being given for visiting British prospective Liberal Party candidates for the European Parliament. During coffee I remind them that we have something in common – I am a labour man with strong conservative tendencies and liberal leanings! Then back to my office to discuss current work in the social affairs groups of the European Parliament and the Economic and Social Committee, where some of our proposals on labour legislation are being discussed. We draw up our plans for explaining and defending our proposals at these sessions. A meeting with the Commission's legal services is fixed for the following week and I agree to talk to Irish trade unionists about redundancy. The rain still pours and I hear that one of my officers is down with 'flu and that an organization of airline pilots wishes to see me urgently. It is 6.30 p.m. I have a quick wash, then dine with a group of industrialists who wish to discuss future trends in European industrial relations. Then I drive home. I feel a slight tightening of my belt and suspect a slight hardening of the arteries. The rain has stopped. I kiss my wife and she says: 'Did you have a good day?'

Jack Peel, November 1978

Of more long-term use is the gradual coordination of the actions of official committees, pressure groups, public bodies and Member Governments. Community social policy encourages them to treat social problems in a context wider than a national one.

In addition to the attempt to promote full employment, the Community has an obligation to promote better employment. It has developed the policy of freedom of movement of workers. This policy enables Community citizens to move anywhere within the European Community in search of a job. In addition, trades and professions can be practised in any of the nine member countries. The standardization of qualifications is being extended to an increasing number of occupations. The main obstacle to freedom of movement in the skilled trades and professions is still, and will remain, the language barrier. Yet in spite of this, over 1.5 million Community workers and their families live in countries other than their own.

Equal pay and equal treatment of men and women as regards employment opportunity has been accepted and the effects of this are now felt in the United Kingdom. Also, in 1978, the Council adopted a directive on the equal treatment of men and women in matters of social security. Directives have been adopted on employee rights in the event of a merger or transfer and protection for workers in the event of collective redundancies.

Improvement of living and working conditions

The Social Action Programme of 1974 listed a number of measures for the improvement of living and working conditions, the preparation of a European social budget, the progressive extension of social protection and specific measures to combat poverty. Success has been limited to date, although many key issues in the social field have been highlighted. As a result of these different activities, the Commission has established for itself a catalytic role in the process of developing both a European awareness and European solutions to many of the social problems which the Community faces.

Economic integration will only come about if problems such as employment and redeployment, education and social justice, are resolved in a humane fashion, and in a way acceptable to the broad majority of individuals in the Community as well as their governments.

Involvement of both sides of industry in decision-making and participation

The Commission has been active in encouraging the 'social partners', as the two sides of industry are known, to come together to develop common European policies. There are two major developments on employee participation. The first is the draft statute for a European company and the second, the Fifth Directive proposal and the green paper produced by the Commission on Employment, Participation and Company Structure.

The European company statute sets out an industrial relations framework for companies which might wish to opt for European status when a European company form is finally accepted. The idea of a European company grew out of the realization that cross-frontier mergers in Europe were desirable, but that a major obstacle was the problem of different legal requirements in the Member States which made these mergers difficult, if not impossible.

Figure 14 Euromarches. The main Commission building, the Berlaymont, is the scene of demonstrations and marches. These will doubtless become more frequent as European trades unions develop and co-ordinate their actions

The idea of the European company was complex from its inception, and developments in the area of worker participation made it more so. Germany already had an evolved system of worker participation and insisted that the proposed European company should have similar provisions. The Draft Statute in 1975 was therefore based largely on the German system with a two-tier board and worker representatives on the board.

The Fifth Directive was also largely based on the German system. It proposed (1) that any firm employing more than 500 people must have a supervisory board on which employees would be represented, and that (2) the two-tier system should be introduced, that is a board of management and a supervisory board. The Commission does not see the necessity for laying down exactly how worker representatives on the supervisory board should be appointed, but suggests that member states should respect common principles to ensure that delegates to the supervisory board are genuinely representative of the workers of the firm in question.

The work on the Fifth Directive and the proposal for a European company has not culminated in proposals acceptable to the Community. The Commission's role has been important in moving and coordinating the thinking of member states on the question of participation, but the problem is too large and too complicated to be resolved easily by a directive in the short term. The Commission's approach in recent times, as is often the case when progress cannot easily be made, is to go for agreement on the principle and on the ends to be achieved and leave the means to member states. While this may be a satisfactory and, indeed, the only way of making progress in worker participation, the problem for the European company is more severe. European industrial integration will remain a pipe-dream while it is impossible to set up a company which can operate effectively across the legal and tax frontiers of the Community. Yet, until a system of employee participation acceptable to all member states is established, it is difficult, if not impossible, to draw up a European company law statute.

Progress on worker participation and on European company law needs to be monitored by companies, but it is likely to be a slow process. It looks as if the European type of company will not be possible for some years yet.

In October 1978, the Council of Ministers approved a directive setting out common rules for the merger of limited liability companies in the Community. The purpose is to establish an equivalent level of protection throughout the Community for the associates, creditors and employees of the companies involved in mergers. This directive, and an earlier one dealing specifically with the rights of workers when companies merge, indicate that some progress is being made.

Current preoccupations in industrial relations

Much work is being done by the Commission in the field of industrial relations. Although it does not necessarily result in legislation, it is important for the social and industrial integration of the Community. The system of joint committees of representatives of both sides of industry is a recent innovation. These joint committees have been set up in a number of industries and the effect has been to encourage both managers and workers to look at some of their problems in a Community context.

Other preoccupations are unemployment, which is always prominent, protective legislation, worker participation, incomes policy and the concept of Euro-bargaining. The Social Affairs Directorate-General of the Commission is in close contact with trades union officials from the Nine and has encouraged the development of a European consciousness in trade union affairs. One result of this is that just as employers are working closer together in the Community, employees too are likely to find advantages in mutual exchanges of information and support. Information on pay and conditions, new plants and possible closures, on productivity and costs is increasingly available across the Community.

Box 83

A step nearer Eurobargaining?

Euro trade unions

To promote European trade unionism, the European Trade Union Confederation has set up – with the support of the European Commission – a European Trade Union Institute. 500 000 EUA has been written into the Community budget as the annual contribution for 1978.

Source: Euroforum, No. 27/78, 11 July 1978, p. 5

It is inevitable that some form of Euro-bargaining will develop as unions work closer together, but how this will come about remains unclear. Given the current complication of bargaining and negotiating in the antiquated industrial and political frameworks of some of the nations of the Nine, it could be advantageous to all concerned to ensure that Euro-bargaining, if it is to come, is developed within a coherent framework and not allowed to develop haphazardly as national bargaining has done.

The development of social policy in the Community needs not only to be studied carefully by larger companies. Some thought must also be given to ways in which they can ensure that a coherent social framework is developed which enables the social partners to work together to achieve the common end of a European-wide industrial base to generate wealth across the Community.

Bibliography

Callund, D. (1975) *Employee Benefits in Europe*, Gower Economic Publications
Lawson, R. and Reed, B. (1975) *Social Security in the European Community*, European Series No. 23

Official Publications

Annual Report on the Development of the Social Situation in the Community. From 1958 to present

Employee Participation and Company Structure in the European Community. Bulletin Supplement 8/1975

The Employment of Women and the Problem it raises in the Member States of the European Community, Evelyn Sullerot 1972

18 Other policies affecting business: energy, economic and monetary union, political cooperation

> If it means removing power to increase prosperity the
> House will have to decide whether it wishes to remain
> poor and independent or is willing to sacrifice some
> power in order to be more prosperous
> *The Rt. Hon. James Callaghan, UK Prime Minister,*
> *on the new European Monetary Arrangement, in*
> *the House of Commons on 10 July 1978.*

Each year a considerable number of European laws are added to the statute book. As the volumes of the Official Journal grow the implications for business become increasingly obvious. From fairly modest beginnings, even a relatively minor initiative such as consumer policy is beginning to have some effect (see Chapter 20) and the proposed Community law on liability for defective products has major implications for companies. In the future these laws will be made in closer collaboration and consultation with interested manufacturers and their representatives. More active initiatives will perhaps be taken by industry, in contrast to the somewhat passive role it has played until now.

The next three chapters deal in a few paragraphs with a number of Community policies, some of which are fundamental to the development of the Community, but are not discussed in depth because of limitations on time and space. At the end of each chapter there are references to documents which will explain the policies in detail. The reader should be able to select the ones he wants and order them using the addresses and telephone numbers in Chapter 28.

Energy policy

Energy policy in the Community is in its infancy. Very little progress has been made in implementing its objectives which are:

(1) To guarantee security of supply by reducing the Community's dependency on imported energy. This dependency amounted to about 60 per cent of total requirements in 1975.
(2) To preserve the unity of the Common Market in the event of a crisis in energy supplies.

These objectives were accepted by the Council of Ministers in 1974 when it adopted the Commission's 'Community Energy Policy Objectives for 1985'.

179

The intention of the resolution was to reduce the Community's dependence on imported energy from about 60 per cent in 1975 to 50 per cent, or possibly even 40 per cent, by 1985. The pattern of demand in 1985 will then be as in *Box 84*.

Oil imports would be reduced by maintaining coal production at current levels and nuclear energy encouraged as a source of electricity. Energy would also be saved by using it more efficiently.

Box 84

Demand for energy: 1985

The overall pattern of demand for primary energy in 1985 as compared with the earlier forecasts:

Solid fuels	17% instead of 10%
Oil	47% instead of 64%
Natural gas	20% instead of 15%
Hydroelectric and geothermal energy	3% instead of 2%
Nuclear energy	13% instead of 9%

Source: The European Community and the Energy Problem, European Documentation 1978/1

In fact the energy situation in the Community is still deteriorating. In 1977, the situation in member states was that neither natural gas output nor the move towards increasing the use of nuclear energy were progressing at the forecast rate. The Commission maintained that the aims set out in 1974 were still valid. If dependence is not reduced by 1985, so that imported sources of energy are less than 50 per cent, and oil is less than 50 per cent of all requirements, then continuous economic growth might be threatened. In 1978 the Commission suggested that more positive policies on conservation were required and more urgent action needed to support the Community coal industry. The role of nuclear energy is stressed and, in this respect, the Community work carried out by the Joint European Torus Project (JET) at Culham near Oxford will be of considerable long-term importance.

In the medium term there is some cause for concern at the lack of progress. There is broad agreement on the need for sharing energy supplies in the event of oil supply difficulties, but no agreement has been reached on the fixing of a minimum safeguard price for imported sources of energy. This is of particular interest to the United Kingdom as it would underwrite its investment in North Sea oil, and the possibility of exploiting the vast coal resources of the country. Others would argue that a floor price for oil is not so important for the United Kingdom as is sometimes claimed. There will always be a strong market for local supplies of energy on security grounds, and in any case there is no real possibility of the price of oil falling significantly during the rest of the century.

Recent OECD estimates are pessimistic about the development of nuclear capacity and estimate that little more than half the objectives for nuclear energy will have been met by 1985 if present developments continue. If world consumption of oil continues at its present level, it is by no means certain that oil supplies will be available from outside the Community even at 1979 prices. It is estimated that the Community energy deficit in 1985, to be made up by importing oil, could be as much as $60 000 m. This is a very large amount of money even assuming the oil will be available.

Box 85

Energy policy

Objectives

Planning and organization of procurement and distribution of secure, cheap and adequate energy supplies for industry and public at Community level. Account taken of the following basic situations:

different economic and technical bases in the competition between energy sources (coal, oil, nuclear power, natural gas, hydroelectric power)

high investments with long amortization period necessary

so far, activity by states predominantly in accordance with national criteria

energy policy at European Community level still only in its infancy

Energy statistics for 1975 (in million tonnes of coal equivalent)

Primary energy	Production	Gross internal consumption	Degree of dependence on foreign supply %
United Kingdom	175	289	43
FR of Germany	170	345	55
Netherlands	104	84	−25
France	58	235	74
Italy	35	182	79
Belgium	9	59	85
Ireland	2	9	85
Denmark	0	25	99
Luxembourg	0	6	100
European Community	553	1236	57

Source: European Parliament Handbook 1978

Business interest in a Community energy policy is therefore a strategic one. Companies need to forecast their energy costs as a key factor of their future operations. A community policy, by securing sources of supply, may help to make this forecasting a little more reliable.

Inevitably, there must be considerable developments in this policy area as the Community will find it more advantageous to negotiate for its oil supplies as an entity rather than bilaterally. There are also substantial opportunities for trade-offs and mutual support within the Community. The United Kingdom should be in a strong position, given the size of her oil and coal reserves, compared to the rest of the Nine. For the UK manufacturer it is evident that transport costs will increase considerably over the next ten years. In deciding location policy in the Community, the cost of transporting goods of great size or weight must obviously be considered and so also must the advantages of regional production and regional depots.

Energy policy will only develop when the political will is there to promote it. There is little doubt though that there will be even more discussions about

Box 86

A common problem

EEC, USA and Japan: oil import requirements 1976–78 (millions of tonnes)

	1976	1977	% ± 77/76	1978	% ± 78/77
Consumption (including bunkers)					
EEC	540	530	− 2.0	540	+ 2.0
USA	850	895	+ 5.3	930	+ 3.9
Japan	265	280	+ 5.7	290	+ 3.6
	1655	1705	+ 3.0	1760	+ 3.2
Production					
EEC	21	47		85	
USA	510	515		555	
	531	562	+ 5.8	640	+13.9
Imports					
EEC	519	485	− 6.6	455	− 6.2
USA	340	380	+11.8	375	− 1.3
Japan	265	280	+ 5.7	290	+ 3.6
	1124	1145	+ 1.9	1120	− 2.2

Note: estimate of import requirements excludes imports for stock piling in the United States and Japan.

Sources: EEC: Eurostat and Commission forecasts. USA: Chase Manhattan and Independent Petroleum Association of America. Japan: Petroleum Association of Japan

pooling resources, common purchasing policies, price regulations, supply conservation and the need to establish a Community bargaining position. These are in the range of possible Community strategies for energy, which in spite of current difficulties will in all probability begin to be developed in the next few years.

Economic and monetary union

Political, defence and democratic aspects of the Community may determine in the long term whether it survives, but at present the Community is better known as the Common Market. Economic policies have been central to developments over the first twenty years. The Customs Union — the removing of obstacles to trade, through the application of the competition laws or through the gradual abolition of tariff, non-tariff and technical barriers to trade — the Common Commercial Policy and action in the social and industrial policy fields are all important spheres of Community economic activity.

Monetary and financial policy, medium- and long-term economic policy, 'conjunctural' or general economic policy and economic and monetary union are attempts to describe and develop the economic framework within which the present Community operates.

It is now generally agreed that progress on European integration can only take place if there is a move towards genuine economic and monetary union. Much detailed theoretical work has been done, few practical results have emerged. The failure of the 'Snake in the Tunnel' — European currencies fluctuating narrowly against one another in a tunnel of fluctuation against the dollar — was an early setback. The 'Snake' was meant to be a first and important step towards European monetary union. It failed when currencies such as the lira and sterling could not remain within the 'Snake' because of external, mainly speculative, pressures against them. This occurred in spite of a certain amount of support from the European Central Banking Community.

There followed the belief that perhaps a two-tier Community with a group of rich nations and a group of less rich ones would be more appropriate. But rising inflation, the floating of the dollar and the oil crisis caused the 'Snake' to wriggle too much to stay in the tunnel.

The currencies of richer countries, Germany, Belgium, Holland, Luxembourg and Denmark, have continued within the 'Snake', but economic and monetary union looked a forlorn hope and was not taken too seriously, even when President Jenkins relaunched the idea during his first year as President of the Commission. He saw it as a way, perhaps the only way, to advance the cause of European integration.

At the European Council meeting in Copenhagen in 1978, the German Chancellor, Herr Schmidt, proposed a radical plan for a Community currency zone. The subsequent European Council at Bremen proposed to fix all European

currencies against the European Unit of Account (EUA) which would be re-named the European Currency Unit (ECU). The limits of fluctuation of the new European 'Snake' were ultimately to be only 1 per cent. It would be supported by a revived and enlarged European Monetary Fund which would have large reserves, from member countries, to back it — perhaps one-fifth of their gold and dollar reserves and also national currencies. The total reserves would be about $50 billion.

Although the British government had reservations about the plan, consider-able progress was made at Bremen. It led President Jenkins to comment that the Bremen Council was 'by far the most important and worthwhile European Council I have attended'.

The progress of EMU is a key indicator in the development of the Com-munity. Should there be development towards economic and monetary union then many other, less important, policies will advance. Considerable impetus would be given to European integration.

President Giscard d'Estaing and Chancellor Helmut Schmidt made it clear in mid-1978 that France and Germany attached great significance to the develop-ment of a European Monetary System (EMS). The technicalities of the system were discussed by finance ministers and central bankers in the autumn of 1978. In spite of a reluctance, largely on political grounds, to be closely tied to Com-munity exchange rates, monetary policies and inflation rates, there are signs that government officials and politicians of both major UK parties may go along with the Franco—German initiative and support the principle even though delaying the entry of sterling into the system until such time as it can take the strain of the narrow institution limits. Whatever their decision there will be considerable development in the Community as France and Germany are determined to develop a European Monetary System, with or without the United Kingdom. Nearly all the Community countries would follow leaving the United Kingdom isolated. The principle of the EMS is perhaps more important than the practice and much depends on the United Kingdom's attitude to it during 1979 and 1980 rather more than on the timing of the United Kingdom's full entry into the system. The EMS, which came formally into existence on 13 March 1979, without full United Kingdom participation, was, nevertheless, an important step towards the ultimate goal of economic and monetary union.

The year 1979 is crucial. The European Monetary System, direct elections to the European Parliament and the enlargement of the Community to include

Figure 15 and 16 (opposite) A European currency? It could be a long time before one set of coins replaces the currencies of the Nine, although the 'Europa' or now the 'ECU' are talked about as future replacements for this collection of coins in our pockets. ECU is short for European Currency Unit but happily for Frenchmen, is also the name of a now obsolete French coin. Even if the ECU becomes an everyday word in central banking parlance, it will remain for the present an accounting unit of transfer between central banks and a standard measure of value.

Box 87

Money and Europe — President Jenkins

The prospect of monetary union should be seen as part of the process of recovering the substance of sovereign power. At present we tend to cling to its shadow. These arguments do not run against international co-operation, as for example in the OECD and the IMF. On the contrary, we need to improve the functioning of the international economy by a better shaping of its constituent parts. Monetary disunity in Europe is one of the major flaws in the international system as well as in the functioning of our small to medium-sized states.

On the seventh and final argument, I can be quite short since, like the first, it is a traditional one. It is the straight political argument that monetary union stands on offer as a vehicle for European political integration. Jacques Rueff said in 1949 'L'Europe se fera par la monnaie ou ne se fera pas'. I would not necessarily be quite so categorical. It should, however, be clear that the successful creation of a European monetary union would take Europe over a political threshold. It seems equally clear that Europe today is not prepared to pursue the objective of monetary union uniquely for ideological reasons. To move in this direction Europe also needs materially convincing arguments. I have tried to set out some of the economic arguments.

I summarize as follows. We must change the way we have been looking at monetary union. A few years ago we were looking at a mountain top through powerful binoculars. The summit seemed quite close, and a relatively accessible, smooth, gradual and short approach was marked out. But then an avalanche occurred and swept away this route. The shock was such that more recently it has even seemed as if we have been looking at the summit with the binoculars both the wrong way round and out of focus.

I believe that a new, more compelling and rewarding but still arduous approach is necessary. We must also change the metaphor. Let us think of a long-jumper. He starts with a rapid succession of steps, lengthens his stride, increases his momentum, and then makes his leap.

The creation of a monetary union would be a leap of this kind. Measures to improve the Customs Union and the free circulation of goods, services and persons are important steps. We look for bigger strides in working out external policies, establishing more democratic and thus accountable institutions, elaborating more coherent industrial and regional policies, and giving our financial instruments the means to keep the whole movement on a balanced course. We have to look before we leap, and know when we are to land. But leap we eventually must.

We must not only do what is best in the circumstances. We must give our people an aim beyond the immediately possible. Politics is not only the art of the possible, but as Jean Monnet said, it is also the art of making possible tomorrow what may seem impossible today.

Extract from President Jenkins, The First Jean Monnet Lecture, Europe's present challenge and future opportunity, Florence, 27 October 1977

Greece, Portugal and Spain are three major developments which will shape the development of the Community for many years to come.

Political cooperation

From the beginning of the Community it was clear that an advanced level of economic integration would inevitably lead to increasing political cooperation, particularly as regards the foreign policies of the Member States.

As a result of a number of initiatives, and in particular of the meeting of heads of government in Paris in 1974, it was agreed that the Nine would 'gradually adopt common positions and coordinate their diplomatic action in all areas of international affairs which affect the interest of the European Community'. The Paris meeting led to the founding of the European Council (Chapter 6), which is a most important method of political cooperation, being both an initiating and decision-making body. However, there are other methods through which political cooperation takes place in the Nine.

Conference of ministers of foreign affairs

The Conference now meets at least four times a year. It often meets before or after foreign ministers' meetings for Council of Ministers business. The Conference of Ministers, as well as deliberating on general foreign affairs matters, also executes those decisions taken by the European Council which fall within its jurisdiction. The chairman of the Conference often acts as spokesman for the Nine and this strengthens his position.

In addition there is also a *political committee* which is attended by senior officials of the ministries of foreign affairs of member states. This meets, on average, once a month to study current problems and maintain contacts on a wide range of policies. Occasionally, a *working party* is set up to consider specific problems such as the Middle East or Asia. A working party may study, for example, the current position on détente and the lead up to the Belgrade Conference.

A *group of correspondents* has also been set up with the task of following the implementation of political cooperation. It also prepares the work of the political committee. There is also more frequent and routine communication through a telegraphic system which allows member states to be in regular confidential contact with one another.

There is a further link through the *embassies of the Member States* which meet in third countries throughout the world. In non-member countries the embassy of the Member State, which is currently President of the Council, acts as the secretariat for political cooperation. The embassies of the Nine within the Community also play a role in political cooperation, as do the permanent

Box 88

Political cooperation in Europe of the Nine

In fact, I think that I can affirm that the procedures of political cooperation have become stronger and more demanding than the texts. Between the Nine countries of the Community has developed a sort of customary right which, naturally, is not accompanied by any sanction, but which has the character of a recognized rule which may be broken on occasions, but whose existence is recognized. However, there is fairly strong pressure on our diplomatic machinery that we should help each other, that we should speak with one single voice and that we should avoid discord.

Of course it is interesting to give some thought to the origin of this pressure. It is not, as certain people are still trying to prove, that the partisans of Europe are blind militants of a new orthodoxy whose dogmatic intolerance is trying to deny the realities of our states, our people or our parties. It is high time to leave behind these worn-out and absurd arguments which are still making us live in a hallucinatory world.

What happens, on the contrary, in day-to-day events, is that a double form of pressure emerges and will doubtless continue to emerge increasingly strongly both inside and outside our states; inside our states, because our peoples are becoming increasingly more aware of our joint action in a world which is dominated by the super-powers and also by the automatic majorities in a certain number of international fora; and outside, because the third countries who perceive the world dialogue as being between the large groups, await, expect and sometimes demand to know Europe's collective point of view and to hear its voice. It is this double pressure which is pushing us towards political cooperation and not some kind of European sectarianism.

At the time of drawing up this list, we must neither overestimate nor underestimate what has been done. We must not overestimate it because political cooperation, despite its progress, is not a common foreign policy. It is still exclusively based on the political goodwill of governments which, in this sphere, subject to the transfers of competence which they may have made to the advantage of international organizations, say that they are still sovereign.

We are all free to understand the extent of the illusions in this affirmation. It is also precarious, reversible and susceptible to exceptions. In addition, the shortcomings and weaknesses of the internal construction of Europe impose objective limits to political cooperation. To speak with one voice in the world, we must first be able to recognize the convergence of our own interests amongst ourselves, and this is still not the case in many spheres. But, on the other hand, it is necessary not to overestimate too much the result of our efforts because, in fact, we have managed to achieve a high degree of cooperation between us and because we often manage to present to the outside world a united image of Europe.

Henri Simonet, Belgian Foreign Minister. From a speech made in his capacity as the then President of the Council of Ministers, 14 November 1977

representations to international organizations such as the UN, UNCTAD and OECD.

The European Commission takes part in all ministerial meetings and is represented at meetings of the political committee. COREPER works on problems in which Community affairs and political cooperation questions overlap.

The European Parliament is involved with political cooperation. A yearly report is submitted to it by the chairman in office of the Conference of Ministers of Foreign Affairs. The chairman also meets with the Political Affairs

Box 89

Political cooperation in the Community

(1) The European Council. Meeting of heads of government three times a year.

(2) Conference of Ministers of Foreign Affairs. Meets at least four times a year often on the same day as the Council of Ministers − the same ministers being present on both occasions but wearing different hats. At the Council of Ministers they are representing their government at a Community meeting to decide on Commission proposals. At the Conference meeting they are discussing political cooperation on their own governments' initiative.

(3) Political Committee. Senior officials from the Nine Ministries of Foreign Affairs. Monthly meeting to study current problems.

(4) Group of Correspondents. To monitor the development of political cooperation.

(5) Constant confidential telegraphic communication between the Nine

(6) Meetings of embassy representatives of the Nine wherever they are represented in the world.

Committee of the Parliament every three months. In 1974, the right of the European Parliament to put written or oral questions was extended to cover questions about the conferences of ministers of foreign affairs.

There is, therefore, a complex network of political relationships at the level of Member Governments of the Nine, and these overlap, in places, with Community political activities. The development of political cooperation ultimately depends, however, not on the plethora of committees and systems, but on the political will of the nine member governments which is where the real power still lies.

Perhaps the most interesting fact about political cooperation is how it has grown in a very short time. It shows how European cooperation, given the political will, can come about very rapidly indeed.

Bibliography

Cairncross, A. *et al.* (1974) *Economic Policy for the European Community,* London: Macmillan

OECD (1974) *Energy Prospects to 1985,* (2 vols) Paris: OECD

Official Publications

    The Community and the World Energy Situation, Communication from the Commission to the Council, 9 March 1978

    Economic and Monetary Union by 1980, Report of the Study Group, March 1975

    The Economic Situation in the Community, Quarterly

    Energy for Europe: Research and Development, Bulletin Supplement 5/74

    The European Community and the Energy Problem, European Documentation 1975/2

    Graphs and Notes on the Economic Situation in the Community. Monthly

    Guidelines and Priority Actions under the Community Energy Policy, Bulletin Supplement 6/73

    Medium-term Prospects and Guidelines in the Community Gas Sector, 1972

    Report to the Council and the Commission on the Realization by Stages of Economic and Monetary Union (Werner Report), Bulletin Supplement 11/70

    Summary of Convergence of Economic Policies in 1977, Communication from the Commission to the Council, March 1978

Ray, G.F. (1975) *Western Europe and the Energy Crisis,* Trade Policy Research Centre

Saunders, C., (1975) *From Free Trade to Integration in Western Europe,* Chatham House – PEP, European Series No. 22

19   The Common Agricultural Policy

Blessed be agriculture! If one does not have too much
of it
Charles Warner, My Summer in a Garden, 1871

The Common Agricultural Policy (CAP) is of fundamental importance to the Community. The Policy operates more or less successfully, and the agricultural regime of the Member States is integrated through it. Whether its objectives are the right ones cannot be discussed in such a short chapter, but perhaps two points should be made:

(1) The costs and benefits of the CAP are difficult to quantify. It is doubtful whether many of the simplistic cases made out to defend or support it are accurate assessments. It was developed for a complex range of economic, political and defence reasons.
(2) The CAP should not be judged purely in terms of current costs and benefits. More fundamental questions have to be asked, such as, does Europe need to be more or less dependent on food imports in the future for reasons of security, regionalization of world trade or the increasing competitiveness of Third World industry? The CAP needs to be assessed in terms of ends such as these.

Both means and ends are important, even in financial terms. The CAP took over 75 per cent of the Community budget in 1977. Over 6.5 million units of account out of a total of 8.5 million units of account were devoted to financing it.

The management of agricultural markets is the responsibility of the Community alone now that tariff barriers between markets of member states have been dismantled and trade with non-member countries is subject to Community rules. The CAP protects Community farmers against cheap imports from other countries by a system of import levies. It sets common prices throughout the Common Market and ensures the joint financing of restructuring plans and the operation of the Policy. Only a few products like alcohol of agricultural origin, sheep meat and potatoes have not been brought into the system.

Indicative and intervention prices

The most important prices which are fixed at Community level are: (1) the 'indicative' or 'guide' price which is the wholesale price guaranteed to producers and (2) the 'intervention' price which is a lower price at which the Community is

Box 90

Commissioner Tugendhat on the CAP

It is widely believed in the United Kingdom that the CAP, designed as it was for a Community of Six, has an inherent tendency to produce policies detrimental to the United Kingdom.

Personally I have always contested this. It is my belief that, given the sweeping changes which have occurred in recent years in the world's economy and food supply, and the likely future trends, the question of price stability and security of supply has become sufficiently more important to justify paying a premium in terms of the actual level of prices. As a result the CAP is in fact not such a bad fit for the United Kingdom as it is often supposed.

It is, however, too expensive, takes too large a share of the Community budget, and produces too many surpluses. As I have often said before, it needs to be reformed in a number of ways, some quite far reaching. This need for a close look at the CAP has now been recognized at the highest level, by the Community heads of government at the recent European Council meeting in Bremen. The Commission has been called upon to produce a report on the workings of the Community's agricultural policy.

Extracts from a speech by Christopher Tugendhat, EEC Budgets Commissioner, to the Cheshire Branch of the NFU, Crewe, 20 July 1978

obliged to buy products from farmers if they cannot be sold in Community markets or exported. 'Mountains' of butter or meat occur when the Community intervention price has been set at a level which obliges the Community to buy much of the produce which farmers cannot sell at the intervention price or above. This occurs when there is a good harvest or over-production. The purpose of setting indicative and intervention prices is to ensure that there is a regular supply of produce and that farmers obtain sufficient income to encourage them to produce for a particular market. The agricultural market, under any system, is complicated. It can be influenced by political and economic factors as well as by the weather and the usual problems of a market based on long supply lead times and short-term demand.

When the Community has to buy in produce and a 'mountain' occurs, it is not easy to get rid of it. If it is sold in the Community, it may depress prices even further. It follows that even more produce will not fetch the intervention price and will have to be bought in, thus adding to the 'mountain'. If sold outside the Community, then there are political problems, and possible accusations of dumping or wasting taxpayers' money. The 'mountains', which occur from time to time, have to be seen in context. They do not occur too frequently

Box 91

The price of agricultural goods

The CAP is very complex. There are at least 21 different types of price to regulate it. Among them:

The sluice-gate price (prix d'écluse) is required for calculating the supplementary levy. In the case of goods processed from agricultural products the levy is not equal to the difference between the c.i.f. price and the threshold price; to avoid market disruption in this case a supplementary levy is charged, equal to the difference between the lower free-at-frontier offer price and the sluice-gate price.

The free-at-frontier offer price (prix d'offre franco frontière) is quoted for all products imported from third countries. It is required for calculation of the supplementary levy which is given by the sluice-gate price minus the lower free-at-frontier price.

The second free-at-frontier offer price (second prix d'offre franco frontière) is used as a basis for calculating the supplementary levy (see free-at-frontier offer price) when imports from certain third countries are at abnormally low prices compared with supplies from other third countries.

The reference price (prix de référence) is used in the MO for fruit, vegetables and fishery products for calculating the countervailing charge to be imposed over and above customs duty on goods imported at unusually low prices.

The minimum import price (prix minimum d'importation) serves the same purpose as the reference price and is applied to imports of certain fishery products as a special protection measure.

The intervention price (prix d'intervention) is the price at which intervention centres must buy up produce. It is guaranteed to producers as a minimum return, and is slightly under the target price and slightly higher than the price to the producer (difference – transport costs between the farm and the warehouse of the intervention agency).

The basic intervention price (prix d'intervention de base) is the intervention price of certain kinds of cereal in the area showing the largest deficit. For other intervention centres, the derived intervention price is calculated from the basic intervention price.

Derived intervention prices (prix d'intervention dérivés) are the prices derived for other intervention centres from the basic intervention price at which the intervention agencies buy in produce.

The guaranteed minimum price (prix minimum garanti) is used in the case of durum wheat for the calculation of aid to producers. If the intervention price for the centre in the area with the highest surplus falls short of the guaranteed minimum price, producers receive a subsidy corresponding to the difference.

The buying-in price (prix d'achat) is the intervention price of the MO for pigmeat and the MO for fruit and vegetables. It is derived from the respective basic prices applicable in these COMs.

The withdrawal price (prix de retrait) is the price below which fruit and vegetable producers' organizations will not release onto the market the goods supplied by their members (who receive a payment in compensation).

Source: European Parliament Handbook 1978

and the price represents what has to be paid to ensure security and regularity of supply.

Currency fluctuations and the green pound

A further problem is caused by the fluctuations of Community currencies. When exchange rates were fixed, then so also were Community prices, in terms of the national currencies. Fluctuating exchange rates made the system of levies and subsidies unworkable and so a new system of fixed parities was agreed. The exchange rate parities are adjusted at meetings of the Agricultural Council of Ministers and, in theory, the process balances out what would otherwise be extreme fluctuations in farm incomes. The difficulty is that over time the difference between the 'green pound' rate, as it is called, and the current exchange rate has in some cases become very wide. For some currencies, such as

Box 92

President Jenkins on the green pound

I know that the food industry has had to occupy itself quite a lot in the last few years with the green pound, so that most of you will be perfectly at home when I talk about this imaginary currency. I rather wish that it really existed — perhaps in the form of bank notes signed by the Commissioner for Agriculture so that I could hold one up for you to see. It has recently aroused a good deal of excitement. It still serves, I think, rather like the yellow peril or the red menace, as a useful scapegoat: if you ask the average farmer why he is looking miserable, he will say its because of his low prices caused by the green pound, while the average consumer — a good deal more paradoxically — is quite likely to blame the green pound for the increased cost of his food.

As you know, the green pound — like the green franc, the green mark and the other green currencies — is the rate at which CAP prices are translated into national money in the Member State concerned. Normally speaking, you would expect this to be done at the current rate of exchange on the money markets: after all, that is the rate at which other prices are translated in business and commerce. But it has been accepted in the CAP that, when the value of a currency changes quite substantially because of a devaluation or a revaluation, the effects need not immediately be passed on to the level of farm price support. After all, an overnight change of 10 per cent or more in prices is not necessarily a good thing. So we accept — and the Commission certainly does accept — the use of green rates and the resulting MCAs as a temporary cushion: like the classic device of a transition period, it should allow you to move with least pain from point A to point B.

The trouble comes when the participants in this game are tempted to use the existence of green rates as an excuse for never arriving at point B.

continued

The consequence of that, in the context of the CAP, would be that Member States would apply different levels of farm price support on a permanent basis − and when the gap between levels is of the order of 35−40 per cent, that is a very substantial difference. Now what is wrong with this is not just that it hampers trade and makes life more complicated for you in the food industry because of the proliferation of MCAs − though that is bad enough − and not just that it makes decisions on common prices in Brussels more abstract and remote. What is wrong is that if food producers and processors in the various Member States receive vastly different prices in real terms, it frustrates and makes a mockery of the idea of a common market with equal terms of competition. But we also have to remind the Member States that the common prices are their prices, they have participated in fixing them from year to year: if they deplore the consequences of surplus production resulting from high prices in the Community Member Governments must make an effort to curb them. If they fall head-over-heels into the green trap, they will not achieve the improvements in the CAP which they want.

I have gone into these matters in some detail to try to explain to you why it is that the Commission is in favour of phasing out MCAs and the green pound. It is not because they are expensive, or for the sake of some dogma about the unity of the market, or in order to pick an argument with the British government: it is because we believe their continuation as a permanent feature is not in the long-term interests of Europe or its Member States.

From speech by the President of the Commission, the Rt. Hon. Roy Jenkins, to the Food Manufacturers Federation Conference in London on 27 September 1977

sterling, because of its devaluation in recent years, it is as much as 30 or 40 per cent. Although the farmer would like to see the green pound brought closer to the current exchange rate, because his income would rise correspondingly, the government, particularly in inflationary times, is concerned to keep the cost of food down and hence is under pressure to retain the artificial exchange rate. Countries such as Germany, where the Deutschmark has revalued against other currencies, pay a much larger proportion of the costs of the CAP. They apply constant pressure on governments, such as the United Kingdom, to change the rate, even though in the interests of Community development and solidarity they realize it cannot be done all at once.

A third type of price is the 'reference', entry or floor, price which prevents non-Community imports at too low a level. This is achieved by charging compensatory taxes or levies when the products coming into the Community fall below prices in that market. This form of protection is often criticized, and it is argued that but for the CAP the price of butter, for example, would fall considerably. This is correct in the short run. The problem is that in the medium to long term butter production would fall dramatically in the Community and we would become increasingly dependent on supplies from third countries. The question is whether, given economic uncertainty in the world, this is desirable or not.

Recently, in view of the growing protectionism in the world and the need to maintain employment, the protectionist aspects of Community policies have not been criticized as much as they were. In agriculture, a compromise, probably like that in industrial goods, will be reached. Out of self-interest the Community can see the need for world free trade. This will be encouraged wherever possible. However, it is neither politically possible nor practical economics to allow Community industrial and agricultural production to decline drastically in some products in order to achieve a certain short-term price and cost efficiency. It would cause unemployment, hardship and disruption. It might not even be possible to apply such policies in democratic states, even if it were desirable. If a compromise solution is found somewhere between free competition and total protection, its concomitant will be an increasing role of government in business.

Box 93

Does history repeat itself?

'Critics of the Common Agricultural Policy are urging us to rely on imports of cheap food.

Twenty years ago those who wanted to develop Europe's own energy resources were told to rely on imports of cheap oil.

Verb sap?'

David Walder MP in a letter to The Times, 7 June 1977

In the meantime there is widespread agreement that the CAP needs reform. The problem is that it is the one Community policy which really works. Its operation is highly sophisticated, and it would be practically impossible, even if it were desirable, to dismantle the system entirely. The 'mountains' and the border compensatory amounts, with problems such as the wine war and the need to adapt to the entry of three largely agricultural countries into the Community, make it necessary to urgently seek methods of reform. Meanwhile, the CAP has preserved markets and producers and protected the consumer from too many price fluctuations. More importantly, it has been the testing ground which has shown that European economic integration is possible. It is argued that if this can be achieved in agriculture, then it surely can be achieved in other policy areas.

Bibliography

The Common Agricultural Policy, Commission of the European Communities, December 1977. Pamphlet available free from UK Commission Office

20 Regional policy, environmental policy, consumer policy, and other policies

The more we get out of the world the less we leave,
and in the long run we shall have to pay our debts at
a time that may be very inconvenient for our own
survival
N. Wiener, The Human Use of Human Beings, 1954

Nearly all policies being developed by the Community are of interest to industry to a greater or lesser extent. This section draws attention to the considerable body of European law which already exists and to the likely developments which industry needs to consider both at the strategical and tactical levels.

Regional policy

There are wide disparities between regions of the Community. The differences have increased in recent years. If the Community average per capita gross domestic product is taken as 100, then between 1970 and 1975 that of Ireland fell from 53 per cent to 49 per cent, Italy from 70 per cent to 59 per cent and the United Kingdom from 89 per cent to 77 per cent. This is partly because these countries have had to bear the burden of the redevelopment of large areas of their territories.

The best known part of regional policy is the Regional Fund which between October 1975 and the end of 1977 made £540 million available to nearly 5000 investment projects in the so called assisted areas of member states.

The United Kingdom received nearly 30 per cent of this allocation. It is the second most favoured beneficiary after Italy. The northern region of England was the principal beneficiary with about £45 million. When a grant is approved, it is paid via the national government to the authorities undertaking the project. About 60 per cent of the aid granted to the United Kingdom has been for infrastructure projects. Although the Regional Fund is not very large, it is the equivalent of about 15 per cent of the total amount of the regional aid of member states. In addition, funds have been made available from other financial institutions of the Community, in particular from the European Investment Bank, the Social Fund and funds from the ECSC, and the Agricultural Fund (FEOGA).

197

Box 94

Report on the European Regional Development Fund

Nineteen seventy-seven, the third year of operation of the Fund, brought a considerable increase in the number of projects for which assistance was granted. Out of 2269 projects submitted for grant, 2020 were approved. This compared with 1183 projects approved in 1975, and 1545 in 1976.

Over the whole of the initial three-year period of the Fund, 452.7 million u.a. (35 per cent) of the grants approved were for industrial and services sector projects. Grants for infrastructure projects accounted for 851.4 million u.a. (65 per cent), including 65.6 million u.a. for rural infrastructure. The table summarizes Fund activity in 1977 and over the 1975–77 period.

Regional Fund grants (by Member State)

| | 1977 | | |
	Number of investment projects	Investment involved (million u.a.)	Grants committed (million u.a.)
United Kingdom	505	1 490	145
Italy	736	1 182	192
Germany (FR)	410	893	42
France	184	607	70
Ireland	73	190	30
Denmark	59	38	6
Belgium	47	53	8
Netherlands	5	38	0
Luxembourg	1	3	0
Community	2 020	4 498	504

| | 1975–77 | | | |
	Number of investment projects	Investment involved (million u.a.)	Grants committed (million u.a.)	Payments made (million u.a.)
United Kingdom	1 730	4 038	361	225
Italy	1 192	3 452	520	306
Germany (FR)	670	1 205	72	38
France	625	1 761	193	90
Ireland	267	663	83	47
Denmark	135	144	16	11
Belgium	111	158	19	8
Netherlands	16	179	21	11
Luxembourg	2	7	1	1
Community	4 748	11 711	1 289	740

Source: adapted from the Eleventh General Report of the Commission of the European Community, February 1978

The regional policy of the Community covers four areas:

(1) Less developed regions which are predominantly agricultural and where the farming is low yield and unemployment more or less permanent.
(2) Declining regions. These have an ageing industrial structure and are often dependent on a single industry.
(3) Areas of urban concentration where conditions of living and working create human problems.
(4) Frontier regions between countries where an economic entity is divided by a political frontier.

Regional development is likely to play a more important role in the Community in future. The reason, apart from the need to redress the growing imbalance of the regions, is because the achievement of economic and monetary union is only possible if the disparities between the wealth of regions are diminished. The new world economic order will force the Community into major structural changes. In many areas of change, regional aspects will remain important. Enlargement, which will bring three less developed countries into the Community, will also raise considerable problems of a regional nature.

The Regional Development Fund

In 1977 the Commission made new proposals to the Council. The Regional Development Fund was increased to £370 m in 1978 from £208 m in 1977. Criteria for distributing aid between different Community countries have been modified. In particular, 5 per cent of the total resources of the Regional Fund will not be subject to any national quota, but can be used by the Commission to assist in projects not supported by national authorities. This will give a new flexibility to the Community in matters of regional aid. It is a small move but could have significant long-term effects.

The Regional Policy Committee

This is the other instrument of the Community's regional policy. The role of the Committee, which was set up in 1975 at the same time as the Regional Fund, is to follow the development of the regions, to analyze national regional policies and to gauge their compatibility with each other and with Community objectives.

The Commission also wants from the Council a greater commitment to the regional consequences of Community policies and an increased effort to coordinate national regional policies. It asked for a mechanism for fixing, at Community level, the guidelines and priorities for the coordination of both Community and national regional policies and for a major effort to coordinate the Community's financial instruments. The various funds lend over £1000 m

Box 95

A significant step in regional policy?

A more flexible definition of those infrastructure projects eligible for assistance has been introduced to ensure they are suited to regional needs and regional policy priorities. The maximum level of financing of infrastructure projects by the Fund in certain regions or priority zones has been increased from 30 to 40 per cent.

Distribution criteria

The criteria distributing aid between different Community countries have just been modified. In particular, 5 per cent of the Fund's total resources (approximately 100 million EUA for 1977–80) will not be subject to any prescribed criteria or national quota system. These re-sources can be used by the Community to assist in areas not covered by national authorities, to finance specifically Community projects and to help remedy regional problems which might emerge as a result of the economic crisis. This will give the Community greater flexibility.

The new division of the Fund will be as follows:

Belgium	1%
Denmark	1%
Germany	6%
France	17%
Ireland	6%
Italy	39%
Luxembourg	0%
Netherlands	2%
United Kingdom	27%

units of account each year, and taken together they could have an important impact on the redistribution of economic strength throughout the Community.

Environmental policy

The Community's environmental policy covers both the natural and the man-made environment. The Second Programme on the Environment was adopted in 1977 and covers developments up to 1981. During the First Programme, which lasted from 1973 to 1976, some 40 Commission proposals were accepted by the Council. There has been a steady development of Community-wide legislation. This was facilitated by the fact that national environmental policies have only developed seriously in recent years. As a result Community policy has developed concurrently with national policies and they have been able to influence one another.

The reason for developing Community policies is to solve problems. Apart from the general advantages of working together as a Community there are many environmental problems which do not respect political boundaries. It is, therefore, desirable to treat them on a Community basis and, where they have broader implications, to use the negotiating machinery of the Community to put forward a European view.

Some success has been achieved in the areas of water pollution, air pollution, energy production, noise and waste disposal, all of which affect industry. The Action Programme pays special attention to industrial activities in which the manufacturing processes involve the introduction of pollutants, or nuisances, into the environment. A list of priority industries has been drawn up and proposals have been submitted with regard to the pulp, paper and titanium oxide industries. The Commission is also studying the iron and steel, petrochemical, food and leather industries. These studies have led to a series of directives on detergents, exhaust gases, colourants in food, cosmetics, food preservatives and pesticides.

Box 96

Environmental research

The Commission has just drawn up a revised research programme for the Ministers of the Nine on the protection of man and the environment from certain harmful substances. The new programme would require 20.8 million EUA (1 EUA = 1.2 dollars approx.) and it would run for five years (4.8 million EUA more than the programme adopted in 1976).

Research will be concentrated in four main areas:

The effects of pollution and other harmful substances (heavy metals, chemicals, organic chemicals, oil, heat, noise) on the health of the environment;

The reduction of pollution;

The protection and improvement of the natural environment.

Of particular interest will be the ecological effects of oil-pollution cleaning techniques following supertanker accidents (as with the Amoco Cadiz); the effects on health and the environment of chemicals which are being marketed; the dangers of human exposure to asbestos; the effects of halocarbons used in aerosols on the ozone layer.

Source: Euroforum, No 27, 11 July 1978, p. 5

The abolition of technical barriers to trade overlaps in many cases with the Community's environmental policy. The Community is moving ahead steadily on a wide range of fronts, some of them technical in nature, such as the intention to produce an environmental 'map' of Europe as a base for monitoring developments and for making new policy proposals. Others are of a practical nature – directives which directly affect industry and other sectoral interests in the Community.

Consumer policy

Many of the provisions of the Common Market have been of indirect help to the consumer, but it is only in recent years that the European Parliament has called for an active consumer policy.

Box 97

Seven good years of Euro-research — another Community policy

Between 1970 and 1977 government expenditure on research and development (R & D) in the European Community grew 3.2 per cent per annum in real terms. Only half of total R & D is financed by national authorities.

Whilst expenditure increased in Europe, the American government decreased its own by 1.4 per cent per annum 1970–1976, largely through the cutbacks in the space programme.

The effect of this has been to bring European and US R & D expenditure closer together. In recent years, research outlays have tended to stabilize though in real terms they have increased in the United States.

Average annual increase in R & D expenditure (at constant prices) between 1970 and 1976

	Total (%)	Civil R & D (%)
Ireland	9.4	9.4
Germany	5.4	6.4
Commission	5.2	5.2
Netherlands	4.7	5.0
Denmark	3.7	3.6
EUR 9	3.2	3.4
United Kingdom	2.7	0.7
Belgium	2.2	2.1
France	1.2	1.6
Italy	0.6	1.0

R & D expenditure in 1976 in million EUR (1 European unit of account = ± 1.27 dollars):

Germany	4 070
France	2 910
United Kingdom	2 320
Netherlands	700
Italy	550
Belgium	410
Denmark	190
Ireland	30
Community	11 200

Source: adapted from Euroforum, No. 21/78, 30 May 1978

Articles 85 and 86 of the Treaty have helped protect consumers by forbidding practices which restrict competition or which enable one firm to dominate a particular market. The dismantling of customs duties and the gradual elimination of technical and non-tariff barriers to trade has also worked in the consumers' interest. There is more choice, and prices of consumer goods are probably somewhat lower in the Community than they would have been without the Common Market.

In 1975 the Council adopted a preliminary programme for consumer protection and information policy. It has five objectives:

(1) Effective protection against hazards to consumer health and safety.

(2) Effective protection against damage to consumers' economic interests.

(3) Adequate facilities for advice and redress of complaints.
(4) Consumer information and education.
(5) Consultation and representation of consumers in framing decisions affecting their interests.

The intention is to achieve these objectives by a range of practical measures such as:

(1) Approximation of laws in agricultural, foodstuffs and industrial sectors.
(2) Harmonization of consumer credit.
(3) Protection against false or misleading advertising.
(4) Protection against unfair commercial practices.
(5) Harmonization of the law on product liability.
(6) Improved information on goods and services including comparative tests.

The consumer protection programme should have been completed by 1979. In fact little progress has been made in implementing the programme which itself was to be only the first part of a wider programme.

Consumer representatives have been nominated to the Economic and Social Committee and in 1973 it was agreed to set up a Consumers Consultative Committee. This Committee has the task of representing consumer interests to the Commission and advising on the formulation and implementation of policies relating to consumer protection.

The Commission has certainly been active on the information side and it produces a good deal of published work on European consumers and their rights. However, there has been little legislation.

The Commission has submitted proposals on: labelling and advertising for certain foodstuffs; liability for defective products; consumer protection in door-to-door sales.

The product liability proposals are far reaching and if adopted could be of particular significance to manufacturers. Under existing legislation in the United Kingdom only the retailer is legally liable for the defects of a product he sells. If this legislation is agreed it will mean that the manufacturer will also be liable, but there remains a great deal of further debate.

Consumer organizations are very strongly in favour, but some manufacturers claim that although the principle is sound, the benefit does not justify the cost which ultimately will be borne by the consumer. Consumer policy is relatively new and legislation in most of the Nine is rudimentary. There is therefore considerable scope for Community action, which would be welcomed by the Community's 260 million consumers.

During the next few years a large number of potential consumer protection laws could be passed. The rate at which these proposed directives are put forward by the Commission will depend, to some extent, on the political impetus of the Community. It will be necessary for business to monitor the state of legislation in this area as its effect on business, if it does develop as an important Community policy, will be significant.

Box 98

The Community budget 1979

The money comes from customs duties, agricultural levies and a percentage (currently about 0.6 per cent) of VAT. There is a complicated negotiating procedure involving the Commission, the Council of Ministers and increasingly the European Parliament to determine the amount. Most of the money is disbursed by the Commission and 70 per cent of the total goes on agriculture.

Sector	Appropriations for commit- ment (in mil. EUR) 1979	%	% Variation on 1978
(1) Commission			
(a) Intervention appropriations			
agricultural sector	10 300	70	+12
social sector	100	6	+49
regional sector	600	4	+7
research, energy, industry, transport	600	4	+81
development cooperation sector	700	5	+26
miscellaneous			
	13 000	89	+16
(b) Operating appropriations			
staff	400	3	+8
administration	100	1	+15
information	10		+8
aids and subsidies	50		+7
	600	4	+9
(c) Reserves	60		
(d) Reimbursement to member states from own resources	700	5	
Total commission	14 400	98	+16
(2) Other institutions	300	2	+12
Grand total	14 700	100	+15

EUR = approximately 1.2 dollars. Figures are rounded to nearest million EUR.

A spectacular increase in expenditure has been proposed for the energy sector (+228 per cent in 'appropriations for commitment' and +353 per cent in 'appropriations for payment'). Though regarded as a first rank priority among Community operations, energy policy has never been well endowed with funds despite the Commission's exhortations. In 1979 the accent should be put on the development of Community resources and energy saving measures.

A 49 per cent increase in 'appropriations for commitment' for social

continued

policy has been proposed to expand existing operations and introduce new projects. About half of the funds are earmarked for reducing unemployment, particularly amongst young people. Budget
allocations for victims of disaster areas in the Community have, in
the light of recent events, been doubled.

Areas to receive special attention in the budget are agricultural
structural policy, industrial policy and development aid. Especially
large increases are proposed for social and energy policy. Only a
relatively small increase has been written in for the guarantee section
of the EAGGF (European Agricultural Guidance and Guarantee
Fund) — the organization which finances the management of the
Community agricultural markets and makes up any differences
between world and Community market prices.

Community budget, where the money comes from

Estimates of own resources for 1979 (million EUC)

(1)	Agricultural levies	1 706
(2)	Sugar/isoglucose levies	438
(3)	Customs duties	4 745
(4)	1% of VAT	9 104
(5)	Miscellaneous revenue	158
(6)	Total resources	16 152
(7)	Expenditure	13 859
(8)	VAT rate	0.75%

Triennial estimates of own resources (million EUC)

	1979	1980	1981
Customs duties	4 746	5 050	5 300
percentage change		+6	+5
Agricultural levies and sugar levies	2 144	2 400	2 000
percentage change		−2	−5
1% of VAT	9 104	9 950	10 850
percentage change		+9	+9
Total own resources available	15 994	17 100	18 150
percentage change		+ 7	+ 6

Where the money comes from

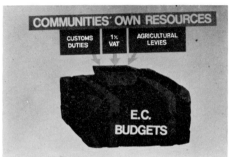

continued

Community budget: where the money goes

COMMUNITY BUDGET
1977

70.70%
AGRICULTURAL
SECTOR

5.11%   SOCIAL SECTOR

3.89%   REGIONAL SECTOR

2.70%   RESEARCH, ENERGY,
INDUSTRY, TRANSPORT

5.03%   DEVELOPMENT AID

3.36%   PERSONNEL

0.05% RUNNING COSTS
0.08% INFORMATION

8.26%   OTHER EXPENSES

*Source: adapted from European Community publications especially
Bulletin of the European Communities, 6–1978*

Other policies

In a book of this length it is not possible to describe all policies which might affect business. Transport policy deserves a chapter (*Box 99*) as does the freedom of establishment, the freedom to provide services to the professions, the new banking regulations, directives on accounting standards, regulations on VAT, public procurement, research and development (*Box 97*), the Community budget. Others can be added to the list according to the interest and the industry.

Box 99

Proceedings of the Council of Ministers: transport

The Council held seven meetings in June 1978 on the following subjects: foreign affairs, transport, economic and financial affairs, agriculture, fisheries and social affairs. The following subjects were among those discussed by the transport council:

Regular coach and bus services: The Council adopted an amendment to simplify the information procedure laid down in the regulation on the introduction of common rules for regular and special regular services by coach and bus between Member States.

continued

Summer time: The Council noted that it would not be possible to decide in time on the application of uniform summer-time arrangements for the whole Community in 1979.

Rhine Navigation Convention: The Council considered the proposal for a decision on the adoption by certain Member States of an additional protocol to the revised Convention for the Navigation of the Rhine of 17 October 1968.

Safety at sea: The Council endorsed a recommendation on the ratification of certain international conventions on safety in shipping.

Liner conferences: The Council reviewed the progress of the proceedings relating to the accession of the Community to the United Nations Convention on a code of conduct for liner conferences.

Costing of railway undertakings: The Council approved the regulation laying down uniform costing principles for railway undertakings.

Austrian transport tax: The Council adopted a statement on the road tax applicable to goods transport in Austria, which was introduced on 1 July 1978.

Railways: In the light of the Commission report on the progress made in the preparation of a programme of cooperation among the railway undertakings of the Nine, the Council considered that the Commission should, in collaboration with the Member States and the railway undertakings, take supplementary measures in certain areas.

Air transport: The Council agreed to the establishment of a work programme covering some ten priority items regarding air transport.

Combined rail/road carriage: After an exchange of views on the subject, the Council called on the Commission to seek ways of stimulating carriers' interest in combined rail/road transport.

Monitoring freight markets: The Council was informed of the Commission's plans for carrying out, for a period of three years from 1 January 1979, an experimental monitoring of the markets for the carriage of goods by rail, road and inland waterways between Member States.

European driving licence: The Council agreed to await the opinion which the Court of Justice is shortly to deliver on certain points concerning the proposal for a directive on the harmonization of the laws governing motor vehicle driving licences: this opinion could have important implications for future proceedings on the matter.

Taxes on commercial road vehicles: The Council agreed in principle on the first directive on the adjustment of national taxation systems for commercial road vehicles.

Source: Bulletin of the European Communities, 6-1978

The above outlines of some of the more important policies will suggest ways of further monitoring their progress and of looking at other policies of interest.

Bibliography

The European Community's Environmental Policy, European Community Documentation
A New Regional Policy for Europe, European Community Documentation
Nielsen, J. (1974) *Regional Policies in the EEC*

The Community is responsible for developing a common external trade policy and towards this the Commission has negotiated trade agreements with nearly every country in the world. Business needs to be aware of these policies as they will affect the context in which trade between the Community and the rest of the world is carried out.

The enlargement of the Community to include Greece, Portugal and Spain is well under way. This will change the face of Europe dramatically and will be one of its major concerns during the next few years. Relationships with the Third World, the North–South dialogue and the Lomé Agreement, which regulates trade and other matters between the Community and 54 developing countries, continue to be important. Lomé II, as the renegotiated treaty is called, will play an important part in developing Community relations with the Third World.

Figure 17 The seven major industrial nations plus one – President Jenkins represents the European Community.

The fourth economic summit meeting of the seven major industrial nations – USA, Canada, Japan, United Kingdom, Italy, France, Federal Republic of Germany – was held in Bonn on 16 and 17 July 1978. The Heads of State and Government of these nations as well as the foreign and finance ministers participated in this meeting. The European Community was represented by the President of the European Commission. Group photograph taken in the park of Palais Schaumburg – from left Jenkins (EC), Fukuda (Japan), Andreotti (Italy), Carter (USA), Schmidt (FRG), Giscard d'Estaing (France), Callaghan (United Kingdom), Trudeau (Canada)

Multinationals and other large companies will continue to be the major means of wealth creation in the next decade, whatever the ends a government and its people will want them to serve. The Community has not thought through its policies towards multinationals but will have to do so during the next few years.

Box 100

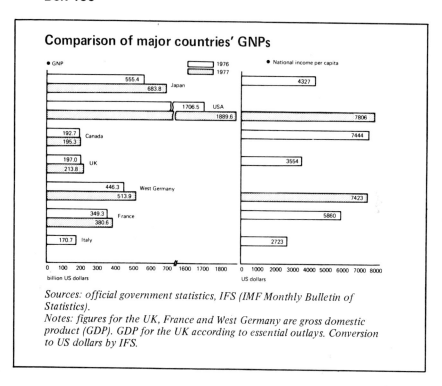

Comparison of major countries' GNPs

Sources: *official government statistics, IFS (IMF Monthly Bulletin of Statistics).*
Notes: *figures for the UK, France and West Germany are gross domestic product (GDP). GDP for the UK according to essential outlays. Conversion to US dollars by IFS.*

Trade with China is perhaps more important politically than it is economically, but there also seems to be better possibilities of increased Community trade with China than perhaps with the Soviet Union and Eastern Europe. These relations are described in this section as is the important triangular relationship which is developing between the Community, Japan and the United States, the three democratic cornerstones of our industrialized society. It is with this relationship that the section begins.

21 Japan and the European Community

Here I must be very frank. In the past there does seem to have been an inbuilt resistance in the Japanese economy to large-scale imports of products that compete directly with the products of Japanese industry. The open world trading system, to which we are all committed, implies acceptance of a growing interdependence between the industrialised countries. Yet unlike the other industrialised countries, imports of industrial goods into Japan only amount to 20 per cent as opposed to more than 50 per cent in the case of the European countries. However, I am glad to say, after my talks at the Keidanren, that there does now seem to be a genuinely more open attitude to imports on the part of Japanese business.

To conclude, the present situation cannot be changed overnight, but I am convinced that it is in the mutual interests of the Community and Japan that we should achieve a better balance in our mutual trade. I am also convinced that protectionist measures are not the solution. With good will we should be able to find satisfactory solutions to our present difficulties since we both want the same thing: to preserve free trade.
Commission Vice-President Haferkamp, Tokyo, May 1977

The fast developing triangular relationship between the Community, Japan and the United States is based on the fact that they are the principal Western industrial powers with market economies. During recent years, and currently, the major problems are the very large trade deficits which both the Community and the United States have with Japan, and the ways in which these deficits can be curbed. Underlying these current problems are the increasingly mutual views on democracy, world peace and stability. All three appreciate the need for closer trilateral cooperation to reinvigorate the world economy, and to practice, in spite of historic and current problems, open and non-discriminatory trade. The management of the North—South development programme, relations with developing countries, and questions of resources, energy and pollution are other policy areas where interests converge.

The relationship between Japan and the Community is the weakest, but its importance and the need to strengthen it is recognized. How to improve these relations is one of the most important problems facing Japan today. For the businessman the key points are:

(1) Both Japan and the Community are actively seeking ways of increasing the amount of manufactured goods which are exported from the European Community to Japan.

(2) The Community has effective powers to ensure that the unfavourable trade balance is at least partly rectified, as Japan needs Community export markets more than the Community needs Japan.

(3) Although the negotiations will be protracted and difficult, and the problems in textiles, shipbuilding, steel and leather goods are likely to prove difficult to solve, there will be an increasing number of spot opportunities for Community exporters. Good quality consumer goods and high technology goods will find markets rapidly, as the Japanese will need to show politically that more Community goods are finding markets in Japan. Every help will be given to the small Community exporter who has quality goods available.

(4) The pattern of Community trade with Japan will be increasingly developed within the parameters of bilateral negotiations between the European Community and Japan.

The Community trade deficit

The growing Community trade deficit with Japan has for some years been a major political problem. In 1970 trade was almost in balance but the deficit has risen year by year until, in 1977, the trade deficit reached over $5200 million and European Community imports were covered by exports only to about 40

Box 101

The trade deficit with Japan

Since the beginning of the 1970s the Community's trade deficit with Japan has increased regularly and the rate at which imports have been covered by exports has decreased, as shown below.

Year	Deficit ($US thousand millions)	Cover ratio* (%)
1970	0.3	
1971	0.8	
1972	1.3	
1973	1.3	67
1974	2.0	63
1975	3.2	46
1976	4.1	42
1977	5.1	39

*Cover ratio = % of Community imports covered by exports to Japan

Source: Bulletin of the European Communities, 3-1978

per cent of the total. The imbalance should perhaps be seen in the light of the fact that Community—Japan trade is only 2 to 3 per cent of their own world-wide trade. The Japanese would argue that they have attracted attention by concentrating on certain key sectors of industry such as cars and electronic goods. They would also argue that Western industrialized nations should accept the concept of free competition. It must be said that in Japan wages are no longer low and, with the strengthening of the Yen and heavy dependence on imported raw materials, the Japanese position is not so strong as it may appear. There is growing competition from South Korea, Mexico and Brazil.

Intensifying Community relations with Japan

Since 1972 the Community has intensified its relations with Japan. Top level discussions are held twice a year with the Japanese government, on similar lines

Box 102

Community dialogue with Japan. Slow progress in 1977

A number of positive aspects are contained in the joint statement issued in Tokyo at the end of the high-level talks held from 22 to 24 March between Mr Haferkamp. Vice-President of the Commission, and Mr Ushiba, Minister of State for International Economic Relations.

The terms of this statement, which were commented on at the press conference held in Tokyo and in Brussels, nevertheless reveal the serious problems raised by the Community's growing trade deficit with Japan. This deficit remains a major source of concern and a major political problem for the Nine, as the Community institutions have frequently made clear in statements made in recent years.

The problem of the trade deficit masks two other problems, as Mr Jenkins pointed out in a speech which he made at the Foreign Correspondents Club in Tokyo in October 1977:

(i) The fact that Japan's exports to the Community are concentrated on a very limited range of products, which are particularly important from the point of view of employment

in the manufacturing industry, which is subject to structural problems caused by the recession. This has provoked reactions. The Community has already made a number of requests to the Japanese to reduce the pressure which they exert on certain sensitive industries: iron and steel, shipbuilding, ballbearings, cars and certain electronic products.

(ii) The difficulty which European products have in penetrating the Japanese market. Despite the relatively low level of the Japanese tariff, there seem to be structural barriers in the Japanese economy which hinder the importation of manufactures, which make up only 20 per cent of Japanese imports, as against 40 to 50 per cent for the other industrialized countries. There are not only administrative and non-tariff barriers, but also structural resistance, stemming partly from the distribution system and partly from social attitudes, to the large-scale importation of manufactures in direct competition with products produced by Japanese industry.

Source: Bulletin of the European Communities, 3-1978

to those held by the Community with the United States. In Tokyo there is a permanent Community delegation whose head has the status of ambassador.

Commissioners now visit Japan regularly, but recent visits have not brought many positive results although both parties agree that they must cooperate in order to deal with the Community's worsening trade deficit. The Community has emphasized the need for further rapid progress to eliminate the non-tariff barriers to Community exports to Japan, and for a sector by sector approach in such areas as agricultural produce, chemicals, pharmaceutical products and diesel engines. Japanese penetration of the Community has concentrated on a few sensitive sectors: cars, steel, shipbuilding, electronic goods and ball bearings. This has affected industrial opinion considerably. Japan has over 4 per cent share of the Community car market (10 per cent in the United Kingdom), while the Community has less than 1 per cent of the Japanese car market. Over 60 per cent of the calculators in the Community come from Japan, and 9 per cent of ball bearings, with no Community penetration in Japan of these products.

Box 103

The causes of the Community's growing deficit

The examples given above (in the working document) do not give an exhaustive picture of the Community sectors experiencing difficulties because of Japanese imports, but they do illustrate the problems which European and North American businessmen face in dealings with their Japanese counterparts: Japanese penetration is concentrated on a few specific sectors, where it causes large-scale disturbances for the corresponding domestic operations. The sectors concerned generally involve intermediate technology, since the advanced industries which need extensive programmes of basic and applied research are comparatively neglected by Japan. In these branches the Japanese create for themselves a privileged position and, in certain cases, a genuine *de facto* monopoly, thanks to the high quality of their goods, the rationalization of their production (the strongest and best organized company is chosen from among the various competitors and

its exports then enjoy facilities offered by the Ministry for International Trade and Industry (MITI)) and the dynamic approach of their export companies. The effort to rationalize production has been further intensified since the energy crisis and the recession of 1974–75.

From now on, Japanese management has set itself the objective of manufacturing in Japan the most sophisticated products — those for which a minimum of raw materials and a qualified workforce are required and which therefore produce very high added value. The industries in those sectors which are slowing down because they are labour-intensive are gradually being abandoned, since they are facing the increasing competition of products from developing countries where wage rates are low.

Source: European Parliament Working Document 570/76. Economic relations between the European Community and Japan

At the end of 1978, the Japanese Automobile Manufacturers Association visited London for talks with the British Society of Motor Manufacturers and Traders. It was suggested that if these talks led to a request by the British for a reduction of Japanese car exports to the United Kingdom this would not be in accordance with Community law which stipulates that only the Community can negotiate with third countries. In practice the British government could claim that the talks were to 'clarify' the situation and this might be accepted by the Community given the particular difficulties of the British automobile industry.

This would be an example of how the Community does not immediately impose the rules on a member country which attempts to trade-off national self- interest with the requirements of Community law. The Commission and other Community institutions accept that haste must often be made slowly, and exceptions allowed to prove the general rule of Community autonomy in external trade relations.

Box 104

EEC and Japan: business aspects

(1) Likely growth of trilateral commercial and political relations — Community—Japan—USA.

(2) Need to monitor European Community—Japan commercial relations which are developing rapidly.

(3) Strength of Community bargaining position because of Japan's greater need to develop European Community—Japan trade relations and current huge surplus with the European Community. This surplus cannot easily be reduced by any significant amount in the short run.

(4) Specific opportunities for exporters in high technology and quality consumer goods as Japan will currently be seeking to show that some progress has been achieved.

Member states of the Community still apply national quantitative restrictions on some 79 industrial products, whereas Japan applies restrictions in only 27 cases, 22 being for agricultural products and 5 for industrial goods. There is more concern, however, about non-tariff barriers — the sheer administrative difficulties of doing business in Japan.

The Community has consistently argued that the best way of securing a more satisfactory balance of trade would be to increase exports rather than impose import restrictions. However, in certain cases where there are sectoral difficulties, the Community has asked Japan to limit exports voluntarily.

Japan has made significant efforts to reduce the Community—Japan trade deficit. In the first eight months of 1978, according to figures supplied to the Commission by Japan, the value of Japanese exports to the European Community fell by 4 per cent while imports rose 12 per cent. This apparent improvement contrasts strongly with the rise in Japan's trade surplus with the United States which, it is claimed, rose 47 per cent over the same period.

It is not clear how much of the improvement is due to Japanese administrative controls on exports. Japan has undertaken to reduce exports in certain areas, and to limit production and increase prices in others — ships for example. There is an awareness in Japan of the pressures to become a good neighbour in terms of trade balances. It is too early to say whether these initial efforts of the Japanese are the beginning of a determined policy to reverse the trend of past years, or simply window-dressing to appease those demanding stricter Community measures.

Bibliography

Economic Relations between the European Community and Japan, European Parliament Working Document 570/76

Japan and the European Community 164/77, Information Directorate-General

Europeans, North Americans and Japanese have in
common a democratic industrial society. Internation-
ally we Europeans have been bearing an increasingly
important part of the burden of responsibility for its
maintenance and development. It means that in the
eyes of the second and third worlds there is more than
one source of Western power. We are seen to practice
on the international scale what we preach on the
national scale about plurality of choice. Thus, the
values which we share, and our joint international
economic responsibilities, combine, not just to add to
our mutual strength but to play complementary parts
in facing up to the present structural problems of the
world economy.
President Jenkins. Speech to the American Club,
Brussels, 1 December 1977

The strongest relationship is the triangle between the Community, Japan and
the United States, is that between the United States and the Community. It is
stronger because of historical and cultural links, and through the close relationships within the North Atlantic Treaty Organization (NATO) of countries with
similar political interests and ideals.

Commercial policies

In terms of business, the relationship between the Community and the United
States may not at first seem to be so significant as that of the Community with
Japan, and it is certainly less often in the news. The commercial policies of the
United States and the Community, in spite of a few areas of divergence, are very
close. Both sides are pressing for substantial progress in the Tokyo Round of
the General Agreement on Tariffs and Trade (GATT). The intention is to lower
world tariff levels even further. There is agreement also on trade preferences for
the less developed countries, on the principle of a common fund and other issues
in the North—South dialogue, and a common appreciation of the long-term
problems of energy, raw materials and world food supplies. These broadly
converging commercial and trade policies make a framework within which trade
between the two countries develops.

The closeness of this new special relationship should not be lost on the Member Countries of the European Community and the United States. The US
approval of the European Community was confirmed in January 1978 when
President Carter visited Brussels and took part in a meeting of the European

Commission. Gestures such as this are not made lightly. It was not merely a protocol visit, which it could easily have been, but a working session. Current issues between the two countries were also raised during the subsequent sessions between President Carter's staff and that of the Commission.

There have been trade problems between the Community and the United States. Some of the protectionist lobbies in the United States are very strong and, in spite of the positive attitude of President Carter and his optimism about future trade relations, there was a potential crisis in economic relations at the end of 1978 when the Community and the United States looked set for a confrontation over duties. Congress failed to extend the President's authority to increase countervailing duties on subsidized imports of certain agricultural products from the Community into the United States. The Commission responded in the Tokyo Round of GATT, by linking US—European Community common action to the lifting of the threat of countervailing duties. Both Japan and the Community are concerned about certain protectionist lobbies in the United States which brings closer the threat of a world trade war, with very serious consequences for all countries. These lobbies would argue that both Japan and the Community are no less protectionist in their different ways. The seriousness of the short-term trade problems should not, however, conceal the increasingly close cooperation between the United States and the Community in world trade and financial matters. Twice-yearly consultations take place between the two countries; 23 of them had taken place by the middle of 1978. In June 1978 a new trilateral discussion was initiated in Washington between the United States, Japan and the Community.

United States—Community trade

The main highlight of US—European Community trade relations is the serious imbalance of these relations both in agricultural and industrial products. In the industrial triangle the Community has large deficits with both the United States and Japan, Japan has large surpluses, and the United States has a large deficit with Japan, balanced in part by a large surplus with the European Community.

Since the establishment of the Community in 1957, trade has risen rapidly between the United States and the Community. In each year the United States has had a surplus with the Community, often a substantial one. While the average level of Community and US tariffs on finished and semi-finished industrial products differ only slightly, the Community tariff is much more uniform and few items have a high level of protection. Only 13 per cent of Community tariffs on industrial goods exceed 10 per cent and less than 2.5 per cent exceed 15 per cent. On the other hand, nearly 40 per cent of US industrial tariffs exceed 10 per cent and nearly 25 per cent exceed 15 per cent.

The Community is now the most important trade partner of the United States whose surplus with the Community has risen from EUR 3 to 8 billion

Box 105

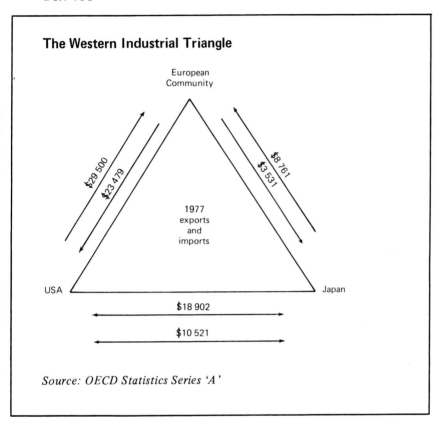

The Western Industrial Triangle

European Community

$29 500
$23 479

$8 761
$3 531

1977 exports and imports

USA

Japan

$18 902

$10 521

Source: OECD Statistics Series 'A'

Box 106

Average tariffs on industrial products and raw materials (%)

	Raw materials	Semi-finished products	Finished products	All industrial products
EEC (Nine)	0.7	7.1	9.2	7.0
USA	3.8	9.1	8.2	7.5
Japan	6.0	9.6	11.5	9.8

Source: Basic Documentation for the Tariff Study, GATT, 1974.

Box 107

US trade with the EEC Nine (EUR billion)

	EEC imports	EEC exports	EEC balance with USA
1958	3.9	2.6	−1.3
1969	10.4	8.5	−1.9
1970	12.3	9.3	−3.0
1971	12.1	10.7	−1.4
1972	11.7	11.5	−1.2
1973	14.4	12.5	−1.9
1974	19.4	15.2	−4.2
1975	19.3	12.4	−6.9
1976	22.2	14.2	−8.0

Source: ECSO (European Community Statistical Office).

from 1970 to 1976. These massive Community trade deficits are due less to large increases in exports to the Community than to the slump in American imports from the Community, which fell some EUR 2.6 billion in 1975 alone.

As well as trade, there has been regular reciprocal investment. The Community accounts for over half of the net direct foreign investment in the United States each year and the United States invests between two and three times as much in the European Community.

The tables in *Box 108* show that in recent years about 30 per cent of US investment abroad has been to the Community. It suggests that while Community investment in the United States has been at about one-third of the rate of US investment in the Community, this situation may now be about to change, and in the next few years there could be some reversal of the direction of investment flow. The popularity of one country rather than another for investment changes over time. It is interesting that 1977–78 showed a significant increase in Community investment in the United States. The only chemical firm investing heavily in Germany in 1977 was ICI of the United Kingdom − most of the German chemical companies (as well as ICI) were investing in the United States.

A relatively large proportion of US investment has been in the United Kingdom and in turn more investment has gone from the United Kingdom to the United States than from any other Community country. Of the $40 billion invested in the Community in 1975, $14 billion went to the United Kingdom, $9 billion to Germany and $6 billion to France. Of the $14 billion Community investment in the United States in the same year, nearly half was from the United Kingdom, the Netherlands was next, and the Federal Republic of Germany only invested $1.3 billion.

The conclusion to draw from these figures is that there is a strong relationship based on trade and commerce. The connection between the two economies is not stagnant and inter-penetration of markets continues. The economic rivalry

Box 108

United States: inward and outward investment

Direct US investment abroad. Net investment at year-end ($ billion)

	1966	1970	1973	1974	1975
World	51	75	103	118	133
of which:					
EEC	13	20	30	35	39
Canada	15	21	25	28	31

Direct foreign investment in the United States. Net investment at year-end ($ billion)

	1970	1973	1974	1975
World	13	18	22	26
of which:				
EEC	7	10	11	13

Source: US Department of Commerce.

---

between the United States and the European Community is, perhaps, healthy for both sides. For example, there was a time when the choice for UK aerospace seemed to be between a European or an American partner. In Europe there is concern that in the aerospace industry access to the large European market should not be granted to the United States without a reciprocal agreement.

The Community needs to build planes but it will buy some from the United States and will be involved in joint ventures with the United States. There is room for cooperation on some projects, but in the longer term there will be pressures within the Community for joint negotiating positions vis-a-vis the United States. The commercial battle will continue and the US–European Community relationship will remain an important, indeed the most important, external relationship of the Community.

The planned development of the world economy depends to a large part on the actions of Europe and the United States in three areas which are interdependent – monetary policy, energy policy and free trade through the Tokyo Round of GATT.

American business and the Community

For American businessmen the Community will increasingly have to be seen as one country, not so much because of present conditions, but because of the way the Community is likely to develop. Community-wide approaches to a growing number of aspects of business will make it necessary for US companies to monitor the progress of European integration. The negotiations to develop US–Community trade will take place with the Commission in Brussels.

American business should consider the Community as a whole and at the same time as nine different countries. It needs to know about:

(1) The Community institutions and policies.
(2) The cultural and business background in the nine different countries.
(3) Strategies for European-wide marketing or investment.

Of these three areas (1) and (3) are covered in this book. The second is best covered by personal visits to target countries. Briefings should be arranged not just with Americans based in Europe but also with Europeans capable of talking about the Community and its countries and policies. Business school courses can be an excellent way of getting to know the national managers of a country and what makes them tick. The attitude of an American to European business should differ very little from that of a UK national looking at the continental market. Many of the cultural and business considerations will be the same for both of them.

The commercial interests of the United States and the Community make it necessary for close relations to be maintained and developed. Commercial rivalry can be helpful provided that the rivalry is seen in terms of mutually developing advanced industrial economies and the underlying need to maintain free trade in the world.

Bibliography

The EEC and the USA: Recent Trends in Trade and Investment. Commission Information Directorate

23 Multinationals and the European Community

> In short, the dramatic improvement in communica-
> tions, the greatly increased mobility of people and
> money, and also the huge concentrations of corporate
> power in the hands of international businesses, taken
> together, demand the establishment of a new dimen-
> sion of international public power.
> *Andrew Shonfield, Europe: Journey to an Unknown*
> *Destination, Pelican, 1973*

Multinationals have been slow to develop their relations with the European Community. This is surprising given that the Treaty of Rome, and the philosophy behind it, supports the concept of transfrontier mergers. The intention has been to encourage larger companies in order to obtain the economies of scale and the appropriate size to service a market of over 260 million consumers. The attitude of the Nine towards multinationals, whether based in the Community or in the United States, has been, in general, favourable. The views popularized by J.J. Servan Schreiber in his book *Le Défi Americain*, which describes and criticizes American influence in Europe through the power of the multinationals, were not so widely held by opinion formers within the Nine, as might have been thought from the initial publicity.

Traditionally, multinationals have maintained a low profile and, until now, this may have been appropriate. The rapid development of communications, and a reading public who want to be informed about the way in which the major institutions of their country operate, has changed this. The demand for more open government, in the widest sense, grows. Multinationals, like government departments, now have to operate in a more open way to achieve their objectives.

Two aspects of European Community—multinational relations

There are two aspects of Community relations with multinationals:

(1) The Treaty of Rome and subsequent secondary legislation. These are important to multinational companies because they affect the ways in which the multinationals operate. Competition policy is particularly relevant, and so is the harmonization programme on company law which covers such subjects as disclosure, safeguarding of share capital, mergers, annual accounts, the structure of public companies and the powers and obligations of their parts.

(2) The second aspect is the general policy and attitude towards multinationals developed by the Community. Both are important. In their own interest, multinational companies should probably take more initiatives and play a

225

more active part in influencing the formation of both specific legislation and general policies affecting business.

Some of the early cases in competition policy in which multinational companies were involved should not, in retrospect, have ever been brought to the Court of Justice. The competition policy of the Community was clear from the start. Any possible infringements of the law should have been discussed with the Commission and phased out gradually with the blessing of the authorities rather than waiting for them to act. The situation has changed, and is still changing, although perhaps still not fast enough.

The Commission proposal for guidelines for companies operating in South Africa, for example, were quickly accepted by the Council of Ministers in September 1977. Many multinational companies were neither aware early enough of the implications of these guidelines nor able to respond effectively to them when they appeared. It would have been more satisfactory for all parties concerned if there had been more formal, as well as informal, discussions of the implications of the guidelines as they were being drawn up.

Large companies in particular cannot afford first to hear of directives affecting their business just as they are about to be published in the Official Journal. It is essential that they receive as much pipeline information as possible so that they can adapt to new situations and help influence current ones.

Companies need to ask themselves what sort of legislation is likely to be passed over the next few years and to devise their own proposals for developing it. After all a major concern of the Community is to provide a strong industrial base from which companies can operate. The aspirations and objectives of large companies and the Community therefore overlap.

Multinational undertakings: the 1973 Commission document

As regards the second aspect, general policies towards multinationals, the Community and multinational companies got off to a bad start. In 1973 the Commission sent to the Council of Ministers a communication entitled 'Multinational Undertakings and the Community'. It contained a draft resolution (*Box 109*), an introductory report and a summary of the various proposals which the Commission intended to put forward to resolve the economic and social problems raised by the activities of multinationals. There was also an analysis of the problems raised by the development of multinational undertakings. The whole tone of the communication, whether intentional or not, is somewhat hostile towards the multinationals. This is evidence in itself of the lack of contact and influence that existed at that time between representatives of the Commission in particular and multinational companies.

The one-time anti-multinational bias of the Commission was, if anything, overcompensated by a briefing note on the European Parliament entitled 'The

Box 109

Multinationals and the Community policy

Draft Resolution of the Council on the measures to be taken by the Community in order to resolve the problems raised by the development of multinational undertakings

The Council of the European Communities

Having regard to the communication of November 1973 from the Commission on the problems raised by the development of multinational undertakings;

Whereas international economic interpretation may help to promote a more equitable distribution of labour and of technical knowledge in the world, and to harmonize social conditions;

Whereas nevertheless the size of the phenomenon gives rise to concern, in particular in the fields of employment, competition, tax evasion, disturbing movements of capital, the security of supply of certain raw materials, and the economic independence of the developing countries; whereas the Community institutions must therefore take the necessary initiatives to ensure that multinational undertakings in their operations shall respect the economic and social aims of the Community;

Whereas the Community must participate fully in international discussions concerning certain problems of world-wide importance which would be begun within the framework of the various international organizations, for the seeking of resolutions in a spirit of reciprocity.

Whereas measures which may be adopted at the present time are concerned with problems which are not specific to multinational undertakings alone; whereas such measures fall in this different policies adopted or being developed by the Community in accordance with the Treaty of Rome;

(i) Confirms its intention to act within the time limits laid down in the various programmes in particular as regards the proposals concerning large-scale dismissals, protection of existing rights of employers in the case of merger or rationalization, the guaranteeing of investments in third countries, internal company mergers, the European Company Statute, the structure of S.E.'s and the supervision of mergers;

(ii) Considers that decisions have to be taken in particular in the fields set out above and notes the Commission's intention to submit as soon as possible proposals concerning the following:

(a) The protection of employees in the case of the take-over of companies;

(b) The laying down of Community rules in particular concerning stock exchange operations and on the origins of funds for investment.

(c) Cooperation between and amalgamation of national authorities responsible for the supervision of stock exchange operations;

(d) International assistance and cooperation measures in the fields of information, monitoring, and tax recovery, and in particular the drawing up of a joint schedule of transfer prices and licence fees;

(e) A body of law on groups of companies;

(f) The collection of adequate information on the international activity of undertakings.

Source: Multinational undertakings and the Community, 15/73, supplement to the Bulletin of the European Communities

Community and the Multinational Undertaking' (16 PE 48.817) which begins:
'The European Parliament has never taken part in the witch hunt against multinational undertakings. Parliament takes the view that the internationalization of
production is a logical consequence of the development of our economies and, as
such, a positive phenomenon contributing to economic growth and increasing
prosperity.'

The communication on multinationals was never discussed by the Council. It
was lost, as so many Commission proposals are when there is no general agreement on them, in a Committee of the Council of Ministers. Nevertheless, the
communication is significant as an outline of the areas of multinational activity
in which the Community will at some time or other wish to be involved.

The communication stresses:

(1) Protection of employees in the case of take-overs or mergers.
(2) Common rules for Stock Exchange operations and investment.
(3) Better common information on various aspects of multinational companies.
(4) Common rules on 'groups of companies' — a French system of cooperation
    between companies.

The draft resolution aims simply to establish an outline approval, in principle,
for the Commission's approach to multinationals. The Commission wished to
work, in particular, on the following:

(1) Tax problems: work on tax avoidance, special attention to transfer prices
    and licence fees.
(2) Monetary problems: more information about the financial flows associated
    with companies' transnational operations.
(3) Groups of companies: Proposals for a special law on groups of companies
    to provide a framework for uniform management of the group.
(4) Protection of workers: more collective agreements at Community level as a
    counterweight to the centralized management of the larger multinationals.
    Existing Commission proposals on mass dismissals, company mergers and a
    European company statute are also relevant in this connection.
(5) Maintenance of competition: size and power of multinational undertakings
    make it especially important that existing Community rules on competition
    and the abuse of dominant positions should be respected.
(6) Action at international level: the Commission sees the need for action at an
    international level, in particular through OECD for the industrialized world
    and also some attempt to ensure that the operations of multinationals of
    Community origin correspond with the economic and social welfare of the
    developing countries in which they operate.
(7) Better information: more information should be provided on transfer of
    funds, origin and composition of capital, number of jobs created and
    abolished, profits and taxes and research expenditure.

Some of these proposals have already been acted upon. The directives on mass dismissals and the preservation of workers rights in the event of a merger have both become law. Others, like the famous Fifth Draft Directive on Worker Participation and the draft regulation on the statutes for a European company, have not yet been accepted by the Council of Ministers. There is, as yet, insufficient agreement among member states. This is not surprising given the complexity of the subjects and the number of diverse interests at European, national and local levels. Progress has been made on monitoring the multinationals in Europe and some of the first results were published by the Commission in 1976 (*Box 110*).

US Congress and the European Parliament: draft code

After its Committee on Economic and Monetary Affairs submitted a report in 1974 on the question of international production, the European Parliament

Box 110

Community multinationals

Surprise, surprise! A recent survey by the European Commission reveals that more multinationals – defined as large undertakings with 'links' with two or more countries – are based in the Community than in the United States. Who would have thought it! The survey is part of an ambitious project to compile the first-ever world inventory of large, medium-sized and small multinationals. There are approximately 10 000 multinationals in Europe and elsewhere (the main concentration being in the United States) and the survey is the first phase of an attempt by the European Commission to assess the economic, social and political impact of each group in its home country and in each of the countries in which it is established.

The report is based on information obtained directly from the firms concerned and lists a total of 4534 multinationals based in the Community as against 2570 based in the United States. Not only are European multinationals more numerous but, with 49 256 links abroad, they also

seem to be more go-ahead than their American counterparts, who have only 24 177. Of the Community multinationals, 173 have links in more than twenty different countries, while only 113 American multinationals are similarly represented.

But the illusion of European drive and initiative is short-lived. An analysis of economic and financial results, based admittedly on a list which cannot hope to be comprehensive, shows, for example, that 1202 American multinationals in the manufacturing industries achieve a total turnover of 737 000 million units of account (1 u.a. = approximately US $1.1) as compared with a mere 516 000 million units of account for 2493 European multinationals. This means that American multinationals achieve a total turnover which is 43 per cent higher than the turnover of approximately twice as many European firms.

An analysis of the top 200 shows that US-based multinationals are clear leaders, both in terms of numbers (51.5 per cent) and turnover

continued

(50.7 per cent). Only 70 (35 per cent) of the top 200 are based in a Community country and these account for no more than 30.1 per cent of the combined turnover (257 057 million u.a.)

To give some idea of the scale on which these giants operate, the Commission survey points out that in 1973 the combined turnover figure for the top 200 (853 124 million u.a.) represented 32.9 per cent of the combined gross domestic product of OECD countries (2 593 592 million u.a.).

On the employment front, the survey shows that the 5 112 multinationals for which such information was supplied had a combined payroll of 45 922 733 in 1973. The 260 biggest employers had a total payroll of 25 082 516, in other words 12 per cent of the labour force of OECD countries.

The potential impact of multinationals on the economy of their home countries is revealed by calculating their turnover as a percentage of gross domestic product. Estimates for 1973 give the following figures:

Luxembourg:	153.1%
Netherlands:	68.8%
United Kingdom:	52.5%
Japan:	45.8%
United States:	41.0%
Italy:	30.0%
Germany:	27.4%
Switzerland:	23.2%
France:	17.5%
Denmark:	13.2%
Sweden:	9.6%
Belgium:	6.8%
Canada:	3.6%

The percentages for the Netherlands, the United Kingdom, Japan and the United States are particularly striking since they relate solely to the activities of the top 200. As to the figure for Luxembourg, it should be said that it reflects the activities of a single multinational, also one of the top 200.

Source: Euroforum, No. 28/76, 13 July 1976, Annex 1, p. 1

adopted a resolution (OJ No. C5/75) approving the approach of the Commission, but at the same time calling on the Council and the Commission to open negotiations with a view to arriving at 'a general agreement on taxes and investment'.

A more interesting development was the forging of links between the US Congress and the European Parliament. They jointly drew up a working document concerning a draft code of conduct for multinational companies and governments. This draft code was drawn up by a member of Congress and a member of the European Parliament. It suggests that if it is normal practice for companies to carry out more and more activities outside the borders of their own country, then it is also normal and necessary to introduce an international framework to ensure that these activities are regulated effectively while at the same time giving them legal security. The suggestion is that the code should initially be agreed by industrialized countries.

Among the proposals of the draft code:

Information. Annual reports should give as much insight as possible into the activities of firms. Governments should draw up an international standard system of annual accounts which would apply to multinationals. There should be closer cooperation between American and Community anti-trust bodies.

Box 111

Control of multinationals

The European Parliament meeting in Strasbourg on 19 April, decided to ask the Commission and Council of Ministers to establish legally binding agreement to control the activities of multinational companies within the Community.

A draft code of principles for multi-nationals, drawn up by Herr Erwin Lange, a German Social Democrat, and Mr. Sam Gibbons, a US Congress-man, was also accepted by the Parliament as a working document. This code envisages international agreement between the United States and the EEC to impose legally binding obligations on international firms operating in Western Europe and the United States.

Replying to the Parliamentary debate, Mr. Henk Vredeling, the EEC Commissioner for Employment and Social Affairs, said that agreed rules were necessary to regulate the activities of international companies in the Community. 'Perhaps an initial step should be voluntary rules and arrangements, but we should then move on to compulsory statute rules', he added.

The motion passed by the Parliament applauded the establishment of OECD guidelines based on the voluntary implementation of rules by international undertakings. It stressed, however, that binding and legally enforceable rules must be laid down gradually and a framework for the activities of multinationals defined in international agreements.

It called on the Council and the Commission to make legally binding arrangements through negotiations with other governments and the international companies concerned. It stressed that negotiations on this were only likely to succeed if appropriate measures were taken at Community level.

The Lange-Gibbons draft code envisages that multinationals should publish annual reports giving a detailed breakdown of their activities across frontiers. Such reports would include financial and personal links with other concerns, funds invested, reinvested and transferred to the home country, the origin and composition of capital and a breakdown of the taxes paid to individual taxing authorities. In addition, it seeks to regulate what it terms 'pernicious political activities' by multinationals.

Source: Financial Times European Community Information, May 1977

Investment policy. Government must be informed of this policy and there must be greater control over investments.

Tax authorities must have all the necessary information for assessing tax rates. Transfer prices should not be used by multinationals to alter their tax base.

Other provisions include control of transfer prices, policy relating to capital markets and employment policy. It is suggested that at least one national of the host country should be in the management team and workers should be consulted when necessary on problems concerning them. Harmful political activities must be avoided and this includes the influencing of politicians or government officials.

Box 112

The multinationals and European industrial policy

Above all, it means that the multinational companies will have to be harnessed as positive agents of development – a development that must be based on principles other than purely economic-rational ones based on profit maximization by the individual firm. Whether the multinationals can be persuaded into such a role, which their past history and present structure in no way fits them to play, is one of the key questions for the future of European industry in the world.

Whether they are American-based (as more than half are) or European-based, the multinationals are firmly established in Europe – a product of the long period, in the 1950s and 1960s, when European currencies were underpriced in relation to the American dollar, and when European trade and customs policy favoured them. The multinationals have become very sophisticated in manipulating policy: they have split markets and manipulated prices and taxation. Their managements are considerably more sophisticated, flexible and knowledgeable than those of the unions – especially because of the failure so far to develop effective European union organizations. In a world of growing international trade and political relations, the multinationals are a dominating force in technological policy, social change and political influence. Their enormous and growing power has to be controlled, and this can occur only through the development of a European policy developed by European institutions on the basis of agreed European development goals.

The opportunity to do this exists because the structures of a European industrial system are still more open and flexible than those of the constituent national systems; so that conscious planning should be much easier on the European scale. But it is also a danger in that existing national policies may rush in to fill the gap; and these, as we have seen, are based on a quite inadequate understanding of the complexity of the problem. Thus, so far, no generally accepted objective exists for industrial planning within the EEC; rather, without any statement of the final objectives it is desired to achieve, plans of varying degrees of comprehensiveness are being framed on a European, national, regional and individual industry level. To replace this, Europe now needs a plan based on a clear understanding of the role of European industry within the world economic system, both as an agent of change and a recipient of it; the function, role of and conduct of the system in relation to European society and the individual; and the shaping of the organization of the system, of conditions of life and work in the widest sense.

The first essential in this would be an enhanced role for existing supranational agencies, both in the EEC and elsewhere. One way towards this might be through interdisciplinary and multi-European organs of decision for definite problem areas such as inflation, unemployment, alienation at the workplace, and destruction of the environment; such bodies could have temporary and limited powers of decision and control over resources. Additionally, in relations with the world economic system, with economic blocs, or with the multinationals, European industry could be increasingly represented by central supranational bodies. Though individual countries will undoubtedly want to negotiate separately on certain issues, the aim should be to treat these increasingly as exceptions to a general rule.

One problem that is likely to loom

continued

large for any such European supra-body will be that of differences in the strength of different countries and regions within Europe. With increasing integration of the European industrial system, it becomes increasingly difficult to rely on automatic compensating adjustments for weak economies -- as the British example shows in the mid-1970s. As the pattern of trade within Europe moves away from complementary trade (of goods for which one country or region has a particular advantage) and towards exchange trade (in which all countries or regions exchange similar goods), there is an increasing problem of differences in cost structures, wages and capital yields, and competitive strength generally. If structural crises emerge, then certain industries and certain countries may try to compensate by bilateral trade agreements with other industrial nations and the Third World — leading to a trend towards disintegration of the EEC industrial system. To compensate, it may be necessary to pay the price of increasing bureaucratic control and resulting loss of flexibility. This is one likely scenario for European industry in the 1970s and 1980s.

Source: Peter Hall, Europe 2000, pp. 137–8, Duckworth 1977

The draft is of interest even though not all members of the two Houses (Congress and Parliament) were in agreement with it. The Community believes that, wherever possible, legislation or agreements on multinational operations should be drawn up in as wide a forum as possible. The difficulty with the United Nations forum is that the debate tends to polarize between the developing countries and the multinationals most of whose activities occur in industrialized countries. The OECD forum finds favour as its guidelines, which deal with the operation of multinationals in the main industrialized countries, are perhaps a better starting point. The Community is working closely with both the UN and the OECD in drawing up guidelines for multinationals and does not want to develop a strictly Western European approach to these activities.

Given the many different interests which are involved, progress in the area of multinational policy will obviously be slow. The Community will undoubtedly develop policies towards multinational companies and it will be in the interests of these companies to become increasingly involved in working with the Community institutions.

Bibliography

Draft Code on Multinationals, Congress and European Parliament
Franko, L. (1976) *The European Multinational*, London: Harper & Row
Multinational Undertakings and the Community, 15/73, Bulletin of the European Communities Supplement

Joint undertakings stand a better chance when they
benefit both sides.
Euripides Iphigenia in Tauris, 5th Century B.C.

Common policies and common approaches to problems are the rungs of the European Community ladder. Some policies like the competition policy are written into the original Treaty of Rome; others have been developed through secondary legislation, through the progressive harmonization of national legislation or the development of Community policies to complement existing national policies. The Commission tends to be diverted from developing common policies for today into developing future policies. It is more difficult to change existing policies than develop new ones. The Community therefore tends to strengthen the rungs in two areas: where it already has powers and in new areas such as consumerism and environmental policy where national positions are less likely to be deeply entrenched.

This chapter deals with policies which in one sense stem from the relations of former colonial countries with France and the United Kingdom. In another sense they stem from the concern of the Community with the North–South dialogue and its intention to combine two approaches in its Third World policy: (1) specific contractual arrangements some of which have existed for a very long time and (2) action at world level.

Community policy towards the Third World is of interest to businessmen because it is the Community and not the Member States which is responsible for regulating external trade (see Chapter 16). In doing business with Third World countries it could be useful, and may be necessary, to know what treaty arrangements, if any, exist between that country and the Community.

The contractual arrangements often cover a wide range of trade and related matters. As the intention of the Community is to develop its relations with the Third World, it is therefore likely that trade will develop in both directions more rapidly with those developing countries with which the Community already has close contact based on historic ties, cultural connections or current trade relations.

These countries are not necessarily the obvious ones to UK businessmen. Although relations with ex-African colonies of the United Kingdom may be well established, the Lomé Convention, for example, gives access to many French-speaking territories in Africa and the Caribbean.

Box 113

Pressures for a Third World/Community policy

The Third World, now emerged from its colonial chrysalis, diverse, immense, rich in abundant natural and human potential, poor in technological development and economically backward. Its peoples want to make themselves heard; they are no longer ready to remain in the margin of history, and have decided to use their capacities, to group their energies, to merge their wills. Time is short, for more than half of them — a thousand million human beings — are condemned to 'absolute misery', to use the expression of the President of the World Bank. The 'proletarian countries' want to win the right to be themselves, to take part in the definition and the operation of the world economic order.

Will the next decades see a conflict here, either open or concealed? Will the industrialized countries understand that the rising aspirations of the poor people of the world, people who have been inarticulate up till now, people who we had tried to blind, that these aspirations will not be suppressed? Do they understand that the deep-seated reasons which have made possible our own civilizations and the establishment of equality and liberty in our own

world, now compel us to extend to elsewhere the same reasoning and processes which led to the expansion of the free industrial world in the course of the last century?

For Europeans, these questions are in no way academic. On the contrary, their needs, their deficiencies, oblige them to seek a close cooperation with the Third World, an intimate relationship with the people of the South, who want to develop, and who will do so. For the European Community it is at once a moral duty, a political imperative, and a vital economic necessity.

These simple truths are now beginning to be seen more clearly in Europe. It also seems that each one of our Member States is too small to handle the problems, sometimes completely new, which arise from a world in which the economic order is rapidly changing. And, as if by instinct, Europeans have been coming together on this issue. It is therefore hardly surprising that progress in this field on the Community level has been more rapid than in any other sphere of activity.

Claude Cheysson, Commissioner for Development, 1977

The Lomé Convention

Although there are a large number of trade agreements, the main contractual arrangement is the Lomé Convention which has established a special relationship between the Community and 54 African, Caribbean and Pacific countries (the ACP countries). The Convention came into force in 1975. At present negotiations are in progress for Lomé II which will replace the original agreement in 1980.

It is a unique and historic agreement which may well be an example for regional arrangements between developing and developed countries throughout the world. It covers the following areas:

(1) *Trade cooperation.* Practically all products originating in the ACP countries may be imported freely into the Community, but the arrangement is not reciprocal. ACP countries may charge import duties provided that they do not discriminate between member states.

(2) *Financial and technical cooperation.* Funds of $4000 million have been set aside for use up to the year 1980. These funds will finance investment projects proposed by the ACP countries and will be managed jointly. There is also provision for regional cooperation of two or more ACP countries and support for small- and medium-sized firms.

Box 114

Preparing to re-negotiate the Lomé Convention

New issues

Though in force only a short time, the Lomé Convention has already proved its worth to the participating ACP states. Of the £2000 m allotted to them by the Community under the Convention, nearly £750 m had been committed by 30 January 1978. The value of Community imports from ACP countries also rose − by 14 per cent between 1975 and 1976, and by 26 per cent in the first eight months of 1977 compared with the corresponding period in 1976.

The Council agreed last month that the main objective of the new negotiations was to consolidate the work of the Convention but that, in the light of experience and economic circumstances, some innovations were necessary under Lomé II.

The most important of these concern a mechanism to ensure consultation between the Community and its ACP partners over sensitive industrial development, and the protection of foreign investment in ACP countries. While the Council discussed the question of linking human rights to aid under Lomé II it did not decide a formal position on this.

Source: 'European Community', July 1978

---

(3) *Stabilization of export earnings.* The STABEX system compensates ACP states for losses if the volume of exports in their most important products falls below a certain level. The poorest countries do not have to repay the compensatory amounts, but other countries do if the situation improves. The scheme is intended to even out large deficit and surplus positions which have caused such wide price fluctuations that, in some instances, the rational planning of a developing economy has become almost impossible.

(4) *Industrial cooperation.* The intention is to grant aid to help ACP countries to develop and diversify their industrial production, in particular through the

Box 115

A day at the Indian Mission to the Community

There is an air of gratifying expectancy in the Mission. A delegation from the Engineering Export Promotion Council is in town. Two dozen representatives of India's growing engineering industries are responding to a long sought invitation from the Community to explore its markets and to forge two-way links.

The Chairman walks into my room, his face radiant with achievement. He has obviously enjoyed being received by the commissioners and the Commission's officials.

The Chairman's senior colleague is full of praise for the meticulous care with which the delegation's itinerary has been arranged. But some young executives are not sure whether the contacts planned for them are the right ones. An experienced exporter observes that the ground could have been better prepared.

I try to prod the group to be less critical and more constructive. The Commission has after all fulfilled its obligation by bringing 'the operators from the two sides together'. It is now up to the delegation to make the best of the opportunity.

At the reception hosted in their honour by the Commissioner for Development Cooperation, a couple of enthusiastic delegates allow themselves to be too eloquent on the excellence and competitiveness of their wares. This makes their Belgian competitors wonder whether the Commission is wise in promoting competitive imports from distant lands. However, those with wider interests and ability to look beyond their nose do not mind the Community's promotional activity. In fact, they see in it long-term advantage for the Member States, for their industries, and for their citizens.

The Community's policies at any given moment must of necessity represent a delicate balance between diversity in national attitudes and differences in the interests of its Member States. On the whole, the Community manages to speak on commercial matters with one voice to the outside world. But at the same time, it seeks to practice differentiation in its external economic relations with associables, associates, and preferred partners, the most favoured nation treatment being reserved for the rest.

Consequently, a heavy responsibility rests on the Commissioners and their aides. They have a hard time, distinguishing differentiation from discrimination. But they finally triumph. The visitors are convinced of the Community's equal determination to develop profitable exchanges with all parts of the world.

As I return home, a seminal thought from the Indo-EEC CCA's preamble comes to my mind: 'trade is not an end in itself, but a means of achieving wider economic and social objectives'. These can be achieved only if the commercial policy of the world's largest trading unit is truly founded upon the principles of comparative advantage and mutual benefit!

K.B. Lall, Ambassador, 1962–66, 1973–77

transfer of technology. This policy will raise the important question of the Community's obligation to buy the goods which the industries of the Third World produce. This will put pressure on Community industries, in particular very heavy pressure on labour intensive, low-technology industries. It will accelerate their decline and push industry within the Community into higher technologies and more sophisticated services.

(5) *Institutions.* The Lomé Agreement is implemented by a Council of Ministers aided by a Consultative Assembly of Representatives of the ACP countries and the European Parliament. In each of the 54 countries there is a Representative of the Community whose task is to manage the operation of the Convention. Although, at present, only trade relations are involved, there is clearly present the germ of the idea of Community representatives acting more as ambassadors to the ACP countries. It could make individual embassies of the Nine redundant in time.

Community agreements with the Mediterranean countries

The second form of regional agreement is with the Mediterranean countries. Mediterranean agreements refer essentially to the southern shore. The northern litoral Mediterranean countries are seen as different, both in their current and future relations with the Community. The north Mediterranean countries are all actual or potential candidates for membership. The ties of these countries with the Community are historical, or economic, or simply geographical.

The formation of a Mediterranean policy is complex. There is already a range of different agreements with various Mediterranean countries and lists of agreements with individual countries are available. However, even more significant for the businessman is an appreciation of Community future policy towards a particular country. This information can be obtained either from Community or national administration sources, but is unlikely to be written.

The principal agreements between the Community and the Mediterranean countries are: (1) with the Maghreb countries – Algeria, Morocco and Tunisia; (2) with the Mashreq countries – Egypt, Jordan, Syria and Lebanon; and (3) the agreement with Israel. The commercial aspects of the agreements involve free access for industrial goods to the Community and concessions covering the main agricultural products. The agreements are not reciprocal, although in the case of Israel there will be a free trade area for industrial products by 1989.

Arrangements have been made in the agreements to ensure that the nearly 1 million Maghreb workers in the Community benefit from the same pay and conditions of work as Community nationals. A Council of Ministers determines the policies behind the various treaties, but the negotiation and renegotiation of the treaties is the responsibility of the Commission, and in particular of Directorate-General I, which coordinates the views of other Directorate-Generals.

Development aid

In 1974 member states agreed to harmonize their development aid. The target is to allocate 0.7 per cent of the Community Gross National Product to developing countries. As well as aid to developing countries associated with the Community under the Lomé Convention, the Community has granted aid to other developing countries. In particular, it has done so under the Special Action Programme in 1978, which confirmed a Community contribution of $385

Box 116

A month of Europe in the World: some examples

Aid to Angola
The Commission proposes to send 400 metric tons of butteroil and 550 metric tons of milk powder to refugees from Angola, and to provide 150 000 units of account to buy medicines, clothing, and prefabricated housing. Last October, the Commission airlifted to Angola 100 metric tons of powdered milk.

Food aid
The Commission has proposed food aid amounting to 707 850 metric tons of grain for 1976, most of it as direct aid to the developing countries, although some will go through international organizations and some will be held in reserve for emergencies.

EEC–NZ talks
The Commission has held a first round of informal talks with New Zealand on the lines of those regularly held with the United States.

$125-million loan
The Community has just floated a loan of $125 million on the US market, using its powers under the Coal and Steel Community Treaty. This is its seventh such operation, and will be used to finance coal and steel production, coal-based power stations, and the re-employment of workers.

Aid to Portugal
Following a Council decision in the autumn of 1975, the European Investment Bank has offered Portugal credits of 150 million units of account at a special interest rate of only 6.5 per cent. A joint committee representing Portugal and the Community is selecting the projects, which are expected to be mainly infrastructure investments.

Work with Canada
The Community has exchanged letters of cooperation with Canada for joint work on environmental protection.

Hong Kong cuts exports
After talks with the Community, Hong Kong has agreed to limit its 1976 exports to Britain of knitted jerseys, knitted shirts, knitted outer garments, woven trousers, women's coats and jackets, and women's woven blouses. This follows overruns in 1975.

EIB loan in US
The European Investment Bank has floated a $75-million bond issue on the US capital market, consisting of 7-year notes at 9 per cent. This is the Bank's first such operation directed solely at the US market.
Source: 'European Community',
January 1976

million to help meet the immediate needs of low-income countries. Food, financial and technical aid and special aid to non-associated countries are also given by the Community. Aid is also given to the four countries of the Indian sub-continent which did not become members of the Lomé Agreement because the United Kingdom joined the Community at a later stage in its development and the countries, in terms of population, would have greatly increased the size of Lomé.

Community aid is not large compared to the bilateral aid given by the countries of the Nine. However, there now exists a sophisticated and well-developed framework which will enable the Community to increase the size and amount of its aid through existing mechanisms. In an increasing number of Community policy areas these mechanisms now exist, and year by year the Community gains more experience from operating them. The infrastructure of the Community is firmly established, yet the choice of its final design is still open.

Bibliography

The European Community and the Third World, Official Publication, November 1977

The European Community and the Developing Countries, European Documentation, London: HMSO

25 Enlargement of the Community : Greece, Portugal and Spain

> Enlargement is neither a small step, nor a leap in the dark, but it will create a different sort of Community and whether it will be an improved model only time will tell

According to the Treaty of Rome, any European country can apply to join the Community. Greece, Portugal and Spain have recently applied to become members, presenting the Community with one of the greatest challenges, if not the greatest, of its development during the next decade.

The main arguments in favour of the Nine becoming the Twelve are political. It is claimed that accession will strengthen the nascent democracies of Greece, Portugal and Spain. This political imperative argument has led the Community to accept in principle the three applications, and to press on rapidly with the Greek negotiations which are well advanced.

Although enlargement is regarded favourably for political reasons, it will considerably affect the development of the Community, and in retrospect may prove to be a major turning point in its history.

It will pose very severe problems for industry and agriculture. There are already enough difficulties in the steel, shipbuilding, textiles and footwear

Box 117

Enlargement: political imperative v industrial reality

Cherishing parliamentary democracy

The Rt. Hon. Roy Jenkins, President of the Commission, has emphasized, as have others, that the second enlargement of the Community is primarily a matter of political principle. The Community 'was founded in the duty to cherish and nurture parliamentary democracy and individual liberty'. Whatever our difficulties, these remain our entrenched values. 'The recent emergence of new democratic regimes in the three applicant nations', he said 'calls for a direct and full-hearted response from the Community. To fail to give such a response would run the risk of undermining the very democracy for which we stand'.

Address to the Deutsche Gesellschaft für Auswartige Politik, 8 December 1977

continued

Protecting British industry

The principal causes of concern expressed to the Committee, in the order of frequency of mention, are:

(a) the present low level of wage rates of the applicant countries, compared with those in the Nine, which reduce production costs significantly;

(b) the need to ensure that the applicant countries practise 'fair trading' as soon as possible after accession. Apart from high tariffs, the main non-tariff barriers are quotas, import surcharges, cash deposits and administrative delays. The three applicants should not be allowed to shelter behind restrictions to fair trade over a long transitional period;

(c) low social charges and payments in the applicant countries, or rebates of these charges to exporters, which again reduce production costs;

(d) the need for the applicant countries to end production and export subsidies as soon as possible;

(e) the dynamic effects of entry on the textile, footwear, cordage and steel industries in the applicant countries. It is felt that these industries are well poised to expand in the applicant countries, as they have a combination of low labour rates and modern machinery;

(f) concern that three low labour cost countries will for the first time be within the EEC and that their wage rates would have to rise rapidly to nearer the EEC average if UK industries were not to be seriously affected; and

(g) the possible migration of labour from the applicant countries to the UK aggravating the unemployment problem in the UK.

From 17th Report of the House of Lords Select Committee on the European Communities, Session 1977–78 (HL 102): Enlargement of the Community

industries. The necessary adjustments for entry into the Common Market of three countries which have low wage rates, low social charges and payments, many non-tariff barriers such as quotas, import surcharges, cash deposits and administrative delays, will be painful both for the existing members and the applicants.

However, some of the industries already in difficulty are well poised to expand in the applicant countries. The Confederation of British Industry has expressed its concern not so much about the current levels of production in certain applicant country industries, or even projections based on existing plant and equipment, but about the need for adequate safeguards to ensure that the three countries do not expand their industrial base too rapidly. It fears this might be achieved by developing those industries which are already competing strongly with Community industries and which would represent even more of a threat when inside the Common Market. However, the current difficulties in certain Community industries are only in part caused by the potential or actual threat of cheap imports from the applicant countries. More generally, they are caused by conditions of world trade but, nevertheless, some Community industries will strongly oppose enlargement if it is likely to erode their markets even more rapidly.

Figure 18 EUROPA on a bull. The Goddess is surrounded by nine cherubs in this engraving. We can speculate on the nationality of the cherubs pulling the bull's tail and sticking an arrow into it, and also on the three maidens on the left who look as if they would like to be involved. One is clearly in tears – perhaps left out. Plenty of scope for conjecture here!

Concern has also been expressed about the possible increase of immigrants from the three applicant countries. Current, and probably future levels of unemployment in the Nine, make this threat less real than imagined.

Greece and Portugal are not seen by most UK trade associations as potentially very important markets for British goods. On the other hand, they believe Spain offers greater possibilities for trade expansion, provided that tariff and non-tariff barriers are dismantled rapidly and effectively. The relative size of the countries and their trade with the United Kingdom is shown in *Box 118.*

The three countries are already heavily dependent on Community exports and imports. Membership is likely to increase the two-way flow of trade thus contributing to the development of regionalized trade, a trend which has been accelerated by the energy crisis.

From a business viewpoint, it is necessary to assess which industries in the United Kingdom are most likely to be threatened by the membership of the Three. Measures must be taken to ensure that the transitional arrangements provide UK industries with reasonable protection in the short run and in the longer term open up the applicants' markets to UK goods and services in return for phasing out that protection.

Box 118

Trade of applicant countries with the EEC and the United Kingdom

	(1)	(2)	EEC trade as % of total trade (3)	(4)	(5)	Trade with UK £M (6)	
	Popu-lation	GDP per capita $	Exports to EEC	Imports from EEC	Imports from UK	Exports to UK	Trade balance (+ = favourable to UK)
UK	56	3 900	36	37	–	–	–
EEC	259	5 350	–	–	9 249	11 510	−2 261
Greece	9	2 400	50	40	151	71	+80
Portugal	10	1 650	51	42	225	230	−5
Spain	36	2 900	46	33	369	361	+8

All figures are 1976

Source: (1) OECD main economic indicators
(2) OECD national accounts
(3), (4) OECD Statistics of Foreign Trade Series A/Monthly Review of External Trade Statistics No. 28 (UK figures)
(5), (6) Trade and Industry, 10 March 1978/Department of Trade

On the positive side, the Spanish market is of interest, as regards investment and exports. Spain has a more highly developed industrial structure than Greece and Portugal. Its size and growth potential, together with the low degree of trade liberalization so far achieved, present Community industry with considerable opportunities for exports in a wide range of consumer goods and capital equipment. The automotive industry is a good example. Spanish accession would increase export opportunities both for British car and component manufacturers. There will also be opportunities for manufacturers of tobacco, manufactured food products and pharmaceuticals. Imports of pharmaceutical products into Spain at present are almost zero because of non-tariff barriers and yet the pharmaceutical market is larger than that of the United Kingdom. There will also be opportunities for wool and allied industries.

In agriculture the effects of enlargement will be felt quite severely. Mediterranean countries, such as Italy and France, already have over-production difficulties with products such as wine, citrus fruits, tobacco, tomatoes and olive oil. Agriculture is a major part of the economies of the applicant countries. There will be further strain on the CAP as a policy which attempts both to organize the rational marketing of agricultural products and to assist in farm income support

Box 119

Place of agriculture in applicant country economies (1975)

	Spain	Portugal	Greece	EC-9	EC-12
Agricultural employment (millions)	2.8	0.9	1.1	8.7	13.6
Proportion of workforce in agriculture (%)	22.0	28.1	35.4	8.7	11.3
Agricultural GDP ($ billions)	9.0	2.1	3.5	59.5	74.1
Proportion of GDP arising in agriculture (%)	8.9	14.5	16.5	4.4	5.0
Agricultural GDP per worker employed ($,000)	3.2	2.3	3.1	6.8	5.5

Source: calculations based on European Community Commission estimates, dated 9 February 1978.

and structural change in rural areas. There are already signs that French and Italian farmers will not tolerate too generous agricultural concessions if these threaten their livelihood.

Others problems of enlargement

Enlargement will strengthen the Community as a trading bloc, but will, inevitably, affect relations with other trading partners. As the Community's capacity to absorb agricultural and industrial consumer goods is finite then the increase in imports from the Three must affect existing arrangements with other countries, particularly those of the Mediterranean. Unfortunately, sensitive goods, already in world surplus, will be most affected.

The institutions of the Community will also be under considerable strain. It was difficult enough adjusting to the enlargement from Six to Nine. The proposed enlargement will introduce three more languages into a Community where already one EEC employee in three or four is involved in translation or interpretation. Community legislation, since it will apply to all twelve countries, will have to be translated into each of the different languages.

Box 120

Enlargement: House of Lords Select Committee, conclusions on trade and industry

The Committee are of the opinion that given the relatively small size of the industrial sectors in Greece and Portugal, compared to those of the Community, there will be neither great advantages nor disadvantages to UK commercial interests in general by the accession of these two countries.

Specific industries could be adversely affected by three low cost producers joining the Community and very careful transition arrangements must be developed to protect these industries and those working in them. Evidence taken from the textile, footwear and steel trade associations indicates that the interests of these industrial sectors which are already facing considerable difficulties must be sympathetically dealt with during the entry negotiations.

The Committee would expect the Community negotiators to consider increased aid to these industries within the existing Community and to ensure that aid to the nascent economies of the applicant countries should be applied only to those industries where there is not already surplus capacity in the Community.

Spain offers considerable export and investment opportunities. A number of UK industries, notably the pharmaceutical and wool textile sectors, could benefit from the entry and rapid economic growth of that country. The Committee share the concern of British industry that the traditionally heavy protectionist policy of Spanish industry will be relinquished with reluctance and that it will be necessary to monitor closely the reciprocity of transitional arrangements and ensure that derogations permitted from agreed timetables are as few as possible.

The Committee believe that short term problems, which will be serious for some industries, can probably be overcome in the longer term, particularly if the applicant countries can sustain high rates of growth and if wage levels in those countries rise to bring them closer to those of the EEC as a whole. If so, enlargement will benefit Community trade.

From 17th Report of the House of Lords Select Committee on the European Communities, Session 1977–78 (HL 102): Enlargement of the Community.

Technical and legal standards also cannot be applied unless translated officially into the language of each country. One possibility is to ensure that working documents within the Community only appear in a restricted number of languages, but membership of the European Parliament, the Council of Ministers or the Commission cannot be restricted only to those fluent in languages. Language is a matter of national prestige and identity. The distinction between working and official languages is probably the key.

A major overhaul of regional and social policies will have to be carried out. It is likely that there will be a transfer of aid to the Three from countries such as the United Kingdom and Italy. The UK Minister of State, in 1978, estimated that the cost of enlargement to the United Kingdom would be between £90 m and £150 m.

Although there will be severe economic and institutional problems, it looks likely that, on political grounds, the enlargement of the Community will be successful. The challenge is a major one and whatever the outcome, the Community will be changed. However, this should not worry an organization which has developed pragmatically and believes in development by small steps. Enlargement is neither a small step, nor a leap in the dark, but it will create a different sort of Community and whether it will be an improved model only time will tell.

Bibliography

Enlargement of the Community, House of Lords Select Committee on the European Communities, March 1978, London: HMSO

26 Community trade relations with other parts of the world

Trade agreements have been drawn up by the Community with a large number of countries of the world
so that there are now in existence well over 120 trade
agreements of one kind and another with different
countries

Eastern Europe

Since 1973 the Commission has had the responsibility for commercial negotiations with state trading countries and the intention was that as the long-term
trade agreements negotiated by member states with Eastern European countries
expired, they would be replaced by a 'model agreement' which was drawn up in
1974. This envisages long-term non-preferential trade agreements with reciprocal
advantages and obligations, the aim of which is to encourage the development of
trade relations between the two sides.

The problem for Eastern Europe, and the USSR in particular, has been that it
does not recognize the European Community. The official communist view of
the Community is that it is a discriminatory trading bloc and an economic
extension of NATO. Trade relations have therefore been hampered by important
political considerations. The USSR has consistently refused to recognize the
political nature of the Community until forced into it by economic self-interest.

The Community and Comecon

The USSR has repeatedly equated the Community with the Council for Mutual
Economic Assistance (CMEA or Comecon) and the Community has pointed out
the different roles and functions of these two organizations. The Community has
real powers in external trade relations and is a supranational body charged, by
its member states, with sole responsibility for negotiations with third countries.
Comecon is not, legally, a sovereign body and does not have the same powers of
negotiation.

Sir Christopher Soames was the first commissioner to visit a member of
Comecon in 1976 when, as Vice-President of the Commission with responsibility
for External Relations, he clearly stated the Community position. There was no
reason, he said, 'why the development of bilateral relations between the Community and each of the Member Countries of the CMEA should hamper or be
hampered by the development of constructive relations between the European
Community and the CMEA as such'.

The diplomatic wrangling continues, but should not be dismissed as insignificant. What is at stake is the recognition by the USSR of the Community as a sovereign body. The implications of this make it understandable, given the Soviet Union's policy, why there should be such careful preparation of positions. In 1977 the Chairman of the CMEA sent a message, through the UK Ambassador in Poland, to the UK Foreign Secretary, who was also at that time the President of the Council of Ministers, suggesting a meeting. The Community accepted such a meeting, but proposed that the President of the Council should introduce Mr Haferkamp, Vice-President of the Commission, to the Chairman of the CMEA as the Commission would represent the Community at all stages of negotiations.

Practical steps
While the necessary diplomatic procedures were followed, two practical steps were taken. First, there was the new invitation to negotiate the elimination of

Box 121

The Community's trade balance with Eastern European countries (millions u.a.)

	Imports	*Exports*	*Trade balance*
USSR			
1973	2 236	2 126	−110
1974	3 417	3 190	−227
1975	3 672	4 631	+1 059
1976	4 889	4 538	−35
Other Eastern European countries			
1973	2 573	4 277	+704
1974	4 309	6 279	+1 970
1975	4 376	6 408	+2 033
1976	5 075	6 488	+1 413
Total			
1973	5 809	6 403	+594
1974	7 726	9 469	+1 743
1975	7 947	11 039	+3 092
1976	9 904	11 026	+1 062

Source: Statistical Office of the European Communities

quantitative restrictions on textiles on a bilateral basis. This offer was taken up by Rumania first, followed by Poland and Hungary. In spite of this, the original offer and proposal for a model trade agreement was still not accepted. Interim measures to continue trade between the Community and the Eastern bloc had to be established.

Rumania

The 1976 trade agreement with Rumania was the first to be concluded by the Community with an Eastern European country. It applies to the products covered by the Multi-fibre Agreement plus flax, and provides for restraint on Rumanian exports to the Community of 11 categories of products. A further 17 categories are covered by a compulsory consultation clause. Rumania signed the agreement with 25 other countries because otherwise she would have lost all her textile quotas and other arrangements with the Community. They would have been redistributed to the other countries. Hong Kong was one of the last to sign and did so with reluctance, and only because it would have lost all existing arrangements.

The second development was in the fishing industry. The Community declared a 200-mile fishing zone, similar to that declared by almost every other nation. The Council of Ministers brought the decision to the notice of non-member countries, notably the USSR, East Germany and Poland. They were informed that the Community was willing to negotiate new fisheries agreements. A licenced number of fishing boats was proposed. The aim of the Community and the USSR, Poland and East Germany, is to negotiate a framework agreement to regulate reciprocal fishing rights within the 200-mile zones. Negotiations continue. From time to time the interim measures laying down fishing possibilities are extended temporarily, but the ultimate and inevitable outcome will be that the USSR and other Eastern bloc countries will have to accept and agree to negotiate with the Commission which represents the Community.

Pending the negotiation of trade agreements between the Community and the state trading countries, and in order to continue to trade, the Council, in 1975, adopted unilateral import arrangements which fixed quotas for goods, subject to quantitative restrictions, and set out the rules and procedures for any changes in these import arrangements. The quotas have since been increased, except for certain sensitive products, by 5.5 per cent. Although quota restrictions are still important, progress has been made towards liberalization. By 1978, of the 1098 Common Customs Tariff headings, 767 were liberalized as were 99 part headings.

Trade with Eastern Europe has increased steadily during recent years and there has been a positive trade balance for the Community. The percentage of Community trade with Eastern Europe is as follows:

    1973   7.5
    1974   7.4
    1975   8.2
    1976   8.0

For companies within the Community which trade with Eastern Europe, the slow development of trade relations, largely for political reasons, is a disadvantage only if their trade is considerable or capable of rapid development. Smaller companies have been able to operate successfully, and political considerations have not affected them.

Contrary to the commonly held view, trade with state trading countries can be very satisfactory. Agreements are more likely to be adhered to than in many other countries of the world. The word of an Eastern European company is more likely to be kept as it has government backing.

Knowledge of the current state of negotiations between individual countries in the Eastern bloc and the Community will give some indications of future growth patterns. Import quotas are fixed on a country-by-country basis, therefore, in order to take advantage of national quotas it may be possible to export or import from a specific country of the Community through a subsidiary. Once goods are in the Community there are no barriers to their circulating freely, and there is only the need to pay differing rates of VAT between countries. Also goods imported using quota agreements to one country of the Community cannot be re-exported to another Community country.

China

If Community relations with Eastern Europe have been slow to develop for political reasons, they have developed much faster with China for the same reasons.

Although China sees the Community as a capitalist organization, it has nevertheless, since the sixties, emphasized its importance as a strong entity independent of Russia and the United States. Threatened, or feeling threatened by Russia, China sees it in her own interest to have a strong Western Europe on the Soviet bloc's flank.

Chinese interest in the Community was shown by the opening of an embassy in Belgium which took up informal contacts with the Commission. The New China News Agency also opened an office in 1973, and its correspondents were accredited to the Spokesman's Group of the Commission. At the same time, China showed, unlike Eastern Europe, an understanding of the new role of the Commission in negotiating external agreements, once bilateral agreements between member states and third countries ended.

The 'model' or outline agreement which was sent to Eastern European states, but received without comment, was also sent to China which responded by inviting Sir Christopher Soames, as Vice-President of the Commission, to China on an official mission. As a result of this visit it was agreed to nominate a Chinese ambassador to the Community, and also to negotiate a commercial agreement. The first communist ambassador came to Brussels from China in 1975 — the same year as the Soames visit. Chinese internal policies slowed down the rate of growth of relations in 1976, but in 1977 discussions were intensified and China announced its intentions of building up trade with the Community. In 1977, the Council invited the Commission to negotiate a five-year non-preferential trade agreement which was signed in 1978.

At present the Community is China's second most important trading partner after Japan. In 1975 and 1976, Community exports to China were almost 1 per

Box 122

Contrasting attitudes of Eastern Europe and China to the European Community

Commissioner Haferkamp in Moscow, May 1978:

'. . . When we consider the course of developments since the first visit of a delegation of the European communities in 1975, we are obliged to note that the state of our relations is not in line with the development of détente in Europe over these past three years . . .

Today, 111 countries maintain diplomatic relations with the Community. The fact that this is not yet so in the case of our immediate neighbours, is an anachronism. The establishment of normal relations between the individual countries of CMEA and the Community, and between CMEA itself and the Community, is no more than the logical outcome of one of the most significant facts of the closing years of this century.

Chinese Minister for External Trade on signature of European Community/China Trade Agreement, April 1978

After noting that 'the signing of this Agreement marks a new development in political and economic relations between China and the EEC', Mr Li Chiang continued his address as follows:

'. . . The social system of our country is different from that of the states of Western Europe, but we are all faced with a common task, which is to safeguard our independence and sovereignty. We have much in common and should provide each other with mutual support. We support Western Europe in its union for strength and in its struggle against "hegemonism". We want to see a united and powerful Europe, and the countries of Europe, for their part, we are sure, want to see a prosperous and powerful China. We are prepared to make our contribution to the development of cooperation and friendship between our country and the EEC . . .'.

Source: Bulletin of the European Communities, 4,5–1978

---

cent of total exports, which is small in comparison with the 8 or 9 per cent with the Eastern bloc, but there is considerable potential.

The Arab world

The countries of the Arab League are now the largest trading partners of the European Community. This alone underlines the importance of Community relations with this part of the world; in addition there are political, social and cultural relationships between these two areas which may have more long-term interests in common than is at present apparent.

In 1976, over 20 per cent of Arab countries' exports went to the Community, compared with 16 per cent to Japan and 9 per cent to the United States. In the same year over 13 per cent of Community exports went to Arab countries. The main Arab exports were hydrocarbons, but there has been a rapid increase in the value of oil-based exports, and these will continue to grow and probably continue to find their best markets in Western Europe.

The Euro-Arab dialogue could become the keystone in relations between the Community and the Arab League countries. It was launched in 1973 but did not take place at expert level until 1975. The significance of the dialogue is long term rather than short term. The relations between the two areas will continue to be important and based on proximity, complementary economies and the increasing interchange of visitors for business, education and recreational reasons.

The Mediterranean agreements

The Community has built up a series of mainly preferential trading agreements with countries around the Mediterranean (see Chapter 24). They range from Association Agreements with countries such as Greece, Turkey and Portugal.

Box 123

The Euro-Arab dialogue

In December 1973 at the 'Summit' of the Nine in Copenhagen, the heads of government replied to an approach by Arab ministers and confirmed the importance they attached to the search for long-term cooperation in technical, economic and cultural areas.

Despite initial difficulties in getting the dialogue started the Nine managed to conduct a joint negotiating position with the Arab League countries. The subjects discussed covered cooperation in the following fields: industry, infrastructure, agriculture, trade, finance, science and technology and social and labour aspects.

The Euro-Arab dialogue, undertaken jointly by the Nine and the member-states of the Arab League, is a vast long-term project, that could lead to bilateral agreements between Arab and European countries or between Arab countries and the Community (as was the case with the Mediterranean countries, (Algeria, Morocco, etc.). Three Arab League countries have signed the ACP-EEC Lomé Convention—Mauritania, Somalia and the Sudan.

continued

Trade between the EEC and the Arab countries (1975)

	EEC imports (million u.a.)	EEC exports (million u.a.)
World (excluding EEC)	118 608.7 (100%)	116 099.0 (100%)
Arab League	23 530 (19.8%)	14 383 (12.4%)
Saudi Arabia	8 567	1 394
Iraq	2 652	1 744
Libya	2 475	1 851
Kuwait	2 370	562
United Arab Emirates	2 266	740
Algeria	1 972	2 651
Morocco	758	983
Qatar	689	179
Syria	436	549
Oman	360	301
Tunisia	336	667
Egypt	299	1 268
Sudan	158	281
Mauritania	115	100
Lebanon	52	590
Bahrein	44	172
Somalia	11	56
Jordan	8	206
Yemen (PDR)	7	30
Yemen (AR)	2	58

Note: the Arab countries are the Community's leading trade partners (taking 12% of EEC exports, 20% of imports), followed by the United States (11% of exports, 16% of imports), and third East Europe (10% of exports, 7% of imports).
Source: EEC

The EEC's trade balance with the Arab League (million u.a.)

1970	1971	1972	1973	1974	1975	1976
−4 533	−5 605	−5 042	−6 357	−18 747	−9 829	−12 754

Source: SOEC

which envisage ultimate customs unions with the Community, if not member-ship. The renegotiation of these agreements from time to time is a complex task. There are as many political as trade problems involved.

Although these agreements may not be very important in themselves, and some of the provisions are not very effective in developing trade between the countries and the Community, they do provide a framework for the further expansion of the Commission's role in negotiating on behalf of the Community. This role, though in theory restricted to trade relations, increasingly involves political considerations. Through these agreements, and the negotiating of them, Community members learn to work together and to coordinate national policies. This may lead to a gradual political convergence of views.

The European Free Trade Area

The EFTA countries, since 1 July 1977, have had a customs free trade area within the Community. The seven EFTA countries are Austria, Switzerland, Sweden, Portugal, Iceland, Norway and the associate member Finland. The

Box 124

The economic relations of the European Community with countries with which it has contractual agreements

	ACP[1] states	Maghreb[2] countries	Mashreq[3] countries	Israel	Total
Population (in millions)	268	36	48	3	355
Exports of the EEC (1975) in million EUA	7 590	4 301	2 613	1 220	15 724
in % of total exports outside EEC	6.5%	3.7%	2.2%	1.1%	13.5%
Imports of EEC (1975) in million EUA	8 159	3 020	795	538	12 512
in % of total imports of the EEC	6.9%	2.5%	0.7%	0.5%	10.6%
Trade balance of the Community	−569	+1 281	+1 818	+682	+3 212
Financial aid envisaged by the agreements in million EUA	3 444	339	300	30	4 113
Period of application of financial aid	1.4.1976 until 1.3.1980	until 31.10. 1981	until 31.10. 1981	until 31.10. 1981	

[1] 46 ACP States who signed the Lomé Convention on 28 February 1975. There are now 53 (1978)
[2] Algeria, Morocco, Tunisia.
[3] Egypt, Jordan, Lebanon, Syria.

Source: EEC Documentation

EFTA agreements provide for the establishment of a free trade area for industrial products between the Community and each EFTA country. They also grant minor concessions on certain agricultural products. Although trade between the Community and the EFTA countries increased considerably between 1973 and 1976, trade between EFTA and the rest of the world has grown even faster.

The free trade agreements have worked well, so far, but the Community believes that the liberalization of trade must be extended and secured. Although tariff barriers are coming down and quotas are being increased, other obstacles to trade, such as non-tariff barriers, need to be eliminated. Relationships are important between these two great European trading blocs as the Treaty of Rome provides the opportunity for any European state to join the Community. Although at the moment, for a number of different political and commercial reasons, the EFTA countries are not likely to apply for membership, major economic or political crises can change situations rapidly. There is therefore considerable interest in the further development of EFTA–European Community contacts.

Latin America

In 1971 a Community–Latin America dialogue was initiated at ambassador level. It was intended to provide a forum for examining problems of mutual interest. The Community is concerned to develop its relations with Latin America as a

Box 125

Trade between the Community of the Nine and the countries of Latin America has developed as follows between 1968 and 1976 (in $m)

Year	EEC imports	EEC exports	EEC trade balance
1968	3 450	2 711	− 739
1970	4 395	3 360	−1 035
1972	4 815	4 615	− 200
1974	8 315	8 474	+ 159
1975	7 934	9 041	+1 107
1976	9 164	8 240	− 924

Source: IMF Direction of Trade and Statistical Office of the European Communities (1976).

whole and is consequently building up its relations and contacts with the Latin American Free Trade Association (LAFTA). It is also developing relations through bilateral agreements with various Latin American states, and through its general development cooperation policy. One of the aspects of this policy is to promote regional or sub-regional economic integration. An example of this kind of integration in Latin America is the Central American Common Market, or the Andean Pact, which the Community is following with close interest.

Bilateral trade agreements have been signed with Argentina, Brazil and Uruguay and more recently with Mexico. Many of these countries have signed the international agreements for the textiles trade. The agreements restrict the theoretical export capacities of these countries but they also safeguard existing arrangements which might otherwise have been threatened as the demand for protectionist policies in the European Community, as elsewhere, increases.

Aid for regional integration. The Community has gained experience and understanding of integration problems and gives aid to help the process. The motives for this are realistic. Community experience has shown that a large economic entity has greater trading possibilities and also is more stable during a period of crisis. Latin America must, however, be concerned about the way its share of the overall Community import market has fallen off from 7.5 per cent in 1968 to a little over 5 per cent in 1975 and 1976.

The rest of the world

Trade agreements have been drawn up with a large number of countries of the world so that there are now in existence well over 120 agreements of one kind and another with different countries. Some of these framework agreements are not very important, while others are of great significance to either one or both partners. For the first time a group of nations has given to its central negotiating body, the Commission, the right to negotiate trade agreements on its behalf. To the extent that trade and politics are increasingly intertwined there has arisen, through this mechanism, the possibility of a genuine European approach to regions and countries all over the world. It may prove to have been one of the most important developments of the Community to date.

Bibliography

The following pamphlets, and many others in the series, are available from Directorate-General X of the Commission. See Chapter 28 for the address.
The European Community and the Arab World
The European Community and China
The European Community and Eastern Europe
The European Community and Latin America
The European Community and Southern Africa

27 The future of business and the European Community

'As for the future, your task is not to foresee, but to
enable it'.
Saint Exupery, The Wisdom of the Sands, 1948

It is difficult to forecast especially about the future! If you are involved, or may
one day become involved, in corporate strategy you need to have some idea
about the way in which Western Europe, and the European Community in
particular, is developing. You may have to consider whether the instititions are
making progress, whether more power is being given to them by Member
Governments and whether the trend will continue. Also you will have to ask

Figure 19 'As for the future, your task is not to foresee, but to enable it'

Box 126

Future international scenarios

From this mosaic of considerations, some trends stand out as likelier than others. From them, we can perhaps construct a most probable – or at any rate a least improbable – scenario. The superpowers will not retain the monolithic strength of the early post-war years; they will be diverted elsewhere, and for different reasons both are likely to have urgent problems of internal economic development. America will be less concerned with Europe than formerly, but it will not be able or willing to withdraw its military presence. The fundamental dividing line down the centre of Europe will remain, though the currents of trade and knowledge across it will increase.

The leading nation states of Europe will continue as the basic units of power, but all – even the strongest – will face fundamental economic challenge arising from the need to compete with the manufactured products and cheap labour of the Third World. They may not rise to this challenge, especially in the cases of greater structural weakness, such as Italy and Britain. But if they can, it will almost certainly be through technical cooperation under the umbrella of a strengthened EEC, coupled with preferential trade and development agreements with the countries of the Third World.

Some of these nations, especially in the Mediterranean south, may acquire communist governments, but these may well prove independent of Moscow and even aligned to the West. At the same time, many nations will face a further – and in some cases very dangerous – challenge from strong political movements in their own mountainous or peninsular peripheries; and, though this challenge will be arduously resisted, the strong probability is that finally the outcome will be partial devolution. (And this could arise in an opposite way if the central powers decided that their peripheries were too troublesome and too economically burdensome.

Some of the new peripheral units, again, could have radical or left-wing governments, leading to a possible change in the political geography of Western Europe. Though some may find it expedient to join economic groupings others may profess a sturdy independence.

The most likely Europe of the year 2000, then, is a loose confederation of nation states, including a number of small new arrivals, which have surrendered some of their powers to federal European organs; linked in turn to a loose federation of the countries of the Third World, via a series of trade and development agreements; but with many exceptions. Yet the route from our world to that world is rough and uncharted; and progress along it will doubtless be slow, faltering and treacherous.

Source: Peter Hall, Europe 2000, p. 30, Duckworth 1977

whether a genuine common market of 300 million people will emerge, whether many of the technical and legal requirements for exploiting this market will be drawn up in Brussels and whether there will be a European Union. The answers will provide guidelines for future business activities in Europe.

The key decisions about which way the Community will develop, from a business viewpoint, will be made by industry working closely with government.

Business—government relations is a relatively new area of activity, but it is here to stay. A broad range of UK organizations are now operating from a European base. The recent European operations and acquisitions of companies such as GKN, ICI, Lucas and BP show how this process is accelerating.

With smaller firms this type of expansion is expensive and more complex. The smaller companies will continue to serve local markets. Yet the advantages of

Box 127

The President of the Commission, President Jenkins, on its future

In all our activities we must remember our underlying political purposes. Our means are largely economic. But our end is and always has been political. It is to make a European Union. It is to preserve and fortify our peace and liberty. It is to restore to Europe the influence in the world which we have so wantonly thrown away in a generation of European civil wars. Much has already been accomplished. However great may be our present difficulties they are as nothing compared with the problem which confronted those who had to build afresh out of the rubble and bitterness of the late forties.

Let us not bemoan too much. But let us at the same time be aware of the size of the stakes. The values of justice for all, individual freedom and intellectual integrity, which were the norms of a civilized society, and to which can now happily be added a sense of social fairness, are now genuinely at risk. There are not many countries in the world which can be counted upon to sustain them. We represent about half of that number. If our Community cannot be made to work, what can? If we, among the richest and certainly among the most favoured and talented of the populations of the globe, cannot learn to work together, what prospect is there for humanity? Or for a decent civilized life for ordinary men and women? There are the stakes and there are the issues. Let us approach them with an awesome sense of responsibility, but also with a courageous and determined optimism.

From address by the Right Honourable Roy Jenkins, President of the Commission of the European Communities, to the European Parliament. Luxembourg, Tuesday 11 January 1977

cooperation in a European sense are obvious; even small companies are beginning to seize opportunities across the Community.

The future of the European Community matters to business more than has so far been realized. If business considers the Community to be important, and by all the signs it does, then it will need to do more about its Community relations.

Box 128

Jean Monnet, the father of the European Community, on its future

The roots of the Community are strong now, and deep in the soil of Europe. They have survived some hard seasons, and can survive more. On the surface, appearances change. In a quarter-century, naturally, new generations arise, with new ambitions; images of the past disappear; the balance of the world is altered. Yet amid this changing scenery the European idea goes on; and no one seeing it, and seeing how stable the Community institutions are, can doubt that this is a deep and powerful movement on a historic scale.

Can it really be suggested that the wellsprings of that movement are exhausted, or that other rival forces are taking their place? I see no sign of any such rival forces. On the contrary, I see the same necessity acting on our countries – sometimes bringing them together for their mutual benefit, sometimes dividing them to the detriment of all. The moral is clear, and it cannot be gainsaid. It has taken root in our peoples' consciousness, but it is slow to act on their will: it has to overcome the inertia that hinders movement and the habits that resist change. We have to reckon with time.

Where this necessity will lead, and toward what kind of Europe, I cannot say. It is impossible to foresee today the decisions that could be taken in a new context tomorrow. The essential thing is to hold fast to the few fixed principles that have guided us since the beginning: gradually to create among Europeans the broadest common interest, served by common democratic institutions to which the necessary sovereignty has been delegated. This is the dynamic that has never ceased to operate, removing prejudice, doing away with frontiers, enlarging to continental scale, within a few years, the process that took centuries to form our ancient nations.

I have never doubted that one day this process will lead us to the United States of Europe, but see no point in trying to imagine today what political form it will take. The words about which people argue – federation or confederation – are inadequate and imprecise. What we are preparing, through the work of the Community, is probably without precedent. The Community itself is founded on institutions, and they need strengthening; but the true political authority which the democracies of Europe will one day establish still has to be conceived and built . . . .

But time is passing, and Europe is moving only slowly on the course to which she is so deeply committed . . . . We cannot stop, when the whole world around us is on the move. Have I said clearly enough that the Community we have created is not an end in itself? It is a process of change, continuing that same process which in an earlier period of history produced our national forms of life.

Like our provinces in the past, our nations today must learn to live together under common rules and institutions freely arrived at. The sovereign nations of the past can no longer solve the problems of the present: they cannot ensure their own progress or control their own future. And the Community itself is only a stage on the way to the organized world of tomorrow.

Jean Monnet, Memoirs, pp. 523–4, Collins 1978

Times are changing. The next few years will probably see European developments on a scale far greater than envisaged at present. It will take a crisis to bring
together the countries of the Community, but there are signs of crisis everywhere.
There may be a major crisis in employment as industries find they can no longer
compete. The need for Community-scale action to help these industries to adapt
to change becomes more apparent.

While individually powerless, those who read this book can collectively
influence, and perhaps enable, the necessary change. This book is dedicated to
you and to those who have contributed to it, some acknowledged and others
not. The business community is the creator of wealth, the means to our society's
ends. It is through its efforts that the European business community of the
twenty-first century will come about. It is a century which we shall visit, if at all,
for only a little while and which therefore by our efforts now we bequeath to
future generations. We have a challenge to which we can respond.

Bibliography

Hall, P. *et al.* (1977) *Europe 2000,* London:Duckworth
Monnet, Jean (1978) *Memoirs*, London: Collins

Section five
Sources of further information

28 Ten contact addresses and telephone numbers

The following contact points will enable you to find answers to further questions. In particular the EEC Information Unit is outstandingly good value. It has six lines and an excellent staff who spare no effort to ensure that your queries are answered. If the answer cannot be obtained immediately they will phone you back. The service is free.

The UK Office of the Commission is also first class and has the best library on Community affairs in the country. It is a source of general information and does not claim to help businessmen specifically with export or investment information. This should be obtained from the Department of Trade or the British Overseas Trade Board.

(1) *EEC Information Unit.* The EEC Information Unit helps companies of all types and sizes by answering general questions about EEC membership and by guiding them where necessary to more specialized information sources.

1 Victoria Street, London SW1H 0ET, Tel: 01-215 4301

(2) *The Offices of the Commission.* The UK Office represents the Commission of the European Communities and is able to offer both general and specialized information about the work of the Communities.

20 Kensington Palace Gardens, London W8 4QQ, Tel: 01-727 8090

The European Community has press and information offices in most European countries and in other parts of the world. Of particular interest are:

United States. Suite 707, 2100 M Street, N.W., Washington D.C. 20037, Tel: Washington 872-8350; 245 East 47th Street, 1 Dag Hammarskjold Plaza, New York, N.Y. 10017, Tel: New York 3713084

Canada: Suite 1110, 350 Sparks St., Ottawa, Ont. K1B 7S8, Tel: Ottawa 238 6464

Japan. Kowa 25 Building, 8-7 Sanbanche, Chiyoda-Ku, 102 Tokyo, Tel: Tokyo 239-0441

United Kingdom. 4 Cathedral Road, Cardiff CH1 9SG, Tel: (0222) 371631; 7 Alvn Street, Edinburgh EH2 4PH, Tel: 031-225 2058

(3) *The Department of Trade.* Ask for the information department. They will find you the right extension for a general enquiry. For enquiries about export or investment possibilities in different countries, contact the British Overseas Trade Board (see 4 below).

Overseas trade. The Department is responsible for commercial policy and relations with overseas countries and is concerned with economic policies affecting the international position of the United Kingdom. It promotes UK commercial interests overseas, negotiates on trade and commercial matters, and administers UK protective tariffs.

1 Victoria Street, London SW1H 0ET, Tel: 01-215 7877, Telex: 88 11074/5

(4) *The British Overseas Trade Board.* Under the direction of the British Overseas Trade Board, the Department of Trade promotes British exports, providing an export information service to industry and commerce. It has eight regional offices. Also it handles government support for overseas trade fairs.

Export House, 50 Ludgate Hill, London EC4M 7HU, Tel: 01-248 5757, Telex: 886143

(5) *Commission of the European Communities.* Ask for the Information Directorate-General (DG X). The telephonists speak English. The switchboard is often busy so phone early, especially when Brussels is one hour ahead. Remember, Belgium closes down for lunch from 1 until 3. A useful contact point for finding out the name of the official dealing with your particular industry or problem. They will also put you on mailing list of, for example, Trades Union Information or Euroforum (see Chapter 30).

200 Rue de la Roi, 1049 Brussels, Belgium, Tel: Brussels 735 0040, Telex: 21877 Comeur B

(6) *Export Credits Guarantee Department.* A separate government department responsible to the Secretary of State for Trade. ECGD provides credit insurance for UK exporters against non-payment risks, guarantees to banks for export finance, and insurance against political risks on new overseas investments. Support is also available against cost-escalation on certain large capital goods contracts and for performance bonds.

Aldermanbury House, Aldermanbury, London EC2, Tel: 01-606 6699, Telex: 883601

(7) *HMSO.* The sales office for all Commission documents. You can obtain a catalogue of all documents available.

HM Stationery Office, PO Box 569, London SE1 9NH, Tel: 01-928 6977 ext 365

(8) *UKREP.* The UK Representation in Brussels. If you have major business with the European Community, or have arranged meetings with Commission officials, you may wish to talk with a member of UKREP before or after your meeting. You can contact UKREP direct or through the Department of Trade or the Foreign and Commonwealth office.

6 Rond Point Schuman, 1049 Brussels, Belgium, Tel: Brussels 736 9920

(9) *The European Parliament.* If you wish to contact a political party or make arrangements to see a European MP in Luxembourg or Strasbourg, contact can be made direct to the Parliament's secretariat headquarters in Luxembourg.

(10) *Office for Official Publications of the European Communities.* If you cannot get what you want from HMSO, telephone this office in Luxembourg.

Boite Postale 1003, Luxembourg, Tel: Luxembourg 47941

29 Short list of abbreviations and glossary

This is a short list of abbreviations and descriptions of institutions and organizations which managers are most likely to meet in their dealings with the European Community.

ACP The African, Caribbean and Pacific states which make up the 54 countries of the Lomé Convention.

BLEU The Belgo-Luxembourg Economic Union. This Economic and Customs Union was founded in 1921 and involves a pooling of foreign currency and combining balance of payments and foreign trade statistics.

BOTB British Overseas Trade Board. Is responsible for the export promotion of the Department of Trade and Industry.

CAP Common Agricultural Policy of the Community.

CCT Common Customs Tariff. The tariff wall between the Community and third countries.

CEE French for EEC.

Commission The thirteen commissioners under their President Roy Jenkins who collectively propose legislation to the Council. The European conscience of the Community.

COREPER The Committee of Permanent Representatives. It prepares the work of the Council of Ministers. Each country is a member through its representative in Brussels who is effectively ambassador to the Community.

Council of Ministers Ministers of the Nine meeting to agree Community legislation proposed by the Commission.

Decisions Community decrees addressed to a state, a company or an individual but binding on them.

Directives Community legislation binding on Member States but leaving them free to decide how to carry them out.

EAGGF The European Agricultural Guidance and Guarantee Fund which finances the CAP.

EC The European Community − probably the name it will be known by in the future.

ECGD Export Credits Guarantee Department. It provides export credit insurance facilities for British exporters.

ECOSOC or ESC The Economic and Social Committee which gives opinions on Commission proposals. (See Chapter 6.)

ECSC The European Coal and Steel Community. Established in 1951 but its considerable responsibilities have now been taken over by the Commission.

ECU The new proposed European Currency Unit.

EEC The European Economic Community. Established by the Treaty of Rome in 1957.

EFTA The European Free Trade Association. Founded as an alternative to the EEC. Members are Austria, Norway, Portugal, Sweden, Switzerland, Iceland and Finland. The latter is an associate member.

EIB The European Investment Bank. It makes loans and guarantees which facilitate the financing of Community projects.

EMA (EMS) European Monetary Arrangement. The new European monetary proposals put forward initially at the Bremen European Council in 1978. Now known as the European Monetary System (EMS).

EMU Economic and Monetary Union. The Council decided to establish this in 1971. It remains a long-term goal.

ETUC The European Trades Union Confederation.

EUA European Unit of Account.

Euratom The European Atomic Energy Community established in 1957 at the same time as the Treaty of Rome.

The European Council A meeting three times a year of the EEC heads of government. The most powerful body influencing the future developments of the Community.

European Parliament Directly elected Parliament from June 1979. It can influence the Commission and Council of Ministers and will grow in power.

FEOGA French for EAGGF.

GATT General Agreement on Tariffs and Trade. An international body which attempts to reduce tariffs and establish an international code of practice for fair trading.

GSP Generalized System of Preferences under which developed countries grant preferential tariff treatment to most goods originating from developing countries.

Maghreb Algeria, Morocco and Tunisia.

Mashreq Egypt, Jordan, Lebanon and Syria.

NTB Non-tariff barrier.

OECD Organization for Economic Cooperation and Development. The economic club of twenty-three of the world's industrialized nations, most of which are in Europe.

Recommendations Suggestions by the Commission or the Council but with no binding force.

Regulations A form of Community law binding and directly applicable in all Member States.

u.a. Unit of Account. The value of the u.a. is based on gold. The value of the EUA used for the Community budget is determined every day in relation to a basket of all Community currencies.

UNCTAD The United Nations Conference on Trade and Development.

UNICE The Employers Federation Trade Association in Brussels.

30 **Further reading**

Developments in the Community are so rapid that in order to keep up with them it is necessary to go beyond books, unless they are year books or appear regularly in new editions. Most Commission and official government publications are very cheap and some are free.

A suggested basic reference library is shown in *Box 53.*

Newspapers and periodicals

Agence Europe. A daily bulletin which covers all aspects of the Community. It regularly leaks internal Community documents and is essential reading for those involved in carefully monitoring Community developments for their organizations. It is too detailed for the busy businessman. 10 Blvd St Lazar, Botanic Building, 1030 Brussels, Belgium, Tel: Brussels 219 0256

Briefing and background notes on different topics. Produced by the UK Office of the Commission and the Parliament. Some of the best and most readable information coming out of the Community. First-class background information published several times a month. Usually only two or three pages. You can ask just for those dealing with your specific interests. At present free but would be worth paying for. Address: see European Community below.

Bulletin of the European Communities. There are 11 issues a year and an index. The *Bulletin*, together with the supplements on specific topics which appear monthly, provides excellent and abundant background information on what is happening in the Community. It is cheap and comprehensive. Available from HMSO, Tel: 01-928 6977.

The Economist. A weekly section on Europe and the European Community.

Euroforum. Weekly news from the Community mainly on industrial, commercial and social affairs. Available free from the Commission, 200 Rue de la Loi, 1049 Brussels, Belgium, Tel: Brussels 735 0040.

European Community. Journal produced by the UK Office of the Commission. General background; too general for business. Available from 20 Kensington Palace Gardens, London, W8, Tel: 01-727 8090.

European Community Information. A *Financial Times* newsletter available monthly on subscription – good general background on Community developments slanted towards business. The Financial Times, Bracken House, Cannon Street, London EC4, Tel: 01-248 8000.

The Financial Times and *The Times.* Both have daily European pages. *The Financial Times* pages are more business oriented.

House of Lords reports. The House of Lords EEC Scrutiny Committee produces reports several times a year on different aspects of Community legislation. These are comprehensive documents which compile information from a wide variety of sources. They are based on evidence given to the Committee by interested organizations such as the CBI, trade associations, expert witnesses, Commission officials and government departments. They are invaluable reference documents. European MP's have compared them favourably with reports coming from the European Parliament committees. Recent ones of interest to businessmen are on: Shipbuilding, Enlargement, Textiles, CCT and the Customs Union. Available from HMSO.

Newsletter on the Common Agricultural Policy. Available free from the Commission.

Official Journal of the European Communities. The official gazette of the European Communities published in two series. The L (legislation) series contains adopted Community legislation which by its publication comes into force. It appears at least once daily. The C (communications) series contains details of draft legislation and other information of interest including summaries of the proceedings of the European Assembly and the Court of Justice. It appears three times a week. Only of value to the large company — too detailed for normal monitoring purposes and takes up a great deal of shelf space. Available from HMSO.

Report of the results of the business surveys carried out among heads of enterprises in the Community. Results of a monthly enquiry into business conditions in the European Community. Available from HMSO.

Trade and Industry. The official weekly news magazine of the Departments of Industry, Trade, Prices and Consumer Protection. Contains valuable information for exporters, including articles on exporting and overseas markets, brief details of changes in tariffs, customs, import regulations, plus a regular weekly review of new European Community legislation. The monthly supplement, *European Community Commentary*, provides an authoritative interpretation of Community thinking and developments as they affect trade and industry. Available from HMSO, PO Box 569, London SE1 9NH, Tel: 01-928 6977 ext 423/472.

Trade Union Information. Available free from the Commission.

Vachers European Companion. A quarterly with names and addresses of officials within the Community and European national governments. Available from Kerswell Ltd, Tel: 01-586 0135.

Books

Books on the Community, including this one, date rapidly. A few books have been mentioned at the end of some of the chapters. Here are four reading lists which cover between them the whole range of available books and other publications.

The European Community: A Brief Reading List, January 1977, Commission of the European Community, 20 Kensington Palace Gardens, London W8 4QQ

The London Business School Library Monthly Guide to EEC Publications. Sussex Place, Regents Park, London NW1

Doris M. Palmer (ed.) (1979), *Sources of Information on the European Communities*, London: Mansell

A Selected Study Guide to the European Community. European Community Information Service, 2100 M Street, Suite 707, Washington DC

Kenneth Twitchett, *A Study Guide to British Books on the Common Market,* European Studies 22, 1975

Index